Westport

Padraig McLoughlin

First published 2007.

Published on behalf of Westport Golf Club by
Golf Image
Oak Tree House
14 Main Road
Bramfield
Herts SG14 2QJ
England

Designed by Chris Murray, Golf Image.

Golf Image is part of the Allsortz Ltd Group

Printed in the UK by Newnorth Ltd, Bedford.

Contents

The Centenary Committee:

Front: Sal O'Connor, Ann Duffy.

Middle: Cathal Hughes (Chairman), Pat Murphy, Padraig McLoughlin (Author).

Back: Liam Gibbons, Patrick Hopkins, Gar Golden, Liam Friel.

Foreword

Researching and bringing together the information and facts in relation to 100 years of golf in Westport has proved challenging and rewarding. We have discovered stories and events that were long dormant and in this publication we have tried to bring to life the story of golf in Westport.

It is a story of challenge, determination and foresight. It involved three golf courses, great occasions and many heartbreaks. But always the pursuit of golf in Westport was carried on in an atmosphere of friendship and fun.

To our Centenary Book Committee, who left no stone unturned in researching the facts and discovering long lost photographs, our sincere thanks.

To our author and fellow member of Westport Golf Club, Padraig McLoughlin, thank you. Padraig wrote this book with feeling and with insight. In the book he has set out the history with a wonderful sense of time and place.

This history records the work, dedication and effort of many great members, some of whom have passed to their eternal rest. It paints a picture of a club with a reputation for sportsmanship, integrity and friendship.

The next 100 years will bring its own challenges, but in Westport Golf Club we have a membership which will rise to the occasion and continue to bring the club forward with pride and purpose. We salute the past and we look forward with anticipation to the future.

Cathal Hughes
Chairman, Centenary Book Committee

ACKNOWLEDGEMENTS

We wish to thank our main sponsors, Allied Irish Bank plc, Allergan Pharmaceuticals Ltd, The Walsh Family, and the Hughes Group. We further wish to record our thanks to Mr Des Mahon, Mayo County Manager, and all those who gave photographs, information and documents. We wish to thank Mr Liam Lyons, Mr Frank Dolan, and Mr Michael McLoughlin for allowing us to reproduce their photographs. Finally, we wish to thank Westport Golf Club and its members, without whose encouragement this publication would not have happened.

Centenary Club Captain's message

Westport's Centenary Year is a time for reflection and to honour our founder members. These are the people who created the foundation for the wonderful club we have today.

It is also a time to thank every single member, both living and deceased, who have dedicated their time voluntarily either as members of various committees or as officers of the club. The present members have inherited a legacy of which we are very proud of and one which I am sure will be passed on to future generations.

Westport Golf Club today represents one of Westport town's greatest assets. It brings countless visitors to the town ensuring a steady revenue stream throughout the year. Westport Golf Club is an asset that needs to be cherished and nurtured to enable it to show off its true potential and make sure it retains its position as one of Ireland's finest parkland courses.

This book has been a labour of love undertaken by Cathal Hughes and his committee and they have worked incredibly hard over the last four years to produce such a fine publication. I am sure that without this committee a lot of the information and photography would have been consigned to the dust bin. This book will serve generations of Westport people for many years to come and it is a fitting tribute to all current and past members.

Finally, on a more personal note, I would like to express my honour at being chosen as Captain of Westport Golf Club in its Centenary year. This is the greatest tribute any golfer can expect and I am very proud to follow in the footsteps of my grandfather, William J., who was captain in 1944; my father, Liam in 1984; and my brother Liam in 2004. The Walsh family have a long and successful association with Westport Golf Club and I am sure this will continue for many generations to come.

Sean Walsh
Club Captain 2008

Centenary Lady Captain's message

It is a great honour to be Lady Captain of a golf club in any year, but to be Lady Captain in the Centenary Year will be, for me, a great privilege. It's a great milestone in a club's existence to celebrate 100 years. A club is only as good as its members who sat on committees throughout the years and we must thank them for getting us this far in our history. We have a wonderful golf course and our thanks must go to the course committee and workers for making it so.

I am looking forward in the coming year to working together with the Club Captain, Mr. Sean Walsh, the vice captains, and in further responding to the requirements of the members, but of course especially the ladies.

We have all joined the club because of our love of golf and I am keen about playing a role in ensuring that all members enjoy to the full our superb golf course and clubhouse.

I will attempt to carry out the duties which my role affords with competence and enthusiasm and I look forward to your support in making 2008 a successful year for the club and all its members.

Nuala Hopkins
Lady Captain 2008

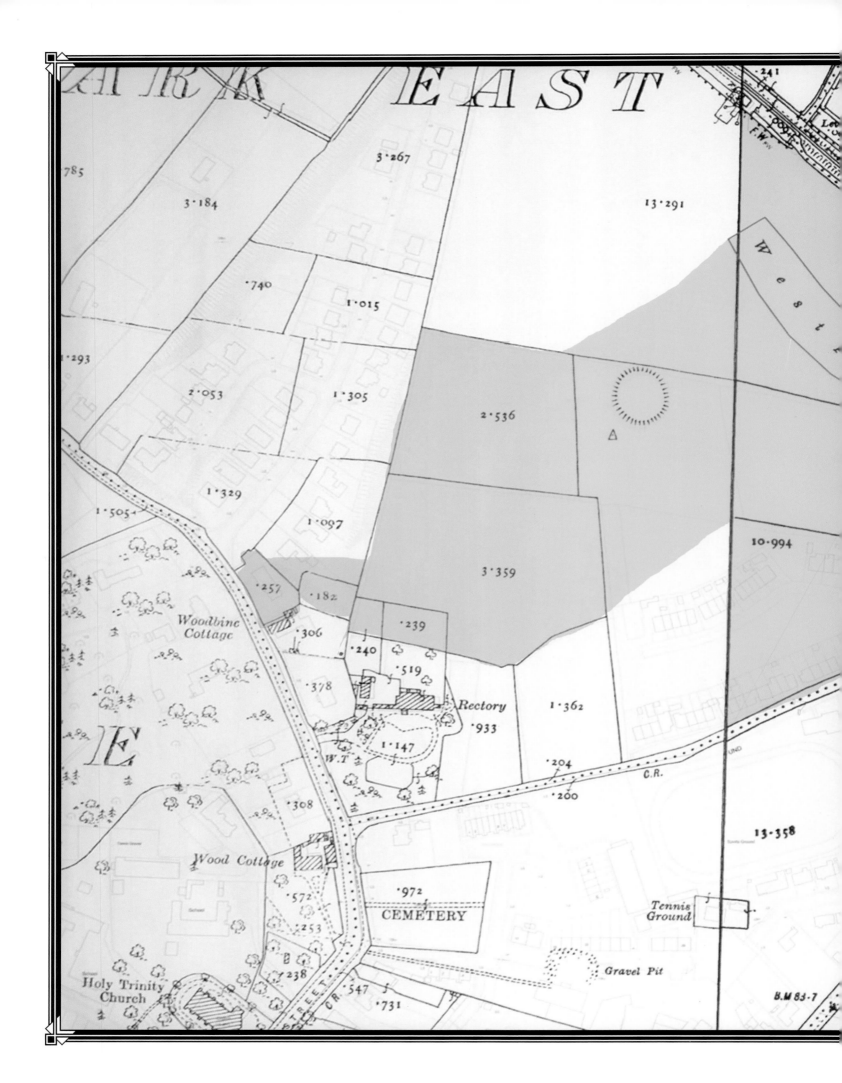

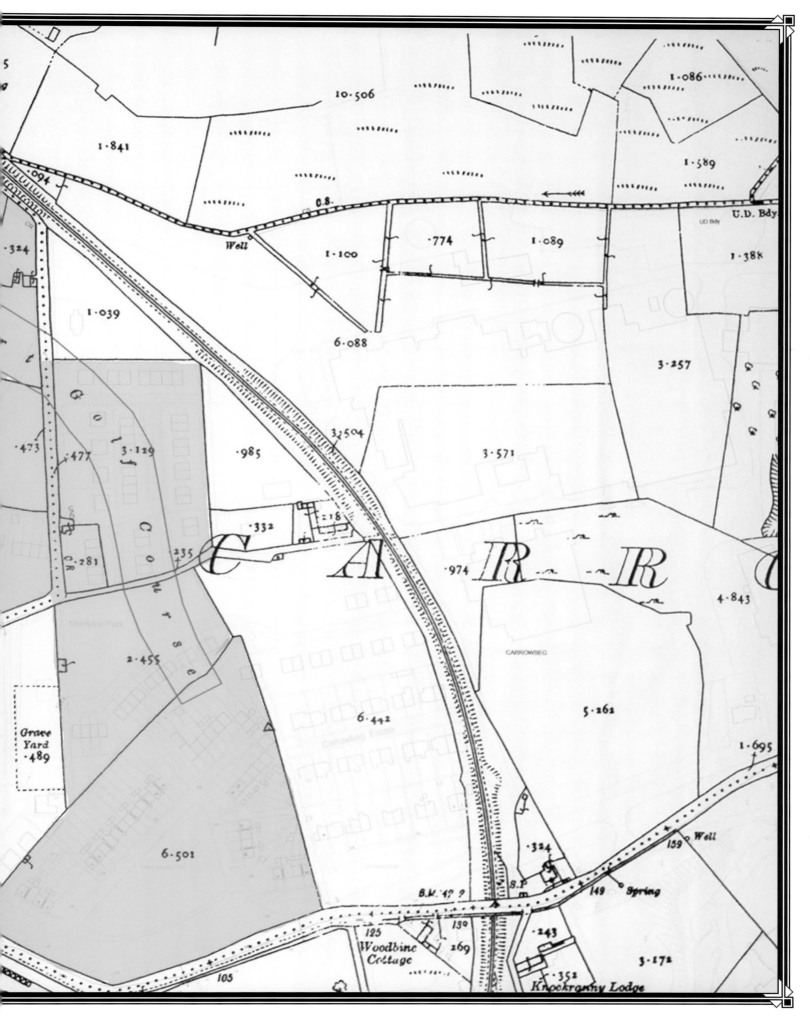

The area coloured green was the location of the first golf course. Set in what was then known as "Trafalgar Park", it covered the area of Fr. Angelus Park, Carrowbeg Estate, Horkans Hill and Deerpark East. The first hole started in Fr. Angelus Park and the 9th green was in the vicinity of Jack Kenny's house on the Newport Road.

Westport's Golf Timeline

1908
Westport Golf Club founded, Trafalgar Park. First captain Henry Darley Livingstone.

1912
A.J. Simpson captain.

1914
Outbreak of World War 1. No entry for Westport Golf Club in Irish Golf Guide.

1915
Club restored at Carrowholly.

1919
August 2: Club re-opens for play.

1927
Membership had reached 80. First pavilion built.

1940
Tom Rooney, professional, shoots course record 61.

1951
Club Secretary, Mr. Lorcan Gill, applied to the Golfing Union of Ireland for a standard scratch score. Par was 68, SSS was given as 67.

1953
The County Cup is hosted for the first time.

1967
Club reopens in May after new lease is agreed.

1914-1918
World War One.

1922-23
Irish Civil War.

1939-45
World War Two.

1966
Club closed once more when the Landlord would not renew the lease.

1919-1921
The Black and Tan War.

1971

John Farrell shoots Carrowholly course record of 68.

1973

Carrowholly closes: On March 22 the 47th and final AGM of Old Carrowholly was held and then the first AGM of the Championship Golf Course.

1975

June 9: New Course was officially opened by the Taoiseach, Mr. Liam Cosgrave.

1980

Westport Wins All Ireland Junior Cup.

1993

History was made at Westport Golf Club when Maureen Flynn became the first ever Westport woman to capture the Connacht Ladies Junior Championship.

2002

Professional Course Record: Paul McGinley – 65 during P.G.A. Tournament.

2004

Westport golf academy opens.

1968

Dublin meeting agrees new course for Westport.

1973

The first holder of the Amateur Course Record was Padraic Higgins (handicap 8) when he had 83 gross in the Gill Cup.

1977

Westport hosts Irish Close Championship.

1985

Westport hosts Irish Close Championship.

1997

Westport hosts Irish Close Championship.

1998

Bord Failte propose a 999 year lease at £450,000.

2005

Amateur Course Record in Irish Close Championship at Westport. Sean McTernan (Co. Sligo) shoots 61 comprising 10 birdies and an eagle for 12 under par.

*History
never seems
like History
When you
are living
through it.*

Chapter 1

THE first COURSE

THE FOUNDING FATHERS PLAY TRAFALGAR PARK 1908-1914.

When the game of golf came to Westport in 1908 the inaugural officers inhabited a society very different from the social order in Westport in 2008.

Politically Ireland was governed directly from Westminster. The Irish Party had reunited after the Parnellite Split but the Irish vote was not needed by the Conservatives or Liberals. Consequently Irish affairs received little attention.

A new Nationalism was stirring within the people inspired by the separatist philosophy espoused by the Gaelic League and the G.A.A. The growth of the separatist movement was evident in the huge interest in the Irish Language. The Language movement was spreading like a bush fire. So much so that one of its principal advocates, P.H. Pearse, arrived in Westport in November 1907 to address a Gaelic League rally. The *Mayo News* (costing 1 penny) reported his speech as follows:

The Mayo News.

"Padraic Pearse, M.A., Dublin, addressed a full capacity audience in Westport Town Hall on Sunday, November 24th on the occasion of the Gaelic League rally there. In his address, Pearse said: "Did you ever in all your life meet an Englishman that could not speak English? Did you ever meet or hear a Frenchman that could not talk French? You never did. Those things do not exist. They are contradictions in terms. You must come to Ireland, the land of contradictions, to find a person professing himself an Irishman, and yet unable to speak a word of the language of Ireland."

The Sinn Fein movement had also begun to preach the doctrine of economic independence from England. The *Mayo News* advertised:

"The Sinn Fein Hotel, James St.
Cuisine – A1, Richard Walsh, prop."

The pivotal Act that inspired the growth of Irish Nationalism was the 1898 Local Government Act. This Act established County Councils, Urban Councils and Rural District Councils. These bodies gave the ordinary people a taste for democracy at local level.

They grew to love the cut and thrust of local elections and the opportunity to influence local affairs. Soon the people would demand democracy at national level.

The Congested Districts Board was also doing good work and by 1912 the tenants on estates were agitating for the C.D.B. to purchase estates. The Murrisk Abbey estate, the Sligo estate and the purchase of the town of Westport inspired agitation.

Despite these indicators that the world of the Ascendancy class was in the process of erosion Westport society in general reflected the anglicisation of Ireland under British Rule. The leaders of this Anglicised world tended to be Protestant and many were Trinity graduates or English educated scholars. Their place of residence was the geographical area of Rosbeg, Belclare and

Murrisk. They mixed in business, in pleasure, and in daily social intercourse. They officiated on the Petty Sessions Bench, the Harbour Board and the Select Vestry of their church.

The education system did not include Irish as a subject on the curriculum. Secondary schooling tended to be the preserve of the few. The scholarly achievements of these students in exams was a news item worthy of publication. The Senior Intermediate results for 1907-1908 were published by the *Mayo News*:

"Walsh, William… passed English, Shorthand, Bookkeeping, Arithmetic, Algebra, Geometry, Experimental Science."

In the Westport Petty Sessions there was the British zero tolerance to "crime" no matter how petty. Fines were severe and costs imposed expensive.

Westport Golf Club's first Captain, W. Henry Darley Livingstone, sat on the judgement bench at the Westport Petty Sessions alongside J.C. Ryan R.M., The Earl of Altamont, Colonel Burke, Colonel Buchanan and Mr. Geo. Taylor. Cases he heard and gave judgement on were:

"Cart after sunset without a light, fine 6s with 5s costs."

"The King at the prosecution of the Head Constable, Cassidy, charged John Burns of Lecanvey with having his 6-day Licence open for sale of drink on Sunday evening, July 26th. Mr. Burns said it was pilgrimage day and people were exhausted from coming down the mountain."

The Old Age Pension Act was instituted in 1908. The problem for many Irish people was how to prove their age.

"Clear proof of the exact age is not possible in this country. Applicants should set down their correct ages to the best of their knowledge and belief. Afterwards they will be visited by the Pensions Officer."

The model T Ford:, a new mode of transport in 1908.

Means not over £21 per annum pension to be paid – 5s. Means not over £31 per annum pension to be paid – 1s. Lloyd George in the House of Commons stated 209,185 had applied for pensions in Ireland.

Transport by rail and sea was characterised by British efficiency, regularity and the philosophy of service to the public. The Western rail line was named the Midland Great Western Railway. It extended from Westport to Achill. Active consideration was given to the opening of a railway line to Rosmoney.

The line would branch off at Barley Hill from the Westport/ Newport line.

Every week the front page of the *Mayo News* carried advertisements for the Laird Line's regular sailings from Westport to Liverpool and Liverpool to Westport.

The White Star Line advertised sailings from Queenstown to New York by British Twin Screw Steamers. Westport Harbour was a very busy business environment.

W. Henry Darley Livingstone was a member of the Westport Harbour Commissioners along-side T.F.Ruttlege. He oversaw the extensive shipping activity at the Quay port. In 1908, 187 vessels of 19,917 tonnes entered the harbour.

A new mode of transport was also emerging. The *Mayo News* carried a news item detailing the killing of a dog in Tourmakeady by a motor carriage. Henry Ford had just begun mass production of the Model T Ford. Each car came off the line in 90 minutes and there was only one colour – black.

In 1908 sport was not a major leisure activity with mass participation. Sporting endeavours tended to be the preserve of the wealthy classes as only they could afford leisure time.

The *Mayo News* sporting reports at this time are very sparse indicating the absence of a sporting culture in society. Westport boasted a hockey club, sailing club , cricket club, soccer club, chess club. Tennis was played on private courts in high summer.

In high summer, also, a regatta took place at Rosmoney. Races were held at Murrisk and Louisburgh. The Louisburgh races received private subscriptions from Lord Sligo and Lady

Wilbraham of £1 each and 10 shillings from W.H.D. Livingstone.

"Westport versus South Mayo in a Ladies hockey match. The match was arranged by Irene Ruttledge." (Ms. Irene Ruttledge was a talented Westport lady golfer in 1915).

"Connacht Cup Hockey Final: Queens College, Galway (now N.U.I.G.) versus Westport."

"Clew Bay Sailing Club A.G.M. H.M. Anketell Jones, Hon.Sec. Burrishoole Lodge.

"Chess … Westport versus Castlebar."

The G.A.A. was in its infancy. One major match was newsworthy in the Sports page: "The Final match… Westport Croagh Patricks v Ballina Stephenite 29th of March at Westport. Special train from Ballina."

Game and Fishing were also leisure pursuits indulged in.

■ Trafalgar Park.

In 1908, W. Henry Darley Livingstone, John Christopher Garvey, Hugh McGonigal, A. J. Simpson, John Murray and P.E. Kelly added another gentlemanly leisure pursuit to sporting life in Westport when they established a golf club in Trafalgar Park.

Westport Golf Club was first listed in the *Irish Golfer's Guide* in 1910. The Guide reported on Westport Golf Club in 1911 as follows:

"Founded 1908. This nine holes inland course is 2.5 miles from Westport Station, M.G.W.R. , and is situated in Trafalgar Park. Hon.Secretary and Treasurer: A.J. Simpson, Bank of Ireland, Westport. Captain: W.H. Darley Livingstone.
Committee: J.C. Garvey; P.E.Kelly; John Murray; Hugh McGonigal.
Membership Fees: Men £1 1s; Ladies, 5s per annum; Family tickets: £2 2s. Membership-70.
Visitors Fees: 1s per day.
Bogey: 36.
Records: Professional, 33; Amateur, 36.
Sunday play allowed.
A short sporting course, with a good number of natural hazards."

Henry Darley
Livingstone,
Captain 1908

Trafalgar Park today is the area known as Horkan's Hill, The Paddock, Fr. Angelus Park and Deerpark East.

The term "bogey" had been used since the very early days of golf in the British Isles and in the 1960's was changed officially to "par".

Bogey now came to mean one stroke over par. The fact that the professional record is listed would indicate that a professional had visited Westport between 1908 and 1911 to teach the members and play the course.

Many courses at this time did not allow Sunday play.

Whitehead golf club, Co. Antrim and Woodenbridge golf club, Co. Wicklow, stated dogmatically:

"No Sunday play allowed".

Waterville G.C. Co. Kerry stated:

" Sunday play optional."

Alongside the report on Westport the Irish Golfer's Guide carried an advertisement for the:

"Portmarnock" Shoe-Best for golfing-
Best for walking-16s/6p".

The cost of this shoe was equivalent to the cost of golf membership for nine months of the year.

The same officers stayed in place until 1912 when Mr. A. J. Simpson became Captain. Thus the names listed from 1908 to 1912 are probably the inaugural officers of the Club.

■ The Course.

The location was within a ten-minute walk of the town centre.

The first hole started in Fr. Angelus Park and the 9th green finished on the Newport Road in the vicinity of the site of the late Jack Kenny's house.

The late Martin McGreal, butcher, Bridge St., drew a map of the course in Trafalgar Park and his recollection shows a nine-hole course criss-crossing O'Malley's field (now Fr. Angelus Park), the Paddock, McCormack's field, McGreal's field (now Conway Housing), Horkan's Hill and Blean's field.

There was no entry for Westport in the 1914 Irish Golf Guide. The club may have become defunct with the outbreak of World War 1.

In 1915 the Club was restarted when a nine-hole course was opened at Carrowholly, 3.5 miles north of Westport.

■ The Founding Fathers.

"The Livingstone family made Westport
and in my time it was a charm"
(J.C. Garvey, Captain 1934.)

Westport's first Captain, Henry Darley Livingstone, came from one of the most important families in Westport for most of the 19th and early 20th centuries.

His great grandfather Richard Livingstone gave birth to trade in Westport in 1800.

His grandfather, William Livingstone J.P. was the first chairman of Westport Town Commissioners.

Besides milling, brewing and distilling the Livingstones were large merchants and imported

large cargoes of grain. In 1830 their distillery was producing 60,000 gallons of whiskey per annum. By the mid 1850s they were operating three breweries, five flour mills, and numerous grain warehouses.

In 1852 one of the Livingstones and the 3rd Marquess of Sligo were asked to be provisional directors for the extension of the railway line to Westport.

In 1873 their landed property extended to 2,223 acres. The Livingstones built and owned Westport Lodge (Sacred Heart School and Rice College) before the Ruttledge family.

In 1894 Henry Darley's Uncle William died, unmarried and aged 61 years.

> "Carriages poured in from all directions.
> The trains brought their contingents of mourners and horsemen arrived from the country districts.
> All the shops in the town were closed and completely shuttered. 200 workmen of the deceased dressed in crapes and sashes.
> There were 110 carriages in the procession and it extended from the Quay into the town, over an English mile."

The *Mayo News* in reporting the funeral paid the following tribute to the Livingstone family:

> "Although differing widely from the great majority of their townsmen in religion and politics William and his father were elected year after year to first place on the Commissioners Board.
> Even in the most troublous times of political excitement there was never a suggestion that this mark of popular favour should be withheld from either of them."

Uncle William had travelled to all parts of the world. He was many times in Russia and the Holy Land.

He was a good linguist and whenever French or Italian sailors had occasion to appeal to the local courts in Westport he was sent for as their interpreter. The *Mayo News* praised his Christian concern for his workers:

> "He was a good friend to his employees.
> When a bad season turned in and people were thrown out of employment he gave them coal at about a quarter what it cost himself.
> When his men were disabled by any cause he paid their full wages.
> When any man got beyond his work he gave them a fair pension during his life."

■ The Guinness connection with Westport Golf Club.

At William's funeral amongst the chief mourners listed were Messrs George Darley Howard Guinness, Gerald Guinness, Mr. and Mrs. Robert Darley Guinness, Fitzwilliam Square. They sent a wreath of "arum lilies, maiden-hair and narcissus."

William's mother and our first captain's grandmother was Henrietta Mary Guinness sister of the late Sir Benjamin Guinness who established the famous brewery in Dublin.

On the death of uncle William the all absorbing question in the district was, " will the business be continued?"

In his will William left £1000 to his nephew Henry Darley Livingstone and £300 "for the increase and improvement of the supply of pure wholesome water for the town of Westport."

The £300 was finally spent in 1901 in making two wells at the Quay Rd. and Mill St.

In 1895 our first Captain's father, Henry Darley Livingstone, J.P., Belclare House, died suddenly aged 66 years.

He was educated at Trinity College, graduating with a B.A. Tributes were paid by the Westport Town Commissioners, Westport Board of Guardians, Westport Magistrates, Louisburgh Magistrates and the Westport Select Vestry. It was stated that it was "his anxious desire at all times to temper justice with mercy."

Wreaths were sent by Mr. and Mrs. Robert

Guinness and Mr. Richard Guinness, London. Amongst the chief mourners listed were Messrs G. Darley and Gerald Guinness (cousins).

■ The Family Values.

The family values thus enshrined in the character of our first Captain were public service to one's community, Christian justice and mercy on the Magistrates bench, Christian concern and charity towards one's employees, and a desire to make Westport a better community for all.

In 1903 our first Captain was appointed High Sheriff for Mayo County.

In 1904 he was a steward at the Achill races.

In 1905 he was on the committee for "Westport Athletic and Cycling Sports in Westport Demesne" (under G.A.A. and I.C.A. rules).

In 1905 he acted as a steward at the Rosmoney regatta. Here he had an interesting controversy to adjudicate on.

> "James Mulholland has lodged a claim to be declared the winner of the race for boats not exceeding 23ft. overall on the grounds that the boat which came in first fouled the turning mark and the men on board caught hold of it to assist the boat in rounding the post. He alleges that the winners also threw out ballast which in itself is enough to disqualify them."

In 1905 the Christian Brothers annual collection listed the following subscribers.

Marquis of Sligo – £3.00
Mrs. H.D. Livingstone – £2-2-0
J.C. Garvey, sol. – £2-2-0
H.McGonigal – £1-1-0
J.Murray, Ulster Bank – 10 shillings.

Ecumenism came naturally to people at this time.

In Feb. 1905 a sorrowful personal tragedy befell Henry Darley. His brother, Arthur Maurice Livingstone, Lieutenant 1st Battalion Connaght Rangers, was killed on the hunting field, aged 25 years and three months. He had fought in the South African War and was awarded the Kings Medal and Queens Medal. He loved hunting. Because of a damaged hand he had been advised not to ride. The horse stumbled approaching a wall throwing him and he fractured his skull on impact.

The *Westmeath Guardian* reported:

> "The meeting took place at Midleton Park, the residence of Mr. And Mrs. A. Boyd Rochford. Owing to his death the Westmeath Hunt Ball to be held at Knockdin Castle, residence of Sir Richard Levinge, has been abandoned."

In 1906, H.G. Black, auctioneer, advertised for sale the property of the Livingstone estate in 11 lots.

Lot 1: 4 x 2 storey slated houses, "The Artisans Dwellings" at Altamont St.
– withdrawn at £475

Lot 2: "The Scotch House" business premises in Centre Bridge St.

Lot 3: Premises in Bridge St.

Lot 4: 2 x houses at the Quay.
Best bid £65 – withdrawn.

Lot 5: Pub in North Mall, house and shop next door, pub in Castlebar St.– postponed.

Lot 6: House used as the "Methodist Manse", South Mall.
Sold to John Clampett for £275.

Lot7: 2 x houses on South side of Castlebar St.
Sold for £155

Lot 8: 2 x superior houses adjoining. Sold £199.

Lot 9: Premises in Bridge St.

Lot 10: "Bridge House" North Mall. Residence of the late Dr. Johnston, Medical Officer for Westport. The fountain on the Fairgreen was later erected in his memory. The house was described as having rooms "large, lofty and airy" with stabling for " 3 horses, 2 coach houses and a fowl house"- postponed.

Lot 11: Beautiful garden with entrance from South Mall formerly held by late Dr. Johnston. Sold for £220 to Richard O'Donnell.

In 1907 John McGreal, Lr. Bridge St., sued W.H.D. Livingstone for injuries received by negligence of his servant. He had been knocked down crossing the street at the present West Bar by a horse and carriage carrying Livingstone's commercial traveller. His traveller had just completed a long drive of 32 miles that day. J.C. Garvey appeared for W. H. D. Livingstone.

In evidence the horse was described as a thoroughbred and:

> "the horse that killed his master,
> young Mr. Livingstone."

In 1908 Henry Darley was a delegate from the Harbour Board to the All-Ireland Industrial Conference in Galway along with Ernest F. Hall.

In 1910 the town was shocked with the news that one of its oldest industries, the Livingstone Brewery, was closing owing to lack of support and the extra duty imposed by the budget. The Mineral Water Factory and the bottling of beer would continue.

Henry Darley wrote to Westport U.D.C. telling them "it was too late to think of re-opening the manufacture of stout and porter." But he would be prepared to consider same on guaranteed support by the traders of the town to the extent of 100 Kilderkins per week. He wrote that:

> "The more support we receive the larger
> number of men we can employ. The traders
> have in their own hands every means of
> supporting us in the mineral waters and
> bottled beer trade to enable us to employ
> a certain number of hands."

W. Doris M.P. Chairman: "I hope the name of Livingstone will not be wiped from the commercial life of Westport altogether. They are in it since Westport became Westport."

He proposed that the traders meet and decide to take a certain proportion of the stout.

J.Walsh: "In the interests of the town I would make the people that do not drink, drink Livingstone's stout and show good example." (laughter)

Chas. Hughes: "Anyone who was down in Cork at the exhibition would be surprised at the support for the local stout, Murphys. In a place like Westport one would imagine they would be able to give the same support."

Mr. Gilboy: "For the sake of labour the traders should support the Livingstone brewery."

However the brewery closed. Livingstones now advertised Guinness Stout and Guinness Extra Stout.

In 1913 Henry Darley knew all about the corporate mantra of 2008 of "being a team player and team bonding".

The *Mayo News* reported as follows:

"WESTPORT MINERAL WATER FACTORY FIRST EXCURSION"
Messrs. Wm. Livingstone Ltd. The brewery, Westport, afforded all their employees an excellent day's outing on Monday last, the Bank Holiday.

They were taken down the Bay in the two motor boats of the Messrs. Jeffers, Westport Railway Hotel. The whole party landed at Inishgort Lighthouse where a picnic was held, kindly provided by Mr. W. H. D. Livingstone, who accompanied his employees in his own motor boat. In the evening the excursionists went over the waters of Newport Bay to the Roigh Hotel where tea was served.

The party got back to Westport Quay about 8 o'clock in the evening after a most enjoyable trip with which all expressed themselves highly pleased."

The Mall, Westport 1908

Henry Darley continued to be conscious of the importance of Livingstones to the town.

In 1914 the *Mayo News* reported on "A Flourishing Mineral Water Factory."

"We notice for the past few months Messrs. Wm. Livingstone Ltd. have added, on an extensive scale, to their Mineral Water plant. They have expended a big amount of money on machinery of the latest and most up-to-date type which includes an expensive "Rotary Filler", capable of filling 100 dozen bottles per hour.

They have also purchased a splendid Thornycroft Motor Lorry which in itself is quite a novelty in the district and enables them to deliver the mineral waters far inland with only a few hours notice.

We congratulate them on their appointment of Mr. P. S. Joyce as a commercial traveller (member of handicap committee in 1917) and compliment them on having an able and courteous manager in the person of Mr. G. F. Durdin. We further congratulate them on behalf of the general public for their strenuous exertions in trying to keep industry alive in Westport."

It is evident then that our first Captain kept faith with the long engrafted traditions of his family in his service to his community, his concern for his employees and his dedication to the well-being of Westport.

■ The Livingstone Brothers and the Great War.

When World War One started in 1914 Henry Darley then decided to serve his country. He joined as a private shortly after war was declared and was promoted to captain. His regiment was the Northumberland Fusiliers.

In May 1915 sorrowful tragedy was to visit the Livingstone family once more. His young brother Harold Gordon Livingstone was killed on the 3rd of May near Ypres.

Harold was the youngest son of Henry Darley and Mary Christina Livingstone. His memorial is in the Duhallow Ads Cemetery, Ypres, Belgium. Grave ref: V11. A. 19. (Mayo Comrades of the Great War). Harold had been educated at Summerfields, Oxford and Harrow. He returned from the Argentine in January to offer his services to his country. He was given a commission in the Royal Field Artillery on 3rd of February.

He had just completed his 34th year.

His Major wrote the following to his mother Mrs. H. D. Livingstone, Belclare House:

> "I hope you will allow me to say how much not only we officers, but also the men of the battery, regret the loss of your boy and how much he had made his mark in the short time he was with us. The battery was shelled very heavily on the morning of the 3rd of May and your boy was struck in the head by a bullet from a shell. He lies buried near the road between Vlanertingh and Ypres, not far from the village of Brielen. We mourn the loss of a good comrade and gallant soldier."

Henry Darley was serving with the Motor Machine Gun Service at the time and he was under immediate orders for the front. Consequently his marriage took place earlier than intended. On the 14th of May 1915 he married Adelaide Lord, only daughter of the late Charles Davol Stickney and Mrs. Sutherland Orr, of Taunton, Mass. U.S.A. The marriage took place very quietly by special licence, at Holy Trinity Church, Brompton, and the bride was given away by General Sir Charles Parsons. The ceremony was performed by his uncle, Canon R.G. Livingstone, Rector of Brinkworth, in the presence of a few relatives.

Try to imagine the rollercoaster of emotions Henry Darley must have been going through at this time in his life. He was lamenting the death of his brother Harold only eleven days earlier. He had been ordered to the frontline and he was anxious to be loved and to love before going over the top. Picture his short time with his new bride and then the inevitable march to the front and possibly the same fate as Harold.

In 1918 his brother Guy Livingstone was honoured by the French Government:

> "The French Government have made Commander Guy Livingstone a Chevalier of the Legion of Honour for sinking a submarine in the Mediterranean and bringing his convoy to safety. Mr. Livingstone is second son of the late Mr. Henry Livingstone, Belclare House, Westport."

■ The world of Westport in 1918.

When the war was over Henry Darley came home to Westport and quietly resumed his seat on the Petty Sessions Bench under his military title, Capt. H.D. Livingstone.

He came home to a Westport world unrecognisable to him politically and socially.

Sinn Fein had triumphed in the 1918 general election winning 73 seats and in the process destroying the Home Rule Party. Every town and village in Mayo had a Sinn Fein Club. The *Mayo News* carried a regular column headed "Sinn Fein News".

> "Edward Moane, Carrabawn (later a T.D.), was arrested and sent to Sligo Jail for 6 weeks on a charge under the Defence of the Realm Act, for singing a song at a concert in Cushlough into which the words, "Up Sinn Fein", were alleged to have been introduced. Mr. Moane held he committed no criminal act."

There was to be no hero's welcome for Henry Darley. No trumpets sounded to honour a returning brave soldier. Although fighting in the Great War for four years and surviving he was seen not as a courageous soldier who had fought for his country as he understood his country to be but rather as someone who had fought for the enemy – Britain.

His mother went to live in Eastbury Manor, Compton, Surrey. Every year without fail up to 1923 she sent £2-2-0 to the annual Christian Brothers collection in Westport.

In June 1923 Henry Darley instructed Wm. Morrisson, auctioneer, Westport and Castlebar to sell by public auction the "Antique and Modern Furniture" of Belclare Lodge.

Westport, Mayo and Ireland had been in political and violent uproar since 1919 with the Black and Tan War and the Civil War. It would appear that like many others of his class Henry Darley had decided to vacate Ireland.

Livingstones mineral waters continued to be advertised in the *Mayo News* until 1933.

The family fortune went into decline in the

early 20th century, due to the demise of Westport harbour and taxation on alcohol.

> "The Livingstones had a whiskey distillery on what is now Distillery Road and a brewery on Bridge Street (now Cosy Joe's). Mr. Livingstone lived in Belclare House and drove a Landau (carriage), fully attired with two horses and liveried horsemen."
> (John Kelly , capt. 1958)

In 1918, W.H.D. Livingstone's only sister, Mary Henrietta (called after her mother and grand-mother) married the Laird of Elderslie, A. A. Speirs, Renfrewshire, Scotland. This Laird leased the land to Elderslie G.C. for their course in 1908. The officers of Elderslie purchased the course, a total of 212 acres, for £125,000 in July 1980.

The pulpit in Holy Trinity Church Westport reads:

> "To the glory of God and in the memory of Henry Darley Livingstone of Belclare."

In 1935 Henry Darley's uncle, Canon. R.G. Livingstone, Rector of Brinkworth for nearly 40 years died aged 98. *The Wilts and Gloucestershire Standard* described him as "England's Oldest Clergyman".

The report stated he never permitted sectarian matters to sway his decision in questions of parochial interest. An extra bell for the Tower of the Church in perpetuation of the Rector's memory was installed bearing the inscription:

> "Given by the parishioners of Brinkworth to commemorate the good work done by Canon Livingstone in this parish."

The Canon's death inspired the following appreciation in the *Mayo News* from J.C. Garvey. Mr Garvey is described by the paper as " a highly respected solicitor in Mayo."

The editor states about the Livingstones:

> "Their passing was a great blow to the prosperity of Westport District and one from which it has never recovered and we endorse every word Mr. Garvey says about them."

Mr. Garvey titled his appreciation, "The Great Livingstone Family":

> "I am an old Westport man and I fear there are few residents in the West who remember the Livingstone family.
>
> When I was a boy I remember Mr. William Livingstone, senior, and his wife who was a member of the distinguished Guinness family. I knew all the sons, Arthur, Richard, Robert, William, George and Henry. One and all were distinguished scholars. I am certain Robert was the most distinguished as early in life he took a scholarship and later a fellowship in classics at Oxford University.
>
> He visited his parents frequently at Westport and often preached in the old and new churches. He always dwelt upon the value of friendship between all creeds and classes and there was not a particle of guile in his spirit. Like myself, he loved the West of Ireland and could talk of Clew Bay, Croaghpatrick and the drive along by the shore to Louisburgh with a freshness and vigour that delighted me. William his brother was a distinguished business man and a fine linguist.
>
> I remember him when he was asked to interpret the evidence of a Spanish crew who could not speak a word of English. A claim was made for salvage which ran into enormous figures and he interpreted the evidence just as if he had been a native of Spain. The Livingstone family made Westport and in my time it was a charm. I hope the memory of that good and great name will be preserved in honour and respect."

The chief mourners listed were:
Miss Isobel Livingstone (daughter);
Mrs. Hagart Spiers (niece/ Henry Darley's sister);
Sir Richard Livingstone (Master of Corpus College, Oxford),
Commander Livingstone,
Captain W.H. Darley Livingstone (nephews);
Mr. Henry Guinness and Mr. Howard Guinness (cousins).

The legacy Westport G.C.'s First Captain bestowed was duty and service to one's society and courage in the face of adversity.

■ Hugh McGonigal, solicitor.

A native of Belfast. He lived in Rosbeg. His father-in-law was A.B. Kelly, "father of the Mayo Bar", Seapoint House, Rosbeg. The main office of the firm was in Castlebar but an office was opened at the Octagon.

Hugh McGonigal was an all-round accomplished sportsman. He played cricket, tennis, soccer and hockey. He also appears to be an originator having presided and served at the inaugural meetings of the soccer and hockey clubs. Considering his prowess with the cricket bat and hockey stick, swinging a brassie or mashie would have attracted his sporting enthusiasm.

In 1894 he presided at the inaugural meeting of the Westport Association Football Club.

> "The inaugural general meeting of the above club was held on Friday evening, Mr. H. McGonigal, presiding. The getting of a suitable field was the chief topic. Committee: Messrs H. McGonigal (chairman). The meeting was a pronounced success from every point of view."

In the same year he played for the Westport Cricket Club v Castlebar. The visitors were victorious in a single innings by 40 to 30. He was the highest scorer on the Westport team with 9 runs. J. Murray was also on the team and he contributed 7 runs.

In 1896 v Ballinrobe Cricket Club the match report stated:

> "McGonigal (capt.) continued to score at a very rapid rate and his play was a treat to witness. Nothing could be more perfect than his leg hits and forward drives and although 6 or 7 different bowlers were tried he treated them all in the same fashion."

In 1897 he played in the Connacht Cricket final. He also starred as a principal contributor in the match v Captain Binghams X1. "The members of the Westport team were entertained to a splendid dinner in the Railway Hotel by the members of Captain Binghams X1 and full justice was done to Mrs. Gibbons excellent table. Music then became the order of the evening with the piano in the capable hands of Messrs. Kilkelly, McHugh and McCormack."

In 1898, H. McGonigal and J. Murray were present at the inaugural meeting of the Hockey Club. "A very largely attended meeting to form a Hockey Club in Westport was held on Saturday last in the News Room. An executive committee was formed and judging by its character the club is certain to be a success. President; E.F.Hall. Vice-Presidents: Messrs. Rev. Mr. Dobbyn, Murray and Counsel. (agent for Bank of Ireland) Committee; McGonigal, Kilkelly, Palmer, Obre, and H. Gallagher. Mr. Hall has kindly given the use of his field for the game and the first practice will take place next week."

In the high summer of 1900, H. McGonigal, J. Murray, J. C. Garvey played in a tennis tournament in Rosbeg. From the names one can picture the charming world of social intercourse inhabited by our founding fathers.

"A very enjoyable American tournament was played off on the 14th and 16th August on the grounds of Seapoint and Summerville, which were kindly placed at the disposal of the players by their respective owners, Mrs. Alfred B. Kelly and Mrs. Yelverton who were: "At Home" to a large number of their friends on above date. The final of the gentleman's singles were played off on Mr. Murray's court on the 25th August."

The following played in the Mixed Doubles;
J.Murray and Miss Garvey – scratch.
Dr. Ellison and Miss R. Garvey, – minus 15;
Rev. J. Collins and Mrs. Yelverton – plus15;
Canon Taylor and Miss Ray – plus 30;
Also competed: S. Hodder and Miss Morse, Rev. J. O. Hannay (writer under the pen name George Bermingham) and Mrs. Vereker; H. Yelverton and Mrs. Murray; H. McGonigal and Mrs. W. B. Kelly; O. Milling and Miss Powell; Mr. Loughlin and Miss Ellison; John C. Garvey and Mrs. Johnston.

In June 1902 Hugh McGonigal received his solicitor's parchment.

"At final exam for apprentices seeking admission as solicitors 37 passed. Mr. Hugh McGonigal of Seapoint House took second place and was awarded a Gold Medal by the Court of Examiners. He served his apprenticeship to his father-in-law, Mr. Alfred B. Kelly, County Solicitor."

In April 1903 he applied for the position of Coroner for West Mayo. Four candidates appeared before the meeting of Mayo County Council: E. Barry, sol; J. Kelly J.P., H. McGonigal and T. F. Kirwan. (Barry, Kelly and McGonigal were members of Westport G.C.)
A statement was made about Hugh McGonigal by one of the Councillors present:

"I have found more kindness and charity and justice done me by Mr. McGonigal than any of the solicitors in Mayo."

He was defeated by J.Kelly by 11 votes to 9.
In January 1912 The *Mayo News* reported his death:

"POPULAR SOLICITOR DEAD"
"Close on a year ago he contracted an illness which was fated to carry him away. He underwent an operation for catarrh. He went to Brighton, England, to seek to recuperate but that dread reaper, death, claimed him there. He leaves a young widow and children."

■ John Christopher Garvey, solicitor.
He was admitted as a solicitor in 1901. His family seat was at Murrisk Abbey estate.
In Feb. 1900 he played hockey for Connacht in the Interprovincials v Leinster. He played forward. He was an avid shooter and his passion was fishing. He kept records in his Game and Fishing Book from 1901 to 1938.
In August 1900 he played in the tennis tournament in Rosbeg.

In 1909 he married Miss Gladys Maud Baker, only daughter of Lieutenant-Colonel Richard Baker of Treenlaur Westport.

The society wedding took place in St. Ann's Church, Dawson St. Dublin.

> "A large portion of the seating accommodation of the church was reserved for invited guests. The bride was accompanied by five bridesmaids – Miss Osborne, Miss Moorhead, Miss Mason, Miss Marie Tomkins and Miss E. Pryor. Her two little trainbearers were Miss Beatrice Warren and Miss Ursula Greer.
>
> The bride wore a lovely gown of white satin souple, trimmed with opal and pearl embroidery and veil of old Limerick lace draped over an orange blossom wreath. Her bouquet was of white heather and stephanotis.
>
> The gifts of the bridegroom to the bridesmaids were Tara brooches. Mr. Henry Darley Livingstone attended the bridegroom. A reception was held in the Royal Hibernian Hotel at which 150 guests attended. The bride and bridegroom left in the afternoon for England en route for the Italian Lakes where the honeymoon will be spent."

In 1911 the Murrisk Horse Races and Sports were held on the Garvey Estate grounds. Permission was kindly given by F.C. Garvey, Murrisk Abbey for this longstanding tradition. The Brass Band of the Westport Temperance Sodality was present.

In the 1st race J. Garvey's "Good Boy" came 2nd (4 runners). In the 2nd race J. Garvey's "Good Boy" came 1st (4 runners).

In July 1912 J. C. Garvey's personal troubles were sensational news. The Lord Chancellor charged him with unprofessional conduct in connection with certain probate proceedings. The Lord Chancellor made an order striking Mr. Garvey's name off the Roll of Solicitors. His Lordship said it was a painful case but it was his absolute duty to the public and the honourable profession of solicitors.

In March 1919 John C. Garvey was re-admitted as a solicitor of the High Court of Justice in Ireland:

> "We understand that owing to pressure of his farming business he cannot for a week or so open an office but he can be consulted at his residence, Murrisk. Mr. Garvey will be practicing in Westport and Castlebar within the next fortnight."
> (*Mayo News,* March 29th, 1919)

In 1933 J. C. Garvey was Deputy Coroner for South Mayo and in 1935 he was Deputy Coroner for West Mayo.

■ A.J. Simpson, Bank of Ireland.

Mr A. J. Simpson, who was sub-agent in the bank, was promoted to agent in 1909 on the transfer of Mr J. A. Brabazon to Dundalk.

In 1911, Mr. Simpson was called to give evidence against a man accused of obtaining the pension under false pretences. The defendant had claimed a pension on the basis that he had only £200 in the Bank. It was discovered by the Revenue Officer in Westport that he had in fact £980 in the Bank. Mr. Simpson when called stated he had sworn an oath not to reveal details of any mans account.

In June 1912, A. J. Simpson was transferred on promotion to Arklow. He was replaced by H. Yelverton who came from Athlone .

■ John Murray, Ulster Bank.

John Murray was manager of the Ulster Bank in 1895. He played cricket, tennis and soccer. He was a member of the Select Vestry.

In July 1919 he died at the Bank House, the Mall, Westport and internment took place in the Westport Protestant Cemetery. He was for 25 years manager of the Ulster Bank and for many years previously he was in Westport as cashier.

> "He leaves a widow and three children to mourn his loss. The massive oak coffin was supplied by Mr. Thomas Navin, Mill St. Westport."

■ Phillip E. Kelly.

Altamont St. Lance-Corporal, 9th North Irish Horse (Royal Irish Fusiliers). His wife was

Elizabeth Constance Louise Kelly, Fairmount House, Mount Vale, York. Phillip was killed in action on the October 10th 1918 aged 29 years.

His memorial is in Dadizeele New British Cemetery, Moorslede, West-Vlaanderen, Belgium. Grave ref: 11.D. 8. (from, " Mayo Comrades of the Great War ")

On October 19th 1918 the *Mayo News* reported the following:

"In the war casualties published during the week we regret very much to observe the name of Colonel Philip E.Kelly who was killed in action in France commanding the 9th Batt. Royal Irish Fusiliers.

He was the only son of the late Mr. Wm. E. Kelly, J.P., D.L. of St. Helens, Rosbeg, Westport.

He was grandson of the late Venerable Archdeacon Cather, Rector, Westport.

Colonel Kelly was a young man of great promise. Early in the present war he won the Military Cross and time after time he was mentioned in dispatches.

He was wounded in Suvla Bay and afterwards in France.

His afflicted mother, Edith May, has the sincere sympathy of the people of his and her native place."

His father was Mr. William E. Kelly D. L., J.P. St. Helens, Rosbeg, Westport.

His father built St. Helens. Later it was the residence of McCormacks.

His father had a brilliant career in London University and then worked as Assistant Engineer to the C. W. Railway of England. When he returned to Ireland he worked as an engineer in the Public Works Department.

He was owner of considerable landed property in West Mayo: "In the most troublous times his relations with his tenants were not unfriendly."

He was member of the Westport Harbour Board where his engineering expertise was invaluable. He was appointed High Sheriff of Mayo in 1898. In 1901 he was made a Deputy Lieutenant.

■ **The impetus towards a golf club.**
Hugh McGonigal, J. C. Garvey, John Murray and P. E. Kelly were active sportsmen playing cricket, hockey, soccer and tennis.

There is no evidence in any sporting reports that W. H. D. Livingstone played cricket or hockey. He more than likely played tennis as tennis nets and equipment were listed as auction items from his house in 1923.

Henry Darley would also be au fait with the sporting world from his stewarding duties at various meets. However it would seem more probable that the impetus to establish a Golf Club would have come from the cricket and hockey players, McGonigal, Murray and Garvey.

In 1914 R. H. Laing, was playing in goal and later at half-back on the Westport hockey team. He was a member of the committee that moved golf to Old Carrowholly in 1915. Mr. W. Edge was playing forward on the hockey team in 1914. He won the first competition held in Old Carrowholly in 1915. It would appear that hockey players became avid golfers.

Thus it maybe that the founding of the Westport Hockey Club in 1898 was to lead eventually to the playing of golf in Westport.

Due to the standing of Henry Darley and the Livingstone family in the community along with the close personal friendships he enjoyed with these men in business and social life he was the obvious choice to be the first Captain of Westport Golf Club.

Just six names from Westport G.C. were listed in the Irish Golf Guide in 1911. Now these pages resound with the self-belief, courage and philosophy of H.D.Livingstone, H. McGonigal, J. Murray, J. C. Garvey, A. J. Simpson and P. E. Kelly. Their imperative echoes through the years:

"Leave a trail in life for others to follow."

Let us celebrate the memory of these men and the world they inhabited. Let us keep faith with their values and outlook on life .

Let us look forward to the next 100 years of golf in Westport with courage in our hearts and vision in our imaginations.

5th Hole

3rd Hole

4th Hole

7th Hole

6th Hole

8

SCHEMATIC LAYOUT OF THE OLD GOLF COURSE AT CARROWHOLLY, WESTPORT.

Chapter 2

PLAYING THE *Kilroy*

GOLF IN OLD CARROWHOLLY

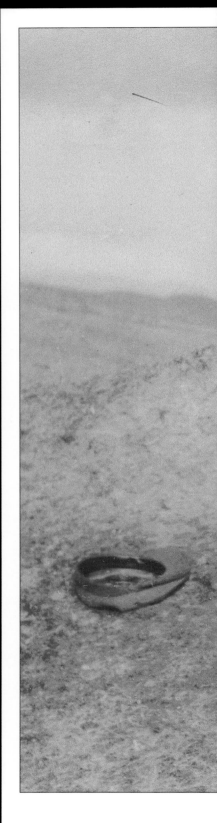

Harry Vardon: He started an explosion of enthusiasm for golf.
PICTURE: SOUTH HERTS GOLF CLUB

■ The Inaugural Meeting

When R.H. (Henri) Laing, F.I.O., Sight Testing Expert, "The Blue Spectacles", Centre Bridge Street, Westport, opened his *Mayo News* on February 6th, 1915 he read about "Peace Vigils" in Balla and Newport. He read the Erris Notes and the presentation to Harry Walshe who was going for training before proceeding to the war front. He read the hearty wish expressed, that Harry and the other gallant fellows who left Erris to back Culture against Kultur, would be spared to return.

But none of these news items really attracted Henri. What excited him and made his heart beat faster was the heading, "Proposed Golf Club for Westport and District."

The advertisement went on to state that a Public Meeting would be held on Tuesday the 9th at 8pm in The Railway Hotel and all who would like to join were invited to attend.

Henri knew plenty about this game of golf. He had read about Francis Quimet, the first Amateur to win the U.S.Open in 1913. Quimet had defeated his hero, Harry Vardon, by five shots.

Henri knew about Vardon and the effect his American visit in 1900 had on golf. Vardon had started an explosion of enthusiasm for this most interesting and healthy game. Henri knew the history of the "Vardon Flyer" golf ball. Spaldings had called it the "Spalding Wizard" but then they

A group of Westport golfers enjoying a day out in Mulranny in 1921:
Back row: B. McGing (High Street), J. Gibbons (North Mall), 2 caddies, G & B Ryan (Castlebar).
Front Row: L. Staunton, Banker, M. McGing, B. Staunton.

realised the importance of marrying a sports product to a glamorous name.

He knew that the "Vardon Flyer" had been overcome by the "Haskell" ball which was livelier and flew further than the guttie. It gave distance and accuracy. Even a mis-hit brought results. He knew that there was no limit to size or weight of the ball used. Some professionals favoured a small heavy ball for driving into the wind while others chose a larger and lighter ball for downwind.

Sometimes when the shop was quiet Henri would rhyme to himself:

" Brassie, Niblick, Mashie,
Niblick, Mashie, Brassie ! "

He loved to say these words. He knew what they stood for. The Brassie was a fairway 2-wood that got its name from the Brass sole plate that protected it from wear. The Niblick was used for the short game (today's wedge). The Mashie was a mid-iron club (the equivalent of the modern 5 iron.)

Henri Laing loved colourful and exciting change. After all he spelt his name Henri, ending with the exotic "i" rather than plain and dull "y". He loved the name he had given to his business, "The Blue Spectacles", because he felt it was a name that best reflected his character. Henri loved to be original. This new game had captured his imagination. He dreamt of hitting a Haskell with a thunderous brassie or a strong mashie or delicately with a niblick .

He was not going to miss this meeting for anything.

When he read his *Mayo News* on February 13th he had the pleasure of seeing his name listed on the committee to act. The attendance had been large and representative and all present had shown a keen interest in the object of the meeting. When he looked around the room he recognised, H. Yelverton, John Kelly, solicitor, Edmund Barry, solicitor, H. G. Black, Patrick Jeffers, P. Tennant, J. Allisser, Postmaster, A. O' Cooper, W. H. Palmer and many more. The first business had been to elect a committee to act. He had been selected unanimously to serve alongside, H. Yelverton, John Kelly, H. J. McTernan, solicitor, F. Gill, P. Jeffers, and W. H. Palmer.

Then they had proceeded to the election of officers. H. J. McTernan, solr. was their choice of Captain. Henri had been proposed for Secretary but declined in favour of J. C. Dudgeon, D.I. The Hon. Treasurer would be A. O' Cooper. They had no lands as yet but hope was high that the club would be in full swing by the end of the month. Henri with the other members would look for the most suitable land for the links.

■ The Suitable Land

By the 6th of March 1915 Henri had already used his brassie, mashie and niblick on the new links. They had found the land very quickly. It was situated about three-and-a-half miles from Westport in the village of Carrowholly. Transport would be a slight problem but once the Minister's Hill was cleared by bicycle it would be practically downhill all the way.

He agreed to use his shop window to post notices about competitions. Until they had their clubhouse they would use the Landlord's House, Mr. T. Ingham, as their base. He loved the course.

Mr. Sullivan, professional, late of Ballybunion and Dollymount, had laid out a course which though a trifle short had everyones approval. From a golfing point of view it would be hard to beat the 2nd, 7th and 8th holes (the Quarry at 8th making a magnificent natural hazard).

Henri adored the scenic view from the 4th and the 5th. They commanded beautiful views of the Holy Hill and the bay. Mr. Sullivan had eliminated the difficulty at the 6th hole and the green could now be reached in three or four shots. This was a great improvement on the first suggested lie for this hole. The 1st, 2nd, 6th, 7th, 8th and 9th greens were now marked out and the work of fencing had begun.

Already there was an excellent six-hole course ready for play. It was very sporting and the turf after a little attention would make an excellent golfing sod. A large number of members had already been out despite the bad weather. Henri was looking forward to the first competition but there would be one major difficulty to overcome. How do you apply handicaps when no one has played the game on this course before?

■ The First Competition

Henri enjoyed reading his *Mayo News* on the 10th of April. They had made a good job of fixing the handicaps as the results returned showed. The first competition had been a stroke sweepstake held on Easter Monday. The course had been in good order but Henri had found the greens at the 3rd, 4th and 5th a trifle erratic. He felt that the finest professional ever born would have had to allow himself three putts per green. No

Michael J Henehan, Captain 1923.

one was surprised at the liberal scores returned. Some of the cards had made interesting reading. Double figures at the 2nd, 3rd and 6th holes were quite fashionable. The winner, Mr. W. Edge with a net score of 94, was congratulated on two consistent rounds. They hoped to hold other competitions shortly and Henri would post details on his windows.

The next competition was a Men's eclectic stroke competition and it was held on Monday 12th of April. The winner was Mr. P. Jeffers with an eclectic score of 39. Mr Edge was second with 41.

Henri loved posting the notices on his window. Members would come in to leave their names with him or to enquire about the next competition. Everyone was bursting with enthusiasm.

Miss Trixie Yelverton, Miss Ruttledge, Miss Barry and Miss Jeffers were regular callers. They would converse about Hickory Drivers, the Vardon grip or Miss Ruttledge's score of 93 which had so far beaten any of the efforts of the men.

He knew he was going to miss all these conversations when the course closed to members from the 1st of May until the end of September. In the meantime there was one more competition to look forward to. Great improvement in the play of beginners had been noticed since these competitions had started. Henri felt his own game had come on. In particular he was now hitting his

mashie really well. He was looking forward to the singles matchplay.

Henri's improvement at this new game was there for all to read in the *Mayo News* of the 1st of May. The report stated that the men's matchplay for 1st and 2nd prizes had been concluded on Wednesday. The final was fought between Mr. R. H. Laing and Mr. Kenneth Murray. Mr. Murray won on the 17th green by 2 and 1. The memory of this battle would have to sustain Henri until October. All he could do until then was to recite his favourite rhyme over and over:

"Brassie, Niblick, Mashie,
Niblick, Mashie, Brassie. "

In roughly 80 days the course had been found, laid out and five competitions played. Henri felt proud of their achievements. But now there would be no golf until October. How did Henri and the Yelvertons, Mr. Edge and Miss Ruttledge pass May. June, July, August and September, the best golfing months weatherwise? How their collective hearts must have pined for fairways and greens under the Holy Hill and with a view of the bay !

In January 1916 an Eclectic competition concluded. The inclement weather prevented the competition from being carried out on St. Stephen's Day. Members were allowed to send in returns when completed. The handicaps were a special club handicap. Mr. P. D. Rees won the Gentlemen's with a good net of 38.

P. D. Rees 45–7 =38; M. J. Quinn 49–7.5 = 41.5; W. J. Edge 47–4=43; L. Murray 45–scr. = 45; J. C. Cuddy 58–11 = 47; K. Murray 51–3 = 48; H. Yelverton 50–2 = 48; R. H. Laing 56–7 = 49; J.C. Dudgeon 50–scr = 50; Rev. Father Owens also competed."

The Annual General Meeting for the election of officers for the ensuing season was held on Saturday 29th of January 1916 in the Railway Hotel.

"Members who did not enter on the 1st of October last are reminded that the subscriptions for the season are due and payable on the 1st. February to the Hon. Treasurer, Mr. W. H. Palmer."

The following officers were elected for the second season beginning on the 1st. of February.

Captain: Mr. H. J. McTernan; Hon. Sec. Mr. H. Yelverton; Asst. Sec. Mr. J. E. Cuddy; Hon. Treas. Mr. W. H. Palmer.

Committee: Messrs. John Kelly, P. S. Joyce, F. Gill, P. Jeffers, R. H. Laing and W. Edge.

"It was arranged that a professional be engaged for the next three months. A handicapping committee was also elected to consist of Messrs. P. S. Joyce; W. Edge; P. Jeffers and the Hon. Sec. Some new members were elected. The prospects of the club appear to be well assured and the number of players should steadily increase for this healthy and attractive game which has "caught on" so well here."

In February 1916 Medal competitions by match play for Ladies and Gentlemen were arranged with an entrance fee of 1s. Play to begin Tuesday 15th of February. Unfortunately the competitions had to be postponed on account of the very bad weather conditions.

It was announced that the club "has secured the services of a first class professional, Mr. W. Mahony, who will give instructions to members from Saturday the 19th inst."

In March 1916 the second competition for men to be decided by match play on revised handicaps was advertised.

"Intending competitors are requested to kindly send in their names with an entry fee of 1s."

In March 1917 Mr. John Kelly was elected Captain and the other officers from 1916 were re-elected. The Committee also remained the same.

"It was decided to hold a stroke competition on St. Patricks Day. Entrance fee 2s 6d. Mr. Laing is kindly presenting a medal. Some new members were elected."

The results of the Stroke Competition on St. Patrick's Day were as follows:

"There was a good entry of 15. Mr. Cuddy won with a good round of 92.

J. E. Cuddy 92-32 =60; Jas. Kelly 96-32=64; P. S. Joyce 97-30=67; W. H. Palmer 101-34=67; W. Edge 101-32=69; M. J. Quinn 101-32=69; John Kelly 111- 40=71; H. Yelverton 103-26=77; H. W. Knox 113-36=77; P. Jeffers 120-40=80; W. Warren 130-46=84; R. H. Laing 126-34=92."

In April 1917 the Captain, John Kelly, donated a prize for a competition at Easter. "The proceeds of the competition to be devoted to the funds of the club. Members entering will be notified when they are expected to play and cards will be left with the caretaker, Mr. Joyce."

In October 1917 The *Mayo News* announced,

" The Links were open for play on the 1st of October. New members may join from that date for the season. They will kindly communicate with the Hon. Secretary, Mr. H. Yelverton."

In February 1919 the Club engaged a professional once more.

"A professional has been engaged and will be in attendance on the Links daily (weather permitting) on and after Tuesday 4th of February for one month. An hour's lesson will be given for 1s 6d. Any member wishing to take a lesson must first produce a ticket from the Hon. Sec. or Mr. R.H. Laing. A ticket will be good for one lesson only. Signed. A.J.W. Moore, Hon. Sec. Westport, 31st Jan 1919."

In September 1919 a valuable prize for a competition to be held immediately was presented by Mr. P. J. O'Malley. The entrance fee 2s 6d. It was also open to ladies.

In 1927 The Club organised a sweep on the Manchester November Handicap in aid of the Club. The first prize, £15, was won by Mr. R. H. Laing.

"It is gratifying to note that the first prize was won by a very popular Westport man."

The Clubhouse pavilion 1927.

The 2nd prize, £10, Supt. O'Dwyer, Castlebar. 3rd prize , £5, Miss C. Maxwell, Longford.

In 1931 R. H. Laing supplied cups and tankards for prizes in Westport G.C.

His bill to the Club for same came to, £18, £23-10-7 and £21-3-4. In 1932 cups from R. H. Laing cost £22-1-5 and prizes for Ladies Day cost £1-1-0.

Inspired by the game Henri had added this service to his sight-testing business.

In 1934 Westport G.C purchased cups from Pringle and Son costing £19-11-5.

What had happened to R. H. Laing?

What we do know is that in 1915 golf was played in Old Carrowholly and R. H. (Henri) Laing contributed a verse.

■ Old Carrowholly

From 1915 until 1973 golf was to be enjoyed in Old Carrowholly by countless numbers. The values enshrined by Henri and the founding fathers were voluntary effort, generous giving, fun competitions, laughter, music, dance, club spirit, social interaction and the game played in the right spirit.

Golf was not business. It was a pure leisure pursuit but its pleasures were not to be kept secret. Beginners were actively pursued, nurtured and guided. Beginners were observed as vital to the future well-being of the club. The future would bring closures and re-openings, interference from wars and regular financial pressures. The members of Old Carrowholly smiled and laughed through everything. Golf had to be played and would be played. If someone was worried about the finances the reply might be:

"The financial position, in the absence of details, is satisfactory."(1958)

Old Carrowholly would become a true members club. Voluntary effort became second nature. The members united in their desire to play the game and enjoy themselves.

They tolerated cattle, sheep and the odd horse on the fairways but their greens were sacred. They were fenced for protection and minded like jewels. Not a year went by but the lawnmower would be sent to Dublin for repair.

Costello, the travelling itinerant, would be hired to sharpen the mower. Difficulties with the landlord would be sorted by their solicitor or a deputation which would include a priest.

Did Henri Laing foresee all this when he attended the meeting on February 9th for the purpose of establishing a Golf Club for Westport? Did he foresee the values enshrined would eventually lead to the New Championship Course in 1973? Robert Frost, the American poet, knew about a beginning and the subsequent journey when he wrote:

" Yet knowing how way leads on to way."
(Road Not Taken)

World War One may have interfered with golf in Old Carrowholly and the club may have closed because the *Connaught Telegraph* reported on August 2nd 1919 that:

"The new Links are now open for play. Intending competitors for stroke competition should apply for cards to the Hon. Secretary. Entrance fee, 1 shilling. All Cards to be handed in on or before Monday 4th of August."

There are no further reports to be found until 1926. Golf was played between 1919 and 1926. Mr. Dan McGing won the Captain's Prize in 1923 when the Captain was Mr. Michael J. Henehan.

Historical events in Ireland would certainly have impinged on the activity. The Black and Tan War 1919-1921 and the Civil War would certainly have interfered with golf.

The dangerous society of that time is borne out by the testimony of J.C. Garvey solicitor (Captain 1934). He turned down the post of "Crown Solicitor" in Mayo in 1921 on the basis:

"Better a live J.C.Garvey than a dead Crown Solicitor."

There is no doubt but the Club existed. This is borne out by an advertisement in the *Mayo News* on July 3rd 1926 stating that a:

"General meeting of this club will be held at the Railway Hotel on Tuesday 6th of July 1926 at 8 o'clock sharp."

The notice was signed by A. W. Fanning, Hon. Sec, (pro-tem) (for the time being).

In August a notice in the *Mayo News* informed the public that:

"Course in Carrowholly is now open for play. Subscriptions should be sent to Geo. Tobin, Esq. Hon. Treas. M &L Bank, Westport."

This would indicate a re-opening. The notice was supported by a news item which referred to the growing popularity of golf.

" The Links at Carrowholly are now open for play. The situation of the Links is ideal.
Like all Clubs in their infancy funds are needed and as Westport has hitherto been in the background as regards facilities for playing this game of world-wide popularity we hope that the club will very soon be prosperous.
We commend membership to all, young and old, desirous of a clean and sporting form of recreation amidst the healthiest of surroundings."

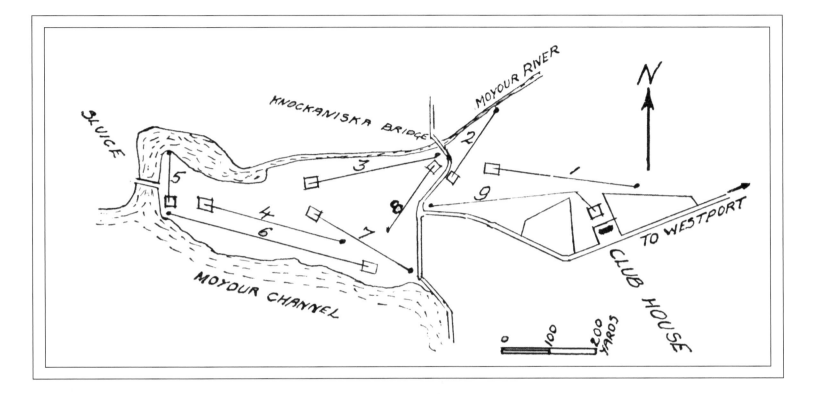

By 1927 membership had reached 80 and the business community began to respond to the growing popularity of the game.

Hughes's Bridge Street offered:

" Golf Hose and Socks" during Irish
Shopping week,
March 15th to 19th, 1927.

The Club now offered an inducement to those who were still hesitating about joining.

"The Committee have decided to admit new members at half subscription from March until the end of the Club's year, 30th of June. It should be noted that after the 30th of June new members will most likely have to pay an entrance fee in addition to the annual subscription."

The suggestion of a future entrance fee might lead one to think an atmosphere of exclusivity pervaded the Club.

While it is true that golf at this time tended to be the preserve of the wealthy classes it is more than likely funds were needed as the Committee:

"Expect to have a comfortable pavilion
erected before the end of May."

In August 1927 the Hon. Sec. J. A. Sheridan, The Manse, Westport, was advertising for tenders in writing for upkeep of greens and tees for three months and for six months. He felt he had to state that personal interviews would not be considered.

T. Stack and J. P. O'Brien were in charge of organising the Captain's Prize for June 12th. The entrance fee was a shilling with another shilling for the Sweepstake but this was optional. There would also be a draw for partners.

In the list of Men's subscriptions for 1928 only two names remain of the original Committee elected to find suitable land in 1915. These names are John Kelly and F. Gill.

The other names from that founding meeting have disappeared. H. J. Mc Ternan, H. Yelverton, P. Jeffers, W. H. Palmer, J. C. Dudgeon, A. O'Cooper, R. H. Laing. Henri Laing was supplying cups in 1931 and 1932 but Henri was not a member in 1928.

So golf had restarted. In May 1931 Westport golfers travelled to Ballina for the Mayo Bankers Meet.

"The entries were large, play was excellent and the weather was ideal."

The cup was won by Mr. J. Duhig, M. and L. Bank, Westport, on a net score of 66. Mr. J. J. O'Regan, Westport, presented the cup. In June 1932 Westport G.C. sent delegates to a Special Meeting of the Connacht Branch of the Golfing Union of Ireland held at the Clubhouse, Claremorris.

Mr. W. A. Murphy and Mr. Adrian de Fleury represented Westport. An apology for absence was read from Mr. J. C. Garvey, Westport.

"A discussion took place as to the clashing of club fixtures in the province and the difficulty of obtaining early dates from secretaries. It was resolved that Major Benson, Secretary of the Union, should be asked to get out a diary card for all the clubs of the province next year and that club secretaries should be asked to co-operate towards this end by sending in their fixture list about February or March."

In May 1937 the qualifying round for the Carrowholly Cup was played. The following qualified: Messrs. E. A. Ryan, G. Gillette, J. J. Glynn, Father Loftus, G. Kenny, D. Landers, W. A. Murphy. Messrs. P. V. Plunkett, J. J. Flatley, Fr. Ruane and W. Clancy tied for 8th place and these four were to play again.

Golf and its pleasures were to continue unabated until 1945. Now the War and restrictions on transport intruded. At the AGM of 1947 it was decided unanimously to carry on with the Club at Carrowholly,

John Kelly recalls: "As now, with all restrictions off transport, it was felt that the Club could soon be brought back to its pre-war strong position. The younger members were very enthusiastic and the older members promised all support necessary. It was decided, having regard to the amount of initial work necessary, to appoint two joint secretaries this year."

The Club closed once more in 1966 when the landlord would not renew the lease. No other suitable land had been found.

It appeared golf in Westport was at an end.

While the groundsman was removing wire from around the greens he was stopped by the landlord and told to contact someone from the

REFLECTIONS FROM JOHN KELLY, CAPTAIN 1958

'John Kelly (1883-1950), my uncle, was Captain in 1926. He moved from the Octagon to Belclare Lodge when he married Madge Malone (whose brother was the manager in the Munster and Leinster Bank on Shop Street) in 1925.

He made a trip to America in 1908 and took on a few novel jobs to tide him over, including one in an ice warehouse, where he proceeded to stick an ice pick in his foot. Subsequently he (rather reluctantly, I would imagine) had to take a job moving corpses in a morgue! Upon grateful receipt of the necessary funds, dispatched by his mother, Sarah, John returned home, whereupon he went to Dublin to study Law. Upon qualification he returned to Westport and opened a practice on the Mall. He did a lot of work for the Land Commission in the 1920's and did well. He was made State Solicitor, and later, County Registrar for Mayo.

James W. Kelly (1889-1957), my father, who ran the family business here on the Octagon was Captain in 1927. He played off a 12 handicap. Bertie Staunton was one of his regular playing partners. My father's sister Eileen (married to M.J.Ryan, Carrabawn) was herself Lady Captain in 1930."

I myself joined the Club in 1947. I picked up a few old hickory-shafted clubs of my father's from behind the hall stand in the house and Lorcan Gill (solicitor) who took over my Uncle John's practice brought me down to Carrowholly and introduced me to Jack Flatley (a teacher in the Quay school) and Willie Walsh (father of Stephen, Liam R.I.P., Cathal and Seamus).

Willie Walsh gave me two golf balls – a very generous gesture given that golf balls were extremely scarce at the time due to post-war rationing. Of course, I broke a few of those old hickory-shafted clubs, so Pierce Gill was going to Dublin and I asked him to buy me some clubs. He went into Elverys at the bottom of Grafton St. and he bought "Horgan Wemack" woods and irons. Horgans were a firm from St. Andrews, beside "Old Tom Morris Green" and they were making clubs for more than two hundred years. They were about £1-7 shillings per club and they were first class.'

The Clubhouse 1966

WESTPORT GOLF CLUB

MEMBERSHIP CARD 1968

SUBSCRIPTION RATES

Men	£7 0 0
Ladies	£3 10 0
Family	£11 0 0
Country	£3 0 0
Beginners	£1 0 0

1967 BEGINNERS

Men £2 10 0, Ladies £2 0 0

OLD COURSE M.Y.

WESTPORT GOLF CLUB

MEMBERSHIP CARD 1972

S.S.S. 63

Membership Fees:

Men	£10.00
Ladies	£4.00
Family	£15.00
Country	£3.50
Juniors (14-21 yrs.)	£4.00
Juveniles (under 14 yrs.)	£1.00
— Daily	£0.35
Weekly	£1.25

payable to either of Joint ...rs before 31st May, 1972.

Club. A new five-year lease was agreed at £150 a year. The official re-opening was fixed for May 21st or 28th 1967. Back to Carrowholly revived the spirit in the Club and brought a renewed burst of activity.

This was reflected in repairs to the clubhouse, installation of a ladies toilet, the attempt to attract young players, golf lessons in the Lecture Hall, and enjoyable social functions like the "Beer and Bones, Crubeens and Ribs". The estimated financial deficit of £175 at year's end did not appear to disturb the returning members.

"This position having been considered by the members it was proposed by N. Ashe and seconded by A. Malone that the sub should remain at its present level of £5. An amendment to raise the sub to £6 was defeated."

The final closure of Old Carrowholly was to take place in 1973 when play started on the New Championship Course in May.

The game of golf in Westport had survived all obstacles, wars, economic depression, transport problems, financial pressures and landlord problems.

Fairways in regulation, silky putting strokes, Dunlops and Warwicks hitting the back of the cups, the Holy Hill, the view of the bay, the clubhouse banter and song and more, much more, had brought serenity of mind and peace of heart to Westport members from 1915 to 1973.

Their golfing lives had been punctuated by the Annual Dance, the Open Day, the Club Day, the fun competitions, A.G.Ms, witty reports in the *Mayo News*, Whist Drives and Silver Circles.

CARROWHOLLY *Diary*

*A taster of the club's social life, from the Annual Dinner through to the thoughts of the witty golf correspondent in the **Mayo News***

■ The Annual Dinner

The Annual Dance became a barometer for a changing society and the breaking down of rank.

1926 The Annual Dance was held at the Town Hall. Music was by the Atlantic Beach Dance Band (J. McGowan, Dublin, Conductor). High class catering was also provided. The tickets were very expensive and their price reflected a clientele of wealth and class. Gentlemen would pay 15 shillings, Ladies 12 shillings and sixpence and Gallery tickets cost 5 shillings. (To put this fee in context the Annual Dinner Dance fee in 1958 cost £1-1-0 and the fee to the Golf Club Dance in 1958 cost 5 shillings.) The civilised ambience of the period is reflected in the descriptive term, "Gentlemen" and the presence of the conductor.

1929 The Annual Dance had moved to the Lecture Hall. Clarke-Barry's Band, personally conducted would perform. Tickets were now 10 shillings.

1937 The price of attendance had dropped to 2 shillings and sixpence and dancing would be to Stephen Garvey's orchestra. Listed as an expense item was the purchase of floor polish at a cost of 2 shillings and three

pence. This would enable the dancers to better "skip the light fandango". In 1938 Jack Power and his Band with the latest "amplifying system" provided the music. More than 100 couples attended with visitors from Castlebar, Ballinrobe and Newport. Mr. Frank Gill, President, thanked those present and added amidst laughter that the bachelor members of the Golf Club had never got such a chance. In November a second dance was held this time in "The Grand Central Hall" James St. Dancing was from 7.30 p.m. and tickets were 2/6 p (Note the starting time for dancing!)

1952 The Dance had moved to the "Pavilion" in the Paddock. Music was by Jackie McNally and Orchestra with dancing from 9 – 1 and admission still 2 shillings and sixpence.

1954 The practice of offering a free Door Prize was begun. This time it would be a 21-piece china tea set. The price of the dance was increased because of this to 3 shillings and the music was by the Resident Band, "Pavilion Orchestra".

1955 The Club became more ambitious in fund raising through their dance. This time they presented ,"Dave Glover and his famous band". There would also be a draw for £100 note at this dance and every 50th person would be admitted free.

Admission was increased to 5 shillings. Obviously this venture had been very successful because on St. Patricks Night they presented an All-Night Dance with dancing from 9-3. Music provided by "Ralph Sylvester's wonderful new band". Each patron was to be included in a draw for £100 note plus a bicycle and radio. The advertisement asked the question:

"Do YOU Want that £100? "

The offer of the £100 note was a crowd winner. In August the Club presented " Alan Beale and his band" from 10-3 for 5 shillings and a free £100 note.

In 1948 during the carnival a nightly golf competition was held on the old tennis court in the Paddock. Mr. Desmond O'Malley, Castlebar St. won the prize of £2 in the Clock Golf Competition with a round of 15 for 9 holes.

In October they announced "The Old Maestro with the Brand New Band"– Stephen Garvey with his full band and organ for an all night dance.

In 1956 they presented "Bobby Mc Caffrey and his 7-piece Orchestra" and in 1957, "Jack Ruane and his Wonderful New Band".

The Club Dance became a valuable fund-raiser through the years. Other fund-raising activities involved the running of Whist Drives, Silver Circles and Carnivals.

In 1935 A Whist Drive realised a profit of £12-10-0. This represented 100 players paying a fee of 2/6p. In 1941 38 tables representing 152 card players participated.

In 1950 the Committee appealed for the whole-hearted co-operation of all members of the Golf Club to help with the Carnival which the Club was running jointly with the Soccer Club. The Carnival was characterised mainly by the holding of Dances. "Gala", "Glorious", and "Grand" were some of the adjectives used to describe the dances.

Ceildhe and Old Time Waltz also featured as did children's matinee, amusements and sideshows. In the pre-television days of the bleak fifties the "Monster Carnival" brought colour and excitement to Westport and much needed finance to both clubs.

In 1959 A Silver Circle produced a financial bonanza. The total intake was £220 with a profit of £120.

The Thoughts of Mayo

■ **On Handicaps 18 +:**
"The competition for Handicaps 18 + is a very popular feature especially as each player is allowed to indulge his individual idiosyncrasies to whatever and wherever the fancy leads him. For example, last Sunday one player smashed his driver, another saw his ball enter the open maw of a waiting well-fed bullock while still another has yet to be revived from high water."(1952)

■ **Autumn Golf (1952)**
Autumn Fourball: to achieve a fair deal no member of 15 handicap or under can pair with a member in the same class.

"Golf in the Autumn is probably golf at its best. There is a whip in the air that seems to get into the club as it comes into the ball. There is also the sense that black winter is three months nearer and there is the hurry to get in as much as you can. The Committee are awarding a bottle of Irish Whiskey to each of the winners. The nip in the bottle allied to the nip of Autumn should encourage keen play and mighty endeavour. The runners-up get each a half-dozen glistening Dunlop 65 gold balls – and probably more than a look at the bottles."

■ The Club Dinner Dance

The Club Dinner Dance was a more sacred event.

It always demanded major discussion as to venue, menu, music, raffle and price of tickets. It was seen as not only an occasion for members to enjoy themselves but also as a valuable way to introduce new people to the club.

In 1959 an Extraordinary General Meeting was called to discuss menu quotations for the Annual Dinner from Newport House and the Travellers Friend Hotel. In 1960 the Annual Dinner was held in the Railway Hotel.

The admission charge was to be £1-1-0. This would include wine.

As regards dancing: "Mr. Jeffers of the Railway Hotel showed the Captain and Sec. the bus waiting room. He had the concrete slab removed and was also to have the floor washed and polished for dancing."

In 1961 the Club was anxious to avoid paying a tax on their Dinner Dance:

"For the purpose of avoiding tax the function was to be called a Dinner. No mention of Dance to be made in the notice."

In 1964 they discussed whether to have a formal or informal dinner.

"Mr. L. Gill said it was unwise to have a formal dinner for two reasons:
(1) Due to the Club's poor financial position.
(2) Because the Club used to be regarded as snobbish and a formal dinner would resurrect that opinion in the town.
A motion was passed that the dinner be informal."

In 1967 the question of paying tax on the Dinner continued to bother the members.

" M. Mulloy is to investigate the possibility of getting out of paying the 10% turnover tax on Annual Dinner."
Later……..

"M. Mulloy reported on his visit to the tax office re. the 10% turnover tax and the result was that we will escape the tax if we promote the Annual Function as a dinner with no advertising. Our advertisement will be placed in the *Mayo News* DISCREETLY."

In 1971 discussion on the Annual Dinner led to the Captain stating that "no committee had the right to bind future committees in any way."

A circular was sent out to 321 people of whom 105 were members of the Golf Club.

CARROWHOLLY *Diary*

■ The Open Day

The Open Day and the Club Day were major events in the golfing life of the Club.
For Open Day every effort was made to show the Club in the best light.

In 1929 erecting a tent for Open Day cost 12 shillings and sixpence. In 1930 work on the course for Open Day involved the hire of a horse and cart for 8 days and this cost £10. The test of the Captain's stewardship was the appearance of the Club for this day.

In 1932 the Captain instructed that 10 shillings extra be awarded to James Ryder for his work in preparing the course for Open Day. This reward would appear to underline the importance to the Captain of having everything ship-shape.

Silver Cups to be played for would be displayed for a week in Mr. John Glynn's shop window in Shop Street. Many businesses in town benefited because of this day. Meat was purchased from Brawns, goods from Dan McGings, Hawkshaws, Lipton, Jeffers, Gavin, Glynn, Feehan and Mc Greal. In 1937 there were up to 50 entries. Entrants came from Ballinrobe, Ballina, Ballyhaunis, Castlebar and Claremorris. Mr. J. Duhig, Athenry, won best nett. In 1938 a Silver Cup was won by J.J.Murphy, Ballina and in the afternoon fourball v bogey Messrs. E.J.Ryan / J.J.Lyons, Westport won two silver cups with 8 up.

■ The Club Day

The Club Day was inaugurated by Mr. De Fleury . Its purpose was to show appreciation to the Ladies of the club for all the fine work they did throughout the year. Mixed foursomes, putting and chipping competitions were held. This day fostered a club spirit and a Club togetherness.

"18th of June 1944, ideal weather, big turnout of members, the Ladies provided a fine tea, everyone thoroughly enjoyed themselves."

On Cup Days the very kind Ladies (such as Mrs. Rees, Mary Mulloy, Mrs. Hall, Mrs. McMahon and Mrs. Gill) supplied lovely teas, usually consisting of bacon and eggs, tarts, cakes etc. Dancing after tea was organised by Ailbhe and Sinead Malone. Ailbhe would stack all the chairs away and sprinkle the dance floor with crystals to facilitate smoother movement of the dancing feet!

Tom "Jap" Walsh (who worked out in Rank's store at the Quay) would supply the music with his piano accordion. He was a wonderful musician- as good as an orchestra! He would have a list of the "Top Ten " of the day beside him which he would proceed to play. He was a very large man, maybe twenty stone and quite a sight as he perspired through the hit parade, with the line of whiskeys waiting on the shelf behind him! The bar turnover was usually about £200 per annum; one memorable Captain's Day the takings came to the staggering amount of £66 which was the talk of the town the next day!"
                                                John Kelly/Capt. 1958)

> In 1938 the G.U.I. Affiliation Fee cost 1 shilling. In 1939 the Club paid £2-4-0 in Affiliation Fees. In 1961 a letter was read from the G.U.I. re. subscriptions. a "Mr. Ashe informed the meeting that we usually pay on 40 members."

■ Golf balls

Golf Balls were expensive items from the beginning. In 1928 a dozen Maxfli cost 17 shillings and a dozen Warwick 13 shillings. The Green Fee rate was 1 shilling and 6 pence. Thus the price of a Maxfli golf ball was nearly that of a green fee for 18 holes! Golf balls became valuable prizes to be won in competition.

"The popular types of ball then were the "Blue Flash" , costing 1s/6p, the Warwick ,costing 1s/10p and the "65" which cost 2s/6p and which was named by Dunlop after Henry Cotton's round of 65 at the British Open."

                                                John Kelly

Mrs. H. McMahon putting on the 9th green in Old Carrowholly with her son, F. McMahon.

Green Fees

In 1926 the Green Fee cost 1 shilling and sixpence. This fee remained unchanged for many years. Between 1929 and 1943 over 726 golfers paid Green Fees.

In 1934 Green Fees realised the sum of 18 shillings equivalent to 12 players at 1/6 each. A Grace O'Malley was responsible for 15 shillings of this sum.

In 1939 Green Fees realised £10-17-0 equivalent to 146 players.

In 1940 Green Fees had dropped to 67 players, 1942 to 12 players and in 1943 to 8 players.

These figures reflect the influence of World War 2 on the Golf Club. There were restrictions on transport and golf balls were difficult to obtain.

The effect of the War is also reflected in a Notice from Livingstone Traders Ltd (Westport):

> "Owing to extreme difficulty in replacing stocks at the present time, customers are requested to ensure that empty cases , bottles, syphons, jars, biscuit tins, sugar bags etc. are ready for our lorries when they call. By doing so customers will assist us in maintaining supplies."

Green Fees and Tourism

In 1960 green fees demanded more thought with the ongoing development of tourism.

"Mr. J. Hughes had three green fee boxes made at a cost of 10 shillings each and he said he would not accept payment until the boxes had paid for themselves. He suggested that a box be placed in each hotel in town and a little printed card be placed on the front giving details of the green fees.

"Each hotel was also to hold a number of cards and to issue one to each visitor who paid green fees. Mr. Hughes suggested that 2/6 per day be charged or 10 shillings per person per week. These suggestions were accepted."

The Thoughts of Mayo

■ On a year of Golf for One Pound (1953)

"During the past year the club framed a very good rule.

Any applicant for membership who never played golf before is charged £1 for the first year. In effect this means that the new member is allowed within the year for a £1 to decide whether he likes the game well enough to continue or resign and perhaps shorten his natural expectation of life by about ten years.

This sum of £1 can be spent faster and to much worse effect than by enjoying the health, fresh air and amusement that Carrowholly provides.

The subscription of a £1 is equal to 7 shillings and 10 pence by 1939 standards. Is there better value in Ireland to-day?"

Fun competitions

The members were imaginative in creating fun competitions. In 1944 a one-club mixed foursomes competition was held. Members turned up in great strength thus making the proceedings most enjoyable. M. Mooney and Miss G.S tack emerged winners with a 39. In 1960 a one-club competition was won by Liam Walsh and he took a dozen golf balls as the prize. A two-club competition and a Secret Holes competition were also organised. In the Secret Holes, only the Captain would know the holes disregarded in arriving at the score. There were also regular "Chip and Putt" competitions.

The members were also very conscious that newcomers needed to be looked after and taught the game. Plenty of competitions were organised for these beginners. A Novices Competition in 1952 was won by M. Mulloy. It was also normal for senior members to invite new members for a fourball competition. A very popular feature was competitions for handicaps 18 +. Every effort was made to immerse the high handicapper in the game of golf and in the Club.

CARROWHOLLY Diary

■ The Professional Visit

Regardless of cost to the Club having a professional visit was sacrosanct to the development of golf within the Club.

In 1929 Murray the professional visited and cost the Club 18 shillings.

In 1936 the Club suffered a nett loss of £1-14-9 on the visit of T. Higgins, Rosses Point.

From 1929 to 1940 professionals Murray, Hana, T. Higgins, F. K. Higgins and T. Rooney visited Westport and gave lessons.

They stayed normally for two weeks.

T. Rooney stayed for two months.

The Officers were determined to improve standards and knowledge of the game. They were obviously aware that subsequent enjoyment would follow therefrom.

They suffered losses gladly on these visits as they were investing in the future.

A certain Bobby Jones was illuminating the world of golf in the thirties and lifting spirits after the Wall St. Crash.

He gave birth to a new phrase, "The Grand Slam" when he won the British Amateur, the British Open, the U.S. Open and the U.S Amateur.

The Officers in Westport during this period knew that the professional visit was vital to the ongoing development of golf.

They showed their appreciation by making a donation of ten shillings in 1943 to the Professionals Benevolent Fund. In 1944 they made a subscription to the Professional Golfers Association costing ten shillings.

Down through the years the Club invested in Golfers Handbooks in order to improve their knowledge of rules.

In 1931 a Golfers Handbook, Edinburgh, cost 8 shillings and 5 pence.

■ Liquor Licence (1947)

"An application on behalf of Westport Golf Club for a Certificate of Registration which would enable the Club to sell liquor was granted.

Mr. John Prendergast B.E. said that he had drawn the sketch (produced) of the Club headquarters. Mr. G. Murphy, Club Secretary, said that there was a licence in force before but it was allowed to lapse owing to a decrease in membership. Membership had grown and was continuing to grow with 80 people registered at present."

The Thoughts of Mayo: 1953

■ On the County Cup:

Carrowholly has the privilege this year of running the County Cup, open to all Mayo Clubs.

Each club sends a team of 10, the best six returns are reckoned and the Cup goes to the lowest total score. It is expected that 80 of Mayo's best players will be seen at Carrowholly. Not the least amongst them will be Padraic Carney the famous Mayo football star.

All this means work for the members who are gallantly responding to the call.

A common sight now is one of the Trustees emerging from the bunkers at the 9th Green covered in sand and glory, the Captain wielding a noble pickaxe at the 1st, the Vice-Captain a spade at the 5th, the Secretary a fork at the 7th and all the Committee with the regulation sugans at the knee putting into practical effect the theory of the land project.

The occasion is historic as this is the first time in the span of golf in Westport that the contest has been held here."

■ Major John McBride Competition : 1916-1966 celebrations

The organisation of this competition underlined the voluntary ethos enshrined in the club.

● The groundsman will be re-employed 3 days a week, costing £4. Two medallions will be presented as prizes.

● Greens to be attended by members of the committee.

● Greens to be allocated to nominated names.

● Drains to be cleared if ground is very wet prior to competition.

● Caravan given by Mr. Gill to be used for purpose of competitors changing.

● A second caravan is considered necessary to accommodate the numbers who will participate.

● Clubhouse to get another coat of Snowcem and doors and windows to be painted.

● Mr. A.de Fleury will change holes before competition.

● Sign for Barley Hill Cross to be erected by P.Cox.

● Mr. E. McBride to be written to and asked to present prizes. Invitation to be sent to McBride. Committee member, Mr. Owen Hughes, to attend.

● Members to participate in the parade on Easter Sunday.

The winners of the Major John McBride Competition Medallions were Dr. Halpenny and Jim McGowan.

■ The Captain's Prize

The Captain's Prize was the unofficial matchplay championship of the club. In 1947 there were 32 entries. A preview stated:

"It is very hard to pick the winner beforehand and while the Mall and Bridge Street both fancy the winner will be among their contingent, there is a strong feeling that the cup will go in the Quay direction, while Castlebar led by that dark horse with the blonde hair, Mr. T. Burke, have a strong interest."

The semi-finals were played sometime in November or December. These months would not have been the best weather-wise to play the final of such a prestigious competition.

In 1948 one had to write applying to play in the Captain's Prize.

"The latest day for accepting applications for the Captain's Prize competition is Friday, June 4th. Intending competitors should write immediately to the Secretary, Mr. G. Murphy, the Mall, Westport."

There were 44 entries.

The draw produced the following matches:

Byes at top: D. P. Landers v T. Johnstone; P. Gill v J. McLoughlin; M. Heverin v J. F. O'Malley; P. J. Dempsey v J. J. Flatley; A. A. Moore v E.Hynes. 1st Round: G. P. Murphy v C. J. Doherty; C. Clune v B. McShane; L. Gill v J. Heraty; T. Stack v John O'Donnell; J. Kelly v John Mulloy; P. Higgins v S. W. Johnstone; James Hughes v P. J. Golden; D. P. Casey v M. D. McCormack; J. Quinlevan v F. I. O'Brien; T. Bourke v T. P. Brennan; S. Wickham v M. J. SugrueJ. J. Warde v J. McBride.

Byes at bottom: B. Jeffers v H. J. Staunton; N. Gill v J. P. Maguire; V. Clarke v P. Flanagan; W. O'Brien v John Thornton; A. de Fleury v W. J. Ryan.

Winner: M. J. Sugrue beat S. W. Johnston 3 and 2

In 1949 the draw for the Captain's Prize took place on the 16th. September. There were 22 entries and "Members are requested to finish their second round matches before the 27th of October."

In 1950 S.W. Johnston defeated Liam Golden 3 and 2 in a 36 hole final.

"Golden was unlucky in losing balls at crucial stages of the game. It must have been extremely disheartening to lose the ball or find it in an almost unplayable lie after hitting some of the finest drives ever seen on the course."

The comments of the Captain, Mr. P. Dempsey, at the presentation are noteworthy,

"In former years the two finalists often came down to play their game without any other member even knowing or caring whether the game was being played or not.

"This year, however, there was an all round revival in the club. More members were playing, competitions were played to schedule, the finances were improved, there were more social events and generally speaking there was an atmosphere of life and progress in the club. He thanked the ladies for providing such an excellent meal at their own expense. He had great pleasure in presenting the prize, a suit length, to the worthy winner."

■ Solidarity March Over Bloody Sunday (1972)

The Troubles in the North of Ireland had erupted in 1969. The shooting dead of 13 people on a Sunday in 1972 brought an emotional response from the entire country.

"The Captain informed the meeting that a protest march was being held in the town on the morrow, Wednesday 2nd February 1972, to show solidarity with the people of

the North following the slaying of 13 people on the previous Sunday. The parade was to assemble on James St. at 11 a.m. and end with Mass at 12 noon. The day had been authorised as a day of National Mourning and the Committee authorised giving the day off to the staff of the Championship Golf Course."

The Thoughts of Mayo

■ On the missing Pavilion Committee: (1954)
"The Club are anxiously seeking news of the whereabouts of the Pavilion Committee. This body was last seen on the middle hill of the 6th fairway the day after the A.G.M.

"Any particulars, however meagre, will be gratefully received by the General Committee"

■ On New Members:
"New members are always welcome and the only qualifications expected by the Club are a patience beyond human reason and a hopefulness beyond human endurance. Such is the game of golf. (1954)"

■ On AGMs (1955)
"Annual General Meetings of golf clubs are queer incidents and Westport is no exception. Your best friend for the previous twelve months will refuse to back you up on a point of procedure.

The whole meeting will rock with laughter at a motion which to you appears reasonable. In other words you are on your own."

More Thoughts of Mayo

■ On the Kilroy

"Carrowholly is acknowledged to be the best laid out nine-hole links in Connacht. The second, fourth and eighth holes are probably as good as one could find in the country. Especially the eighth known to members as "THE KILROY". Many of the players trying time after time to beat this hole with everything they have and not succeeding have been heard to mutter silently and to themselves, "surely Kilroy was here!"

■ On the Tankard Competition/Code of Dress (1954)

"Last Sunday was the first of Spring and it brought from Westport into Carrowholly the usual disarray of weird clothing dear to the hearts of golfers.

It also marked a Tankard Competition. The Tankard is a pint pewter with a glass base. These Tankards hold a pint or if you like three or four balls of malt. If won it is standing proof of the winners quality at golf, at beer-drinking and of his capacity to add to the home furniture at 3 shillings a go."

■ On the Accounts (1956)

"The accounts of the Club for the year 1956 were presented. They disclose the alarming fact that for the first time in twenty-seven years the Club had a very healthy credit balance. Arguments immediately arose as to how this should be spent. One section wanted an extended Pavilion bearing a slight resemblance to London's Crystal Palace. Another section suggested caution, quite properly pointing out that money was money and that it was good to look at for some time. There is still the rule allowing in at a reduced fee of £1 new members who have never played golf before. The Club is open to everyone and to all Codes. The Golf Club welcomes all and for their £1 promises fresh air, a long Sunday and Wednesday walk, bounding health and ample facilities for refreshment."

■ On Born Architects! (1957)

"On the question of reconstructing the Clubhouse every Committee member is a born architect who "has a plan". However the final plan is agreed and the contractor with great courage has undertaken the job. The Club's Bankers did not display the same courage and disagreed with the Committee's theory that money is made to get around and get around fast. The result will be a fine capacious airy clubhouse but a disapproving, credit squeezing bank. As the Club cannot get on without either, they will make very uncomfortable bed fellows."(1957)

■ On the Clubhouse (1957)

"The contractors have just finished the extension, a matter of gleaming windows and sunlight and Carrowholly takes on a new lease of life. There is plenty of room for armchairs and ample time for drowsing in the western sun which is as good a way of using a Clubhouse as filling it with Golf talk."

■ On Burning up the Course (1957)

" Most of last years cups were collected by N. Ashe. A meteoric challenger this year is M. Mulloy who is burning up the course. J. Kelly is playing down to a 5 handicap with ease. P. Cox likewise, to his infinite content. Liam Golden has the distinction of a 3 handicap which means he must play in top form all the time if he is to get anywhere. The rest of us play our game, miss our shots, read more golf articles, buy more expensive golf books and dream of a time when we will conquer Carrowholly with a glorious intoxicating round of 68.

■ On D.P. Landers beating the Kilroy (1952)

"D.P.Landers stood on the Kilroy with the match all square and 2 holes to go. He played to the green 190 yards away. His drive hit the wire going in and the ball trickled onto the green. Local rules allow a substituted shot. No golfer in his place would tempt fortune by taking the second shot. But the jacket and the empty pipe came into play, the shot was taken, the ball landed ten feet from the pin and was duly sunk for a two and a win. Newcomers to the club never believed the legend. But some of them saw the Kilroy being played as it was never played before. And the legend is now to them established fact."

■ On Stroke and Stableford (1957)

"To the uninitiated the terms 'Stableford' and 'Stroke' might be intriguing mysteries. Their explanation is simple. In a stroke competition you deduct from the total number of times you hit or did not hit the ball, your handicap and your net score is the return. Stroke is the exacting, heartbreaking competition during which golf cards are torn up, clubs smashed in temper, and language used which was never learned at school.

Stableford is the joy of the mediocre golfer. Points are allowed for each hole. If you go to glory in one hole, there is always the next to pull you back and the long handicap man is notoriously hopeful."

■ On the delay in playing the Phillips Cup (1957)

"This is rolling much more majestically to its end and the writer confidently predicts the final to take place sometime in the year 1960. In fact the betting has started and one dead-pan member puts his money on the Day of Judgement."

A view of the 6th tee at Old Carrowholly and the fairway, with out of bounds on the sea shore all the way down the right hand side

"Go and have a day at Westport. The Fairways are a sheer delight to walk and play on. What joy there is in a good second off a hanging lie!"

Chapter 3

THE OLD COURSE IN
Carrowholly
1915-1973

■ **The Land.**

Tommie Ingham, Carrowholly, (father of George Ingham) was approached by club members with a view to lease about 70 acres of land in order to develop a golf course.

In the first few years, Ingham's house, "Carrowholly House" was used by the members as their club house. Here they would park their cars (if they had any) or bicycles.

When they had completed their round of golf Mrs. Agnes Ingham (nee Gavin from Clynish Island – mother of George) would serve the golfers tea, sandwiches and scones, before they set off for Westport circa 3.5 miles away.

The first lease was for 30 years @ £30 per year payable by £15 every six months. Money was scarce and sometimes the club would be slow to pay. When those situations arose Mr. Ingham would sometimes let the pedigree short-horn bull loose on the course.

"The Inghams owned the land on which the course was, and if the rent was late getting to Tommy Ingham he would let a few horses loose on the course leaving the place in a nice state! " (John Kelly)

The money would then follow immediately. Mr. Ingham would remove the bull and golf would continue enjoyably.

It was written into the first lease that cattle, sheep and horses could graze on the course and this was the reason why the greens were fenced. In the second lease the horses were not allowed to graze as they damaged the fairways excessively with their hooves.

S.S.S. 63. PAR 68. Total Length: 5,046 yards.

"Carrowholly is acknowledged to be the best laid out nine hole links in Connacht. The second, fourth and eighth holes are probably as good as one could find in the country." (*Mayo News*, 1953)

On the left, Mr. John Kelly, captain 1926, and on the right, his brother Mr. James Kelly, captain 1927.

RULES (Selected) 1926

The annual subscription shall be as follows:

Gentlemen.................£2-2-0
Ladies £1-1-0
Family £4-4-0

Country Members residing over ten miles from Westport.

Gentlemen.................£1-1-0
Ladies 0-10-6
Family £2-2-0
Juvenile Members 0-10-6

Commercial Travellers not residing in the County of Mayo   10s.6d

Green Fees:.......1s. 6d per day.
Weekly Tickets, 5s.
Monthly tickets, 10s.

ELECTION OF MEMBERS:
Shall be in the hands of the committee.

All candidates for membership must be proposed and seconded by two members of the club.

The mode of election to be by ballot and TWO BLACK BEANS IN FIVE TO EXCLUDE.

Country members, lady members and persons under the age of twenty-one shall have no voice in the management of the club. Ladies to be described as Associates without votes and without attendance at general meetings.

Members under 16 years of age shall not be eligible to play in the club competitions.

Any member leaving the district before the expiration of the first half-year shall be entitled to a refund of half his annual subscription.

CLUB TRUSTEES:
The "funds" of the club and the whole of its property, real and personal, shall be vested in the present trustees, called the Club Trustees, which expression shall include their successors, who shall have power:

(a) To invest the funds of the Club in any investments which the Club Trustees deem advisable.
(b) To borrow money on mortgage of said property, or any part thereof, or by the issue of Debentures secured by the said funds and property, or any part thereof, provided that the Club Trustees shall not exercise the said power to borrow money until a resolution to that effect is passed at a General Meeting of the Club.

The Club Trustees shall be members of the Committee.

A Club Trustee shall be deemed to have resigned on ceasing to be a member of the Club or on ceasing to permanently reside in SAORSTAT EIREANN.

■ Groundsmen.

Mr. Tommie Ingham had the contract for Caretaker and he employed a man called, "Monaghan" to look after the grounds and the fences.

After five years Mr. James (Birdie) Ryder undertook the Greenkeeper/Caretaker job and he worked on the course for 25 years.

James Ryder was responsible for building tees and improving the course. He built the large elevated 6th tee, over beside the Barrier. James Ryder cut all the tees and greens with a push lawnmower. (warm work!)

In 1928 his wages were £1 per week. Occasionally extra men were employed. In 1931 wages to James Ryder and Pat Casey came to £31-4 shillings.

In 1932, on the Captain's instructions, James Ryder was to receive 10 shillings for his work in preparing the course for Open Day.

In 1939 the Club allowed £2 for the purchase of a wedding present for James Ryder.

In 1940 extra men were employed once more. F.Browne was employed for 7 days @ 5 shillings plus 2 shillings and 6 pence overtime. M. Casey was employed for 75 days.

In 1941 M.Casey for 25 days and in 1943 wages totalled £57-17-6 including £4 to James Ryder for cutting fairways.

In 1953 the County Cup was hosted for the first time. The groundsmen were Willie and Jim Kelly who were praised for having "worked wonders with the greens and fairways."

In 1959 some difficulties began to emerge with the grounds staff. The groundsman "Staunton" resigned. His replacement was criticised for only cutting greens: "No attention to Course. He should be called in to ascertain if he is prepared to carry out the work specified. Offer him £28 and explain he will get a further £17 if he is prepared to bring work up to standard as set out on commencement of his employment to satisfaction of committee."

In 1960 the appointment of Pat Golden as groundsman was proposed by S. Fahy and seconded by P. Cox. A work-sheet was laid out for the groundsman as follows:

"Tuesday – general work. Tuesday afternoon

and Wednesday morning — greens. Wednesday afternoon — general work. Friday — fairways. Saturday — greens and tees."

Dick Gill was also employed in 1960.

In 1961 Pat Golden, Kilmeena, was unable to give time to the care of the Links and Tony Joyce was appointed in his place. In 1962 concern was expressed that the groundsman might be led into temptation:

" The Sec. read a letter from the Lady Captain asking that the groundsman be asked to sweep

Mr. Tom Stack, captain 1930/31 in front of the club trophies and the hip flask he won in the Captains Prize of 1927.

THE STANDARD SCRATCH SCORE

The Standard Scratch Score of a course is the score which is expected on that course from a Scratch player playing from the medal tees under spring and autumn conditions of weather, with fairways and greens in good order and without wind. It is important to remember that these conditions apply throughout and all tests must be made under them.

In 1951, the Club Secretary, Mr. Lorcan Gill, applied to the Golfing Union of Ireland for a standard scratch score. The following findings emerged.

Course: 9 holes
Average run 15 yds.
How measured: Tape.
3 balls from Tee.
Group: 2.
Drive: Only a slope at a point 215 yds from tee is to be considered.

The Final Result:
Playing Length of Hole:

1.	337	Par 4.
2.	147	Par 3
3.	276	Par 4
4.	301	Par 4
5.	122	Par 3
6.	488	Par 5
7.	263	Par 4
8.	193	Par 3
9.	376	Par 4

Standard Par = 68
Length Adjustment : – 1
Course Value: +1
Putting Adjustment: – 1
Standard Scratch Score: 67.

and tidy the clubhouse after all functions. It was decided to inform the Lady Captain that such a suggestion however desirable was not quite feasible as the groundsman must not be led into temptation by asking him to wash glasses etc. in the bar except under supervision."

In 1966 the groundsman was S. Gibbons. "The groundsman, S.Gibbons, was instructed to remove wire from around greens." Also in 1966 Chas Cannon began work as the groundsman.

In 1970 Chas Cannon continued to be listed as the groundsman.

■ **Golf balls.**

The favoured golf ball was the Dunlop "65". In April 1955 Mr. Lorcan Gill wrote to the Irish Dunlop Co. requesting very urgently 4 doz. Dunlop 65s costing nearly £6. In January 1956 The Irish Dunlop Co. wrote regretting that "it has become necessary to revise our selling prices for golf balls due to increases in costs."

They quoted the following price changes:

Dunlop "65" (English size)
Trade per doz=30s/6p; Retail each=3s/6p.

Dunlop "65" (American size)
Trade per doz=32s/3p;
Retail each=3s/9p.

Warwick(English size)
Trade per doz.=24s; Retail each=2s/9.

Warwick (American size)
Trade per doz=25s/9; Retail =3s.

■ **Professionals.**

In 1928 the Professional cost £3-3-0 and half Professionals expenses per Golfing Union of Ireland cost £2-4-6.

In 1929 the Professional, Murray cost 18 shillings and the car to Carrowholly with the Professional cost 8 shillings and two pence. In 1933 and 1934 the services of Mr. William Hana from Bray were obtained. He charged £6 for two weeks and his travelling expenses cost £2-10 shillings.

Photo 1939: Left to right: Pierce Gill (Captain 1949), Mrs. E. Gill (Lady Captain 1950), Frank Gill, Noel Gill (Captain 1953), Frank McCourt.

In 1936 the services of Mr. T. Higgins, Rosses Point, Sligo were obtained. He charged 1 shilling and 6 pence per half hour. The Club had a nett loss on his services of £1-14s-9p. In 1937 Mr. F. K. Higgins was employed for four weeks at a cost of £3 per week.

In 1939 the Professional obtained was Mr. T. Rooney. He came again in 1940 and stayed two months successfully coaching. He left for Castlebar but was booked again for 1941.

In 1953 Cecil Connolly of Howth was booked for the last two weeks of April.

In 1966 it was decided to invite Mr. Gus Murphy for a week and to arrange accommodation for him.

In 1968 Gus Murphy was asked to bring a selection of golf equipment with him for display and sale. In 1971 it was agreed that Mr. Murphy was an excellent teacher of golf. In 1974 it was agreed that Mr. Murphy would be appointed Club Professional.

However later it was unanimously agreed that the club could not pay Mr. Murphy a retainer and consequently that he should be let go. He was to be given a £100 in appreciation of his work and any stock, (excluding clubs) he wished to sell would be bought by the club. The appointment of a professional would be reviewed again .

■ Caddies.

The golfers created employment for locals in times when there was no work to be found. Locals were hired as caddies.

They received an old threepenny bit (the one with the corners) or a tanner (sixpence) as payment.

The large families in Carrowholly at that time were grateful to the golfers for the money earned from caddying.

The going rate for caddying was usually a tanner. The locals would also sell golf balls they found back to the golfers for a penny or twopence depending on the humour of the purchaser.

The caddies would often go straight to the golf course after school and when they got paid they would go down to Gibbons Post Office and buy "farthing" biscuits.

One could purchase two huge 6-inch digestive biscuits for a "farthing" or a fistful of NKM toffees for a wing (penny).

Every year the golfers would have an "Open" meeting and golfers came from all over the county. They would play all day and then have food in the clubhouse. The caddies would be fed also on that occasion. In the evenings when the golf members would be gone home the caddies (local boys and girls) would play their own golf rounds.

One of the great caddies was John "Bomber" Browne. He stood 6 feet and 4 inches in height. He weighed in at about 16 stones and he could hit the golf ball incredible distances.

> " Many a good caddy roamed the course in the early years including the Gibbons, the Heratys – Dick and Paddy, and John "Bomber" Browne – my caddy, a lovely, natural golfer as good as the best member we had and an extremely pleasant man. You would see a few caddies there on the bridge at Carrowholly and if you wanted their services it was a half crown." (John Kelly)

In 1939 a number of queries were put to the Hon. Sec. Mr. E. B. Bolger, under the National Health and Unemployment Insurance Acts regarding caddies.

"What is the exact procedure adopted at your club when a player wishes to engage a caddy?"

Reply: Caddies are engaged by a player.

" Who is in charge of the caddies?"

Reply: No one.

"Has a player to whom a caddy has been assigned the right to dismiss such caddy during the round for incompetence, or any other reason?"

Reply: Ignored.

"Is there any obligation upon the caddies, or any of them, to attend at the course or do they merely attend on the chance of getting a job when their services are likely to be required?"

Reply: They attend on the chance of getting a job.

"Does the player pay the Caddy Master, or other person in charge, for the services of the caddy, and, if so, does the Caddy Master retain any portion of the caddie's fee, either for himself or for the club?"

Reply: Pay caddie.

■ Hole-in-one.

1949 P. J. Golden at 2nd hole.

1963 Michael Hastings (Post Office) Turkey competition, 20th Oct. 1963.

1968 M. Henehan at 5th-112 yds.

John Kelly at 8th-188 yds.

1969 G. Hall at 2nd- 160 yds.

■ Honorary Members.

1961 – Mr. & Mrs. Gus Gibbons

1967 – Mr. & Mrs.Gus Gibbons

       Mr. & Mrs. George Ingham.

1970 – Mr. Donal Landers

1971 – Missionary Priests – meaning all priests who are natives of the area and who are at present ministering in foreign parts. It was unanimously carried that the local members of the Irish Christian Brothers be conferred with Honorary Membership.

■ Rossyveragh Cup controversy and missionary priests (1961).

"Mr. Liam Golden then asked the captain why Fr. Fitzgerald and Fr. McGovern were not allowed to play in the Rossyveragh Cup and the captain replied that the reason was in his opinion it was unfair that anyone here for only 2 or 3 months should enter and have the chance of winning a major competition.

As a result of a ruling by the committee Fr. Fitzgerald and Fr. McGovern did in fact play in the competition but apparently took great exception to the original ruling of the Captain.

After further discussion it was decided that all missionary priests of local origin home on holidays would automatically become Hon. Members and be entitled to all facilities of the club including entry to all club competitions.

■ Course record.

The existing course record was 63 held by Dan Murray who was formerly professional at Skerries. In 1940 Tom Rooney, professional, broke the record when shooting 61.

In 1971 John Farrell shot 68 gross. This was the best score since the course was altered five years before by lengthening the 3rd hole.

"This record likely to be permanent as the course will be vacated shortly for the new course." (*Mayo News*)

■ Course Infringements – Cattle, Lambs, Horse And Football.

In 1959 fences and greens were damaged by stock and the "meeting authorised the expenditure of up to £50 for the provision of posts and wire for greens."

In 1960, "the Captain informed the meeting that Mr.T.Ingham had complained that one of his lambs had been injured by a golf ball and had to be sold at a loss. It was decided to pay 25 shillings. Mr. Fahy said the lamb was sold for £3-5-0 at a fair and he had got £4-10-0 for others. Mr.Gill thought we were covered by insurance."

In 1961 a letter was received from Mr. T. Ingham claiming damages for a lamb killed on the course. As there was no evidence that the lamb had been killed by a member of the club the committee did not feel responsible and the matter was dropped.

Mr A de Fleury, Captain in 1945.

"Mr. Hall brought to the notice of the meeting that G. Ingham was galloping a horse on the course. L. Gill was to bring Mr. Ingham's attention to the clause in the agreement which stated that no horse be permitted on the course."

In 1962 an urgent note in minutes said:

"See L. Gill esq. re. horse on course presently." In 1964 it was agreed "to write to Mr. Ingham protesting about the use of a tractor and the two horses loose on the course."

In 1967 the Captain reported that a sign prohibiting football on the course was to be erected. He also reported serious damage to the 9th and 1st greens by cattle breaking down the wires. Proof of malicious damage was inconclusive so it was decided to let things lie for the time being.

In 1968 the landlord Mr. George Ingham presented 3 dozen golf balls for a beginners competition. A letter of thanks was to be forwarded to him.

In 1969 it was decided to take action to prevent football being played on the second fairway.

■ Local rules.

1. A ball striking a wire or post on entering a green may be dropped and replaced without penalty. A ball lying within three clubs' length of the wire surrounding the green may be dropped not nearer the hole, without penalty.
2. If a cut drain interferes with a player's stance the ball may be dropped within three clubs' length not nearer the hole without penalty.
3. A ball which lies in a hole and cannot be touched by the centre of a club laid horizontally in all directions over the ball can be dropped, not nearer the hole, without penalty.
4. A ball lying in animal droppings may be dropped within three clubs' length, but not nearer the hole without penalty.

■ Course maintenance and rulings.

The lawnmower was sent to McKenzie and Sons , Dublin, for repair. This happened on a regular basis. In 1935 this cost £1-13-0 with rail carriage costing 5s and 4pence. A green rake cost the

7th tee box at Old Carrowholly: M. McMahon on the tee watched by A. Malone, G. Hall and M. McMahon's daughter-in-law.

considerable sum of £7-14-6 with carriage and Customs duty on the rake costing £1-0-4p.

In 1937 Costello, an itinerant, was paid 15 shillings for sharpening and setting the mowing machine.

In 1941 for sharpening and overhauling the lawnmower Costello was paid 10 shillings and for sharpening the mower one pound.

In 1958 it was suggested that members on days when golf cannot be played overhaul the fairway mower themselves.

> " It was Adrian de Fleury that built the old sixth tee. He was manager in Pollexfens (Quay Mills) so he got some of the men from the Mill down. They built the tee. It took them a couple of weeks. A couple of times a year he would get the men down again and they would re-cut the bunkers and fill them with new sand, and do all kinds of jobs like that. There were no wooden tees then; there was a tee-box on each tee and you would take a pinch of sand and form a little mound and put the ball on top of it." (John Kelly/Capt. 1958)

In 1962 it was felt that a shelter was needed on the 6th hole-

"Mr McMahon has a container which may be suitable for erection as a shelter on the 6th if the landlord has no objection. If found to be suitable the Captain is at liberty to buy it." (Mr. McMahon – local station master)

However C.I.E. had decided not to sell the container referred to by Mr McMahon so:

"P. Golden was to be asked to erect a temporary shelter on the 6th."

In 1963 an instruction was given that "the greens were to be farm manured for one week."

In 1968 the minutes report that " Vice-Capt. Hugh Murphy and John O'Brien had inspected greens and had drawn up a schedule for application of fertiliser and weed-killer. This work to commence in January. Blade of mower to be raised to allow more grass on greens."

In 1970 serious concern was expressed about the financial cost of maintaining the course.

"As the preparation of the course with the gang mower had proved so costly last year indiscriminate use of the gang-mower would have to be avoided and the competitions sub-committee would have to dovetail major competitions with fairway cuttings."

Later "it was suggested that other methods of operating the gang-mower be looked into such as hiring a tractor and seeking voluntary labour among golf club members au fait with the operation of tractors or any other method which would reduce the cost of fairway cuttings."

57

■ Rulings.

In 1963 a temporary rule was introduced:

> "In the event of a ball hitting the wires on the
> 9th green the player may play another.
> Proposed by J. Kelly, seconded by M. Mulloy."

In 1967 it was discovered that the out-of-bounds markers were themselves out-of-bounds!

"The stones marking out of bounds are themselves out of bounds. Boundary is defined by inside line. The rule applying to telegraph wires is the same as one applying to wires around greens."

In 1970 the question of casual water was raised by John Kelly. He stated that it was the original intention that no relief whatever be afforded to a player in the rough. It now appeared that a player could drop without penalty out of casual water.

He was not at all happy about this particularly in the case of Carrowholly where casual water in the rough abounds. It was pointed out that the casual water rule is a rule of golf and that a bye law in conflict with Royal and Ancient rules could not be made by a local committee.

It was agreed that all rough be regarded as a water hazard and relief therein could only be obtained under rule 33(2) and / or (3). Rule 32 (casual water) would not be applicable to the rough. This would necessitate some amendments to the scorecard and the sub-committee were asked to go into the local rules in detail with a view to re-erecting posts etc. on the course which are mentioned on the card but are no longer there.

In 1971 the question of Saturday and Sunday play was discussed:

> "It was the feeling of some that if
> morning and afternoon play was allowed
> on Sunday with the chance of varying
> weather conditions then there did not
> seem to be anything to preclude
> Saturday play. It was the majority deci-
> sion that Saturday and Sunday play be
> permitted with a recommendation that
> as many as possible play on Sundays but
> it was not intended that this decision be
> binding on the Committee for all time."

■ Handicaps.

Stars of the Club included Canon Gunnigan (administrator in Westport) playing of a 2 handicap, Pierce Gill (4); Liam Golden (4); Gerry Murphy (5); John Rafferty (6); David Rees (9); Pat Higgins (Ulster Bank) (4); Adrian de Fleury (5); Dan Landers (5); Pat Cox, Tom "Tyler" Kelly, Maurice Mulloy and myself all played off about 12" (John Kelly / Capt. 1958)

In 1964 the G.U.I. requested an engineer's measurement of the course.

"The main item on the agenda is a letter received from the Golfing Union of Ireland requesting a certified engineers measurement of the course and also a card of the course. It was decided to ask Mr. Malone to measure the course."

In 1965 the Golfing Union issued a directive:

> "In view of direction from Golfing Union
> of Ireland, letter dated 28/10/65, it was
> decided by this meeting that handicaps
> of all members be advanced by two
> strokes from 7/12/65."

In 1968 the G.U.I. complained in a letter that handicaps were too generous."

The main points made by the G.U.I. were that handicaps were too generous and that handicaps should be set on general performance and not only adjusted on competition results.

The G.U.I. expressed the opinion that S.S.S. was often set too low and that a period of 12 months should elapse usually before handicaps have strokes added to them.

It was agreed that the Handicap Committee should undertake to revise handicaps and that general performance at Carrowholly would be the main guide to be used and that possible performance on other courses should "not be a major factor in deciding on handicaps."

The G.U.I. letter caused immediate concern to club members.

> "Mr. Tom Kelly had approached the Vice-Capt.
> Hugh Murphy in connection with reduction of his
> handicap. The handicap committee would
> consider the matter if he would like to put
> forward his case. It was decided to display the
> G.U.I. letter on the noticeboard."

HANDICAPS (MAY 1969)

Adams, C. – 14; Ashe, N. – 13;
Beatty, D. – 24; Bree, P. – 24;
Brady, P.J. – 24;
Blackstock, R. – 24; Clarke, A. – 24;
Carolan, T. – 18; Cox, P. – 14;
Coakley, V. – 18; Cahir, T.J. – 24;
Crimmins, M.J. – 24;
Colbert, G. – 20;
Campbell, J.P. – 24; Cox, Tom. – 24;
Cavanaugh, M. – 24;
Dever, M. – 24; Doherty, P. – 24;
Daly, J. – 24; Downes, M. – 24;
Fitzgerald, Rev. Fr. P. – 14;
Farrell, H. – 18; Farrell, John. – 10;
Greally, Rev. Fr. D. – 18;
Golden, L. – 4; Golden, G. –9;
Gill, L. – 22; Gill, P. – 22;
Golden, Rev. Fr. M. ; Hall, G.– 17;
Hastings, M. – 16;
Henehan, M. – 5;
Hingerton, L. – 18; Hope, F. – 12;
Higgins, P. – 17; Higgins, J. – 24;
Hughes,C. – 24; Hoey, J. – 24;
Horvath, P. – 24;
Johnston, Rev. Bro. M. J. – 18;
Joyce, T. – 6; Kelly, J. – 1 2;
Kelly, Tom. – 9; Kelly, G. – 24;
Kelly, H. – 24; Kelly, P.J. – 22;
King, M. – 13;
Killeen, Rev. Bro. J.B. – 24;
Landers, D. – 22; Lambert, N. – 24;
Mulloy, M. – 15; Malone, A. – 21;
Murphy, H. – 17; Minish, L.T. – 18;
Masterson, J. – 24;
Moran, Michael – 24;

Mumford-Smith, H. – 22;
Murphy, T. – 24; McAleer, G. – 9;
McLaughlin, P. – 18;
McMahon, M. – 19;
McMahon, D. F. – 9 ;
McMahon, A. J. – 24;
McHale, C. – 24; McGonagle, C. – 24;
McDonnell, P. J. –24;
McGreal, J. –24; McGuire, Jim. – 24;
Nolan, T. J. – 24; O'Brien, M. F. – 24;
O'Connor, B.- 24; O'Malley, B. – 18;
O'Malley, Rev. Fr. E. – 20;
Rafferty, J. –24; Rees, D. – 18;
Ryan, H. – 24; Roughan, V. – 12;
Redmond, A. – 18; Reilly, P. – 24;
Staunton, M. – 20; Staunton, H. J. –22;
Stevens, J. – 24; Spicer, J. – 24;
Tobin, S. – 12; Tyndall, A. – 24;
Walsh, L. – 18.

COUNTRY MEMBERS:
Hanley,P. – 16; Hopkins, P. – 9;
Kenny, C. – 12;
O'Malley, R. – 10; Quinn, P. – 18.

JUVENILES:
Breheny, S. – 24; Cannon, C. – 24;
Dyar, G. – 24; Fadden, M. – 24;
Fadden, P. – 24; Gibbons, L. – 24;
Gibbons, J. – 24; Hoban, P. – 24;
King, A. – 24; Kelly, L. – 24;
Kavanagh, S. – 24; Moran, V. – 24;
McLoughlin, J. – 24; O'Donnell, M. – 24;
Tiernan, M. – 24;
O'Donnell, J. – 24.

The level of complaints increased. The Handicap Committee had to become more professional in order to handle complaints.

"A scores register should be maintained and monthly meetings held by Handicap Committee to review handicaps. The Handicap Committee must adopt a more stringent and factual approach towards reducing the handicap of a player who brings in a return lower than the standard scratch score of the day and the Handicap Committee have power to reduce handicaps on general form irrespective of scores returned. The basic S.S.S. should be increased by 1 , 2, or 3 strokes when conditions warrant it. It seemed that the S.S.S. at Carrowholly should be 64 instead of 63. It was decided to investigate the matter further."

However the Club members continued to be very unhappy about their handicaps.

In 1970 the minutes report:

"Mr. John Kelly recalled that they had been given two tasks to perform team selection and adjustment of handicaps. He considered that they had performed with credit in the matter of team selection as witnessed by a County Cup win and a very successful run in the Connacht Shield. After the Captain's Prize an adjustment of handicaps had become necessary and the sub-committee had been CRUCIFIED for their efforts. Mr. Hugh Murphy referred to a letter which had been received from the Captain and regarded its contents as a " bringing to heel" of the sub-committee. A long and heated discussion took place on this whole matter and it was decided on this occasion the adjustments should stand. Letters from C.Q.M.S. Nicholas Lambert and Martin Halpin were read and referred to the handicap sub-committee for their further consideration."

Individuals handicaps continued to cause concern for the sub-committee.

In 1971:

"The question of Gerry McAleer's handicap was causing concern. Mr. McAleer's problem was that he was allotted a handicap of 8 in Westport and a handicap of 6 in Mulrany and it was his contention that a player could not have two handicaps and this is accepted. It was a difficult one to discuss and solve. According to the Rules of Golf, a players home club controls his handicap and there was no intimation as to what club Mr. McAleer regarded as his home club, whether Westport or Mulrany. It was assumed however that he would regard Westport as his home club and if that were so his handicap must stand at 8. A communication in writing was invited from Mr. McAleer setting out his views on the subject. No reply was received. One would only hope that this matter might be amicably settled as one deplores any altercation with one who has always been regarded as among the finest members of Westport Golf Club."

Later Captain David O'Regan of the Handicap

Committee had a discussion with Mr.McAleer and he would be glad to consider for handicapping purposes any cards returned by Mr.McAleer in Mulrany if the Hon. Sec of Mulrany would return such cards to Westport.

■ The Clubhouse.

In 1927 the minutes recorded that the committee expected to have a comfortable pavilion erected before the end of May.

John Kelly said: "Packie O'Donnell (of O'Donnell Builders, the Mall) built the pavilion for £100 and it still stands. It is currently a private residence, near Gus Gibbons shop."

In 1957 it was decided to reconstruct the clubhouse, and in 1958 alterations were made:

"The meeting decided to proceed with alterations, the transference of bar and gents dressing room, the provision of hatch, main room counter and means of securing stock. Mr. Cox's estimate of £30 for this work was accepted. A Silver Circle will be run to pay debts."

In 1960 problems with the bar hours and visitors attending functions emerged.

"The Captain mentioned that there should be a definite closing time for the bar. Mr.Fahy was of the opinion that if the bar closed early the takings would fall considerably. Mr.Cox proposed that 12 o'clock be closing time. Mr.Walsh asked if each member was entitled to introduce one visitor at any function in the clubhouse. The Chairman ruled that this was not so. Members could only bring visitors to Carrowholly if these visitors were residents of the town of Westport and the Carrowholly area."

In 1962 concern was expressed about undesirables crashing functions, "in order to restrain the illegal entrance of undesirables or others during functions it was decided to place a wire cage on the window of the men's locker room."

An imperative followed in the minutes to:

"Get L. Gill to word a circular to the effect that members may not bring locals as guests. Only non-residents of Westport are considered guests of members."

In 1967 another ruling on this issue was given:

"Members were advised that they could invite friends to functions. Any casual caller to a function must be signed in by a member, said member being responsible for said visitor."

In 1967 on returning to Carrowholly it was felt repairs were needed:

"To the gable ends of the Clubhouse. These would be put in hand when the materials become available. Mr.Cox is to be notified to deliver the requisite materials for the Ladies toilet as soon as convenient. Mr.Cox is to supply a list of the materials needed as some members may have some of the items themselves."

In 1969 the Ladies were asked to carry out alterations to the clubhouse:

"The provision of extra lighting such as wall lamps is to be investigated also such other repairs and renovations to improve the clubhouse in general."

In 1971 the minutes record that:

" A total of eight bar exemptions had been given in to Mr. Lorcan Gills office.These were for the Presidents Cup, Ladies County Cup, Guinness Masters, Lady Captain's Prize, Captain's Prize, Rossyveragh Cup, Ladies Day, Cavanaugh Hotel Trophy.

Presidents Cup 1960.
Back: left to right:
A Malone, F.McMahon, Fr. F.Fitzgerald, P. Cox, L. Gill.

Middle: Mrs. Staunton, P. Shanley, Mrs. E. Rabbitte, Mrs. E. Hughes, E. O'Malley.

Front : Mrs. L. Doherty, M.McMahon, not known, B. Staunton (president), S. Fahy, J. Hughes (captain).

Carrowholly Club Teams Through The Years

In 1937 at the Open Tournament in Ballina Rev. M. Hopkins (11) Westport, brought in the best nett with a 68.

JUNIOR CUP TEAM 1949:
A. de Fleury, P. J. Golden, S. W. Johnston, Pierce Gill, Gerry Murphy.

COUNTY CUP TEAM 1959:
L. Golden, P. Golden, Rev. F. Fitzgerald, F. O'Callaghan, P. Cox, M. Cox, J. Kelly, S. Fahy, N. Ashe, D. Landers, P. Golden (Carrowholly)

COUNTY CUP TEAM 1963:
E. McCrea, M. Henehan, T. Joyce, Gar Golden, M. Mulloy, G. Hall, J. Kelly, D. McMahon, G. McAleer, D. Landers.

COUNTY CUP TEAM 1964:
G. McAleer, P. Cox, F. McMahon, E. McCrea, J. Kelly, T. Joyce, M. McMahon, M. King, D. Landers, M. Henehan
Res: M. Staunton, M. Mulloy.

CONNACHT SHIELD TEAM 1964:
D. Landers & E. McCrea, T. Joyce & M.Henehan, L. Golden & P. Cox, A. de Fleury & D. McMahon, J. Kelly & G. Hall, Res: M. McMahon & M. Staunton.

CONNACHT SHIELD TEAM 1965:
F. McMahon & A.de Fleury, M.Mulloy & P.Cox, T. Joyce & N. Ashe, J. Kelly & G. Hall, G. McAleer & M. Henehan

CONNACHT SHIELD TEAM 1966:
T. Joyce(9) & J. Kelly(15), T. Kelly (14) & M. Henehan (12), G. McAleer (11) & A.de Fleury (15), M. King (18) & A. Malone (18), D. McAllister (12) & M. Mulloy (18).

COUNTY CUP TEAM 1967:
T. Joyce (10), G. McAleer (11), M. Henehan (12), F. McMahon (12), T. Kelly (14), F. Hope (13), J. Kelly (15), T. Wallace (16), M. Mulloy (17), M. King (17), H. Murphy (18).

CONNACHT SHIELD TEAM 1967:
T. Joyce & T. Wallace, F. Hope & G. McAleer, M. Henehan & T. Kelly, P. Cox & J. Kelly, M. King & M. Mulloy.

FRIENDLY WITH CASTLEBAR IN 1968.
12 teams from each club playing foursomes. 1 golf ball to the winner. Soup and sandwiches to be provided by the Ladies for 48 @ 2 shillings per head. Probable cost to Westport members 4 shillings. Competitors to start at various holes. Teams:
T. Joyce(9) & Fr. Tobin (18),
G. McAleer (9) & Tom Wallace (14),
Tom Kelly (10) & B. O'Malley (20),
F. McMahon(12) & F. Hope(13),
M. Henehan (10) & M. King (13),
J. Kelly (13) & G. Hall (17),
M. Mulloy (16) & Fr. Greally (20),
A. Malone (21)& Pat Cox (16),
M. Hastings (18) & Hugh Murphy (21),
Myles Staunton (21) & M. McMahon sr.(19),
Tommie Nolan (24) & P. Higgins (20),
P. McLaughlin (22) & Tom Carolan (20).

WINNING COUNTY CUP TEAM 1970:
Tony Joyce(5), John Farrell (8),
Gerry McAleer (9), Gar Golden (9),
Maurice Mulloy (15), John Kelly (16),
Hugh Murphy (17), Padraig Higgins (17) ,
Perry O'Reilly (18), Niall Halpin (19).

Miss M. Gill (lady captain 1943).

Mrs. B. Golden (lady captain 1935/36)

Membership Through The Years: (Selected)

1915
Ms. May Ruttledge,
Mrs. Yelverton, Ms. Barry,
Irene Ruttledge,
Trixie Yelverton, Ms. Jeffers

1926
A. W. Fanning (Hon. Sec.)

1927
J. A. Sheridan (Hon. Sec.)

1928
Dan McGing, P. Walsh,
J. L. Hartley Thomson, F. Gill,
P. D. Rees, M.G. Kenny,
W. A. Murphy, Paddy Joyce,
J. C. Garvey, J. P. O'Brien,
Tom Stack, John Kelly,
Rev. John Gibbons, W. Morrison,
B. Staunton, P. Cafferky,
A.G. Gardiner, F. S. Fallon,
W. Malone, J. Sheridan,
G. R. Anderson, R. B. Donovan,
C. Hughes, M. Moran,
John O'Donoghue, M. Coyle,
M. Henehan, W. J. Walsh,
W. Whyte, G. Tobin, J. Duhig, F.
M. Casey, P. A. Moran,
J. O'Donnell, P. Golden,
Jas. Kelly, F. Mulloy, A. de Fleury,
J. Ryan, J. Kelly, Tony King,
Thomas McGreevey, Waters,
Shanskshaft, O'Gorman,

Landers, J. J. Glynn, R. O'Malley,
Madden, E. R. Hartley,
J. Thomson, D. Anderson,
C. Anderson, C. Mortell,
Dr. McGreal.
Family: McGings, Brownes.
Ladies: Mrs. Egan, May Walsh,
May McGing, G. Hartley,
Mrs. Rees, Mrs. Kenny,
Miss Gibbons, Mrs. Joyce,
Judith Garvey, Mrs. O'Brien,
Miss Stack, Mrs. Duncan,
Mrs. John Kelly, Mrs. Hughes,
Mrs. Hadnett, Mrs. W. J. Walsh,
Mrs. Whyte, Mrs. Tobin,
Mrs. Murphy, Mrs. Mulloy,
Mrs. P. Golden, A. Ryan,
Mrs. Jas Kelly, May King,
Mrs. A. de Fleury, Miss E. Dineen,
E. Hughes, F. Casey, Mrs. Waters,
Miss Lynskey, Miss Connolly,
Mrs. O'Gorman, Mrs. Coen,
Mrs. Hartley, Mrs. F.Tue.

1932
Sgt. Taylor (Castlebar), M. Coyle
(Livingstones), S. Lovett (school
inspector-half year),
Rev. J. Loftus (Tourmakeady),
Men 42, Ladies 20, Family 5.

1933
T.Power (Garda), Garda Nolan
(Mulrany), M. G. Kenny (Land

Commission), S. McKenzie
(Ulster Bank), F. E. Barry
(Munster & Leinster Bank),
6 staff members from Bank of
Ireland.
Men 37, Ladies 12, Family 3

1934
Marquess of Sligo appears on
membership list.
Men 35, Ladies 12, Family 3.

1935
Rev. M. Malone (Tuam),
Rev. Jas Gibbons,
Rev .J. Gunnigan,
Rev. C. Gibbons,
Rev. M.J. Browne, Three
Custom and Excise men-
Leneghan, Oakley, McMahon.
Marquess of Sligo not listed.
Men 40, Ladies 13, Family 4.

1936
Marquess of Sligo, J. J. Glynn,
Men 32, Ladies 17, Family 4.

1937
Marquess of Sligo, Doctor
Murphy, Mental Hospital
Castlebar listed as Lady
Member., Rev. M. Hopkins,
P. V. Plunkett, H. J. Staunton,
J. J. Lyons, J. Kelly.

Ms. Brady, Ms. Kenny,
Mrs. O'Regan, Mrs. McGreal,
Mrs. Golden, Ms. Dineen.
Men 39, Ladies 21

1938
W. J. Walsh, Frank Gill,
Fr. Ruane, Fr. Gunnigan C.C.,
E. J. Ryan, P. Dempsey,
Men 39, Ladies 20, Family 2.

1939
L. Gill, Mrs. Maher,
Men 43, Ladies 19, Family 2.

1940
J. Flatley, Patsy Golden & Liam
Golden (juveniles),
Ms. Eldridge, Mrs. A.de Fleury,
Ms. Nancy Murphy, Ms. Sheila
McBride, Men 42, Ladies 24.

1941
T. F. Maher ,
Men 48, Ladies 23, Family 2.

1942
Men 42, Ladies 25, Family 3.

1943
New members:
Chas. Shanley, Desmond
McCormack, John Mulloy, James
Ward, J. F. O'Malley,

Mrs. E. Ryan
(lady captain
1930).

Mr. F. Gill (president
1926-1951). with
Mrs E. Gill (lady
captain 1950).

Ms. Girsha Stack, Ms. O'Connell,
Men 49, Ladies 24, Family 3
(A.A.Moore, Murphy, F.Gill)

1944

P. Gill, Ms. N. Murphy,
Ms. E. A. Maher, E. A. Roycroft,
J. E. McCourt, L. Golden,
W. J. Walsh, Ms. G. Stack, N. Gill,
J. S. Hegarty, Ms. Canavan,
Mrs. McGreal, C. McKinney,
A. de Fleury, Mrs. Mooney.

1945

Ms.G. Stack, E.J. Timoney.

1946

No reports due to restrictions
on transport.

1947

C. J. Doherty, J. Lehane,
J. J. Flatley, J. McBride,
E. J. Timoney, S. W. Johnson,
G. P. Murphy, Ms. C. O'Connell.

1948

Liam Golden, D. P. Landers,
T. Johnstone, J. McLoughlin,
M. Heverin, P. J. Dempsey,
A. A. Moore, E. Hynes, C. Clune,
B. McShane, John O' Donnell,
P. Higgins, James Hughes,
D. P. Casey,

M. D. McCormack,
J. Quinlevan, F.I. O'Brien,
T. P. Brennan, S. Wickham,
M. J. Sugrue, B. Jeffers,
J. P. Maguire, V. Clarke,
W. O'Brien, John Thornton,
W. J. Ryan.

1949

Pierce Gill, J. Mulloy,
Jas. J. Warde, J. F. O'Malley,
G. P. Murphy,
Lorcan Gill, Liam Golden,
V. Clarke, T. P. Maher,
M. Gilmartin, E. L. Hynes.

1950

P. Dempsey, P. J. Golden,
W. O'Brien, S. W. Johnston,
J. McBride, T. Stack,
H.J. Staunton, W. J. Walsh,
Mrs. F. Gill, Ms. Mulloy, Ms. Gill,
Mr S. Johnstone, Ms. Nestor,
Ms. Murphy, Mrs. Blennerhasset,
Ms. N.O'Malley.

1951

P. Naughton, E. L. Hynes,
M. Gilmartin, J. McBride,
Noel Gill, Joe Mulloy.

1952

P. McEvilly, Paddy Cox,
P. J. Kelly jr., Thomas Kelly, J.

Twohig, P. O Driscoll,
Ms. Noreen Golden,
Mrs. J. Mulloy.

1953

Noel Gill

1954

J. Rafferty, M. Golden,
G. Hall, M. Landers.

1955

F. O'Callaghan, M. J. McMahon,
E. A. Kinch, J. Healy, C. Boland,

1956

M. J. McMahon, T. Ryan,
F. O'Callaghan.

1957

J. Hughes, D. Rees, G. Hall,
N. Ashe, J. F. O'Malley, P. Cox,

S. Walsh, J. Cowley,
M. Staunton.

1958

J. Kelly, V. Clarke,
Frank O'Callaghan, Tom Kelly,
Mrs. J. Hughes, Ms. M. Burns,
Ms. N. O'Regan, Mrs. Rabbette,
Mrs. D. Rees, Ms. E. O'Malley,
Mrs. Doherty.

1959

S. Fahy, N. Ashe, H. Sheridan,
Mr & Mrs Andy Moran,
Martin Cox.

1960

W. Scott, A. Malone, E. McCrea,
M. King, S. Walsh.
Larry Hingerton,
Mrs. Joseph King (Ayle),
Mrs. C. Lydon.

1961
A. McGinty, J. Rooney, Fr. Tobin, P. Fitzgerald (Buckfield), B. Kelly & P. Fadden (Carrowholly)

1962
S. McTiernan, Myles Staunton, A. Joyce, G. McAleer, F. McMahon, T. Wallace, Mr. & Mrs. Denis Egan, Mrs. Joseph King and son, Alan.

1963
Mickey Hastings, Cecil Adams, Mrs. Tyndall, G. Butt, Michael Browne, Peter Hopkins, Tony Joyce, Mrs. Wallace, Mrs. Ashe, Ms. J. Ryan.

1964
T. Wallace, M. Henehan, V. Burrows, Frank O' Donovan, M. Crowley.

1965
M. Hastings, G. McAleer, M. King, N. Ashe, Sinead Bean Ui Mhaoleoin.

1966
D. McAllister, H. Murphy, Fergal Hope, Mrs. E. Hughes.

1967
T. Nolan, F. Hope, C. Adams, Chris Lavelle, Mrs. Rose Golden, Ms. T. Landers.

1968
P. McLaughlin, A. Clarke, T. Nolan, Fr. Greally, Tom Carolan Charles Kenny, L. T. Minish, John Stevens, James Daly, R. Blackstock, Harry Kelly, Michael Downes, Robert Lawlor, James Lyons, S. Breheny

(junior), J. McLoughlin (junior), Niall Mulhern, Ms. Pat Fallon, Ms.Nuala Moran, P. Doherty, Rev. Br. J.Killeen, Corinne McGonagle, Jack Hoey, Cyril McHale, Ms. Mary Cannon, Ms. Colette O'Brien, Mary A. Kelly, Nicholas Lambert, G. Colbert, A. Redmond. Juveniles: Alan King, Liam Gibbons, John Gibbons, Cathal Cannon, Liam Kelly, Martin Fadden, Pat Fadden, S. Kavanagh, Sheila Gibbons.

1969
N. Lambert, Dr. Tobin, V. Roughan, R. Blackstock, M. Cavanaugh, T. Cox, P. J. Masterson & Mrs. Masterson, Ms. B. Whelan, Mr. Michael Moran & Ms. Eileen Moran, Mr. John Farrell, Mr. Jim Spicer, Mr. Perry O'Reilly, Mr. Tom Murphy, Mr. Niall Halpin, Mr. Frank Kenny (Louisburgh)

1970
Fr. Eamon O'Malley, Dr. Sean Tobin, Cormac Hughes, Brian Ruddy, J. P. Campbell, Gar Golden, Rory Daly, Michael F. O'Brien, Padraig Higgins, Liam Walsh (Newport), Thomas Higgins, Captain David O'Regan, Sean O'Malley, Austin and Miss May O'Malley, Jimmy Ward, Brendan Hughes, Michael Stewart, Dr. Betty O'Malley, Supt. Sean Murray, Ms. Elizabeth Fahy, Mr. Elwyn Dunkerley, Lorcan Clifford, John O'Brien, Ms. Margaret Adams, Ms. Ann Hope, Ms. Kay Downes, Ms.Eimear Hughes,

Dr. M. J. Casey, (Clifden), Rev. Peter Waldron, Garda Frank Murphy (Clifden), Rev. Anthony King, Maurice Landers, Patrick Moran,(Cloonkeen), Gerry Hughes, Peter Finnegan, (Reliable Shoe Company), Finbarr Bruen, Ms. Una Quinn, Ms. Loretta O'Malley, Ms. Irene Finnegan, E. S. Bateman (Suffolk), Mattie Reidy, Liam Kelly (C'bar St.), Shay O'Donoghue, Harry Wight (Jury's Hotel), Tony Kennedy (Hotel Westport), Dr. John Campbell, Rev. Vincent Kelly, Mr. & Mrs. Phillip Curran, Edward Kelly, Fr. John Walsh, Ms Eithne Chambers (Newport), Mrs. Jean McAleer, Ms. Barbara Madigan, Mrs. Babs Nolan.

1971
Aidan Redmond, Michael Moran, Vincent Roughan, Michael Loughrey (E.S.B.), Ms.Eileen Carson, N.T. Castlebar, Ms.Kay O'Regan, Dr. Des Kelly & Ms. Pat Kelly, Ms. Peggy Cadden, Jack Dunne(E.S.B.) John McMahon, Ms. Mary O'Brien, Rosbeg and her brother Mr. Gussie O'Malley of Galway, Fr. Jack Garvey, Aughagower, Fr. John Cosgrave, Don Gibbons, Kylemore, Ms. Maureen Ryan, Ms. Angela Crimmins, Ms. Mary Sammon, Ms. Greta Garvey,

Mr. Chris Farrell, Ms. Catherine O'Brien, Mr. & Mrs. Padraig Conlon, Ms. M. Gibbons, Mrs. Peg Clarke, Mrs. M. Tobin, Ms. A. Coyne.

1972
Ms Finola Hughes, Ms. Mary McBride, John McGill, Eddie O'Brien, Mr. & Mrs. P.I. Houlihan, Ms. Marion Hughes, Jim Lyons, Michael Halpin, Martin Halpin, Eileen Lynskey, Alastair Hendry, Liam Walsh (Quay Rd.-family), Robert Shaw (film actor-Jaws),

1973
Bro. P.K. Maher, Joe Lally, Regional Manager W.R.T.O., Dermot Blythe & Mrs. Brenda Blythe, Stephen Walsh, Vincent Coakley, Ms. Bridin Walsh, Willie Hopkins, Charlie Garavan, Joe Langan, Leo Tuohy, Dick Quinn, Ms. Annie McDonagh, Brian Moylette, Roddy Gillen, Peter Ryan, Padraic Joyce & Joan Joyce, Clifden, Nora King, Padraig Hughes, Cathal Hughes,Seamus Hughes, Pat Hughes, Ann Hughes, Marion Hughes, Jim Quigley (Ballina), William J. Flynn, Frank Gill jr., Pierce Gill, Pat & Rita O'Connell, Angela Colgan, Nora McCormack, Castlebar, Gerard Hannon, Bridie Hughes, Pat Hanley (Rooskey), Jim McCann, Denis Carroll, T. J. Hughes, Rev J. Waldron, Claremorris, Rev Sean Blake, Castlebar, J.S. Colbert, Rev M. Newell (Claremorris), Ms. Sal Lawlor,

Rev. Albert Lyons (Achill),
Ms. Mary Jennings, Travellers
Friend ,Castlebar.
Terry Sheridan, H. McGuinness,
Tom Hoban, C. M. Lawlor,
Paul Menton, Dr. G. C. Fenelon
(Dublin), Ms. Pamela Walsh,
J. P. Moylett (Pinewoods),
M. J. Brooker, Mrs.B. Tobin,
Seamus Walsh, Douglas & Mrs.
Jan B. Scott, Billy Bourke
(C/bar) Rev. R. Lyons,
Eddie Egan, Ms. A. Golden,
P. Horkan (Surrey), Greg Dyar,
Nancy O'Brien,
Eamonn Dowling,
Patricia Dowling,
Michael Cannon (Carrowholly),
Seamus Cannon,
Sean Joyce, Thomas Gill,
Ms. Irene Reidy, Matt Farrell,
Roderick Tobin, Ailbhe Tobin,
Rose Higgins, Michael Higgins,
P. C. O'Callaghan, Terry Rafferty,
Ms. T. Rafferty, Vivian Kenny,
Mr. & Mrs. Don Drennan,
Ms. Hazel Dawson,
Chris Hingerton, Ray O'Malley,
Guy Johnston,
Charlie and Edward Lydon,
Ms. Maeve Lawlor,
Brian McDonald, Tom Moylett,
Michael Kilcourse,
Fr. Quinn, Louisburgh,
Ken Church (Hotel Westport),
Jack Staunton,
J. Burke (Louisburgh)
Jean Colomban, Jeff O'Malley.

1968 Letter to members

In February 1968 the following letter was sent to each member. The tone of voice is respectful and courteous. The importance of the member is stressed and the member is made to feel it is his/her club. What is also noteworthy is that the letter is signed by all the Officers, Committee members and Trustees.

Dear Member,
Every four years the Royal and Ancient Golf Club of St.Andrews revises the rules of golf. A new edition is then printed and distributed by the Royal Insurance Co., Liverpool, at a small charge. The Committee has great pleasure in presenting you with your copy of the 21st edition of the *"Rules of Golf"*.

At the Annual General Meeting of Westport Golf Club, held on the 26th January, the decision that most affects us, and one which, we may add, was reluctantly taken, was that the annual subscription would have to be increased. After considerable discussion the following scale of fees was agreed upon; (the old fees are in brackets)

Men £7 (£5);
Ladies £3-10-0 (£2-10-0).
Full Family £11 (£8-10-0).
Country £3 (2gns)
Beginners (i.e. newcomers to golf) £1 (no change)
Men who were beginners in 1967 £2-10-0 (£1)
Ladies who were beginners in 1967 £2 (£1)

In respect of the last two grades an exception was made. Normally one who is a beginner one year pays full fees the next.

However, we had such a wonderful influx of new members in 1967, both ladies and men, that we felt they should get special treatment in appreciation of their having joined us, and in the solid hope of their remaining with us. Therefore their fees are being raised gradually by increments.

The Club as you know is in debt. It is felt however that this debt can be substantially reduced without using extraordinary means , but only with the co-operation of the members. Therefore we would be deeply grateful if each member would consider the following points;

1. If you are a member please continue to be one. We must not lose a single member.
2. If you know of any prospective member would you please approach him/her with a view to joining.
3. In order to keep the interest on our overdraft as low as possible, would you please consider paying your annual subscription as soon as you conveniently can.

We thank you for your continued loyalty to the club.

H.J. Staunton (President)
Michael Tobin, C.C. (Captain)
Brendan O'Malley (Vice-Captain)
Philip McLaughlin (Secretary)
Michael Henehan (Treasurer)
Trustees: H.J. Staunton, P. Cox,
L. Gill, L. Golden, J. Kelly.
Committee: C. Adams, A. Clarke,
M. Hastings, M. King, G. McAleer,
D.F. McMahon, M. Mulloy, H. Murphy,
T.J. Nolan, A. O'Maoileoin.

Chapter 4

Searching
FOR A GOLF COURSE

I n 1959 gloomy bleakness had infected Westport Golf Club. The Club Secretary, Mr. M. J. McMahon, painted a picture of apathy in his report to the AGM

"The various competitions were badly supported and two competitions, the Phillips Cup and Carrowholly Cup were not played. The latter was awarded to Phillip McLaughlin, the sole entrant in the competition. Apathy was also evident in the running of the Silver Circle. Membership is more or less static for the past few years and it is remarkable that practically no young people show an interest in playing golf. If the decline in interest is an indication of things to come then the outlook is indeed gloomy."

What the Secretary didn't know was that in the background both nationally and locally there were people who realised that social stagnation could not continue.

The first clubhouse on the Championship course, 1973.

In government circles Taoiseach Sean Lemass, and Department of Finance Secretary T.K. Whitaker were actively planning to bring about dramatic changes in the social landscape of Ireland. Both Sean Lemass and T.K. Whitaker realised that the old economic policies had failed and were continuing to fail. The country under their guidance moved towards a new era of free trade. Foreign Investment was encouraged and welcomed. In 1961 under Lemass's influence Ireland applied to join the E.E.C.

Taoiseach Sean Lemass

An unprecedented increase in the standard of living quickly began to manifest itself. The greatest instrument for change was the arrival of television. In 1961 R.T.E. was launched. New ideas, new ways of thinking, were beamed directly into peoples homes. The atmosphere in the country became decidedly optimistic. Tourism became an important industry as Irish-Americans began to return for holidays. It became apparent that golf tourism properly developed and marketed could provide jobs . When the children returned to school and the beaches emptied golf tourism could extend a tourist season.

In Westport local business people had realised the importance of tourism long before most.

In the late 1940s Westport Soccer club negotiated purchase of a section of the Paddock from Lord Sligo. Over a period of four/five years an army of 50 to 100 men and boys worked hard physically to produce the present day soccer pitch. No machinery was used only spades, shovels, pickaxes and a railway buggy. The pitch opened in 1952. To achieve continuity and a source of income The Pavilion Dance Hall (presently O'Connell's Warehouse) was built with a loan thus proving that Westport people were self-reliant and could do things against the odds.

In turn in the early 50s a move was afoot to promote tourism in the area. The Westport Tourism Development Company was perhaps one of the first Tourism Co. in the country. Bord Fáilte was formed at that time also. Some members of the soccer pitch committee, Jack McGreevey and Tommie Brennan,

were added to the W.T.D Co. and the name was changed to the W.T.D. and Sports Park Committee. This title did not last long and soon reverted back to the Westport Tourism Development Co. Ltd. Twenty Westport people made up the Committee including four golf club members, John Kelly, Liam Golden, Bertie Staunton, and Stephen Walsh. For many years the thrust of the W.T.D. was a two-week Sea Angling Festival which became the largest of its kind in the country over a period of 15 years. This festival was backed by Bord Fáilte and an affinity developed between the W.T.D. and the State body through its executives and directors. The Sea Angling Festival was big news and TV pictures showed hundreds of English, Continental and Irish anglers landing tons of fish.

The W.T.D. meetings were held in the Railway Hotel and they were oftentimes raucous and resignations were accepted and re-established.

The W.T.D. achievements also included the Bertra access road, the Horse Show (J.McGreevey/ M. O'Donnell), singing pubs and Town Hall concerts." (Stephen Walsh/reflections)

Having successfully established the Sea Angling Festival the W.T.D. set about discussing how to vary and lengthen the tourist season. In these discussions a new golf club emerged as one way to do this. The business relationship established with the executives and directors of Bord Fáilte during the Sea Angling Festival, created confidence in both parties abilities to initiate and bring projects to completion. This trust established was to have positive repercussions for the future of golf in Westport.

In Westport Golf Club the Captain of 1960, Mr. James Hughes, foresaw trouble ahead and the possibility that a day would come when golf would no longer be available in Westport. On the first day of July he informed the meeting: "that the present lease in Old Carrowholly had seven years to run and he said it would be a good thing if the renewal was procured soon."

Mr. Stephen Fahy was of the opinion that "Mr. Ingham was not keen to renew the lease."

■ The Search Begins: 1960-1968.
Golf At Belclare:

James Hughes's worries about the lease kick-started a flurry of activity with the aim of finding suitable land for a golf course. Land had become available in Belclare and this plot became a very live possibility.

"The Secretary went with P. Skerrit to look over the land and let us know what area we would require. Also to find out from Mr. King what rent he would require."

In May 1961 the Captain reported on his meeting with P. Skerrit. Skerrit had pointed out the fields they would require for their links. His estimated rent for the course was £400. The Captain and John Kelly along with B. Scott interviewed Mr. King and he mentioned he would require £200. It was estimated that the initial cost of the links and the clubhouse would be in the region of £1400. The problem was where would they get the money?

> "Some of the Committee were in favour of
> going to the bank but it was decided on
> Liam Golden's suggestion that a £10 levy
> be made on each member and then ask
> the balance from the bank."

By June 1961 instructions had been given to Lorcan Gill sol. to include certain clauses in the lease to cover:

(a) making alterations to existing walls etc. in order to construct course.
(b) Renewal of lease after 25 or 50 years.
(c) Sheep only
(d) Construct roadway to clubhouse
(e) Permission to spray fairways.

Everything appeared to be moving along nicely. Golf would be played at Belclare under the usual conditions as of old. Rented land, sheep on fairways, greens fenced.

Then in August 1961 Mr. Tony King changed his mind about leasing. He would sell either all or part of it. This announcement deflated all hopes and expectations. If they would need the Bank to help establish the course at £1400 and this sum alone would cause great difficulty to finance, they certainly could not begin to contemplate purchasing.

"It was decided by the Committee that nothing further could be done, and the matter be dropped."

REFLECTIONS FROM JOHN KELLY, CAPTAIN 1958

'It was known around that WGC was looking for a new location. Many people knew I was a member and so people with land that might fit the bill came in to see about it.

The first man to approach was Tony King (of a family of big cattle jobbers in the Westport region). Tony worked for a relation of his, Andy O' Gorman at the Quay. They were paper factors.

Andy was a very nice elderly gentleman-a prolific poet; wrote utter rubbish (every time I went out to pick up paper bags or whatever for the shop, Andy would give me a bunch of these famous poems.) Tony arrived in one day. He owned 88 acres beside John Healy's Belclare Hotel.

Tony wondered would the Golf Club buy the land so I got a meeting together and told them the proposal and they were all quite excited. Tony wanted about £10,000 for the land.

Now there was a house, two sheds, a yard and 88 acres of good land on the property-stretching from Vincent Bourke's house up to Belclare House Hotel and down to Shivdillagh at the shore.

It was a bit short for 18 holes – we would have had to incorporate some double greens and alternating tees if the project went ahead. The bottom line was we couldn't raise the ante. Tony said the best price was £9000

So I got another meeting called. This time we went out to see John Healy in the hotel. He had his private house there beside the hotel, beautifully appointed. We went in and John opened the cabinet with everything from Drambuie to lemonade in it!

So we asked John was there any way he could come up with a few thousand pounds.

We also asked could he give us a room on the ground floor of the hotel that we could use as a changing room, and then the point being that we could use his hotel bar as our bar, which of course he would profit nicely from.

He came in a few days later and said he was sorry but he couldn't raise a penny.

The next fellow that came into me with a possible location was a man from up around Knappabeg. He said he had some land between Lough Cogeen and Lough Leitirin, near Knappabeg.

So Pat Cox drove a delegation of us out to have a look.

The land was divided nicely between rocky mountain and wet bog. Pat Cox stepped over a wall and went down to his waist in bog the other side and we didn'y need too long to conclude that this wasn't what we were looking for.'

In March 1962 Mr. Michael McMahon suggested that Lord Sligo be approached with a view to providing land for a golf course and this suggestion was unanimously accepted by the meeting.

"Further discussion on this matter at the next committee meeting was thought to be very desirable."

However within the month Belclare was back on the agenda once more. It was announced that King's land was to be auctioned on the 12th of April. There would be 79 acres with no house. On the 4th of April a meeting "on special business" was held in the Central Hotel. There were obviously people in the Club who saw the need for a new golf course and one that the Club would own.

"Captain: The feeling of the Club is that the land is very desirable if it can be got. Of course the stumbling block is finance.
Lorcan Gill: Reserve price would be very high. The members of the town should guarantee the price.
Captain: The Club is very anxious to get this land. Aim at £6000 for a purchase on 20 signatures @ £300 each."
Lorcan Gill: I propose that names be taken to secure the money.

The names given were Liam Golden, H. Staunton , Lorcan Gill.

In this discussion Bord Fáilte was mentioned. If the course was purchased there would be a grant from Bord Fáilte.

The following motion was proposed by Lorcan Gill and seconded by Liam Golden. It was passed unanimously.

"That if a sufficient number of guarantees be found, an approach should be made to the Club bankers for accommodation up to £6000 for the purchase of Belclare lands; that if such accommodation be granted the club should attempt to purchase the said lands within the accommodation."

> *"Would the land earmarked be suitable for golf at all?*
> *"Could a top course if made, be properly run and maintained?*
> *"Who was going to pay for it? "*
>
> LORD SLIGO

It was agreed that further plans be made to fulfill the terms of the motion. This did not happen because at the AGM on Jan 25th 1963 no mention was made about the new links at Belclare. Then suddenly on August 30th 1963 a Special Meeting was called for the Railway Hotel. The subject for discussion:

"Proprietor of lands at Belclare offers
to sell same to the Club for the
purpose of a Golf Club."

No decisions were made about Belclare because in January 1964 there was an urgent call to "see Lord Sligo"

"M. Staunton to find out about the cost of a
club house in Belclare and see Lord Sligo."

While all this activity concerning Belclare was taking place Lord Sligo had been doing some thinking. In an interview he gave in 1970 he stated:

It was in 1964 that it first dawned on me that a championship course might be made on the Westport Estate. The lease of the existing nine hole course was coming to an end and there was no eighteen hole course in the county. Tourism was growing fast and something which could extend our short season was obviously desirable.

"I knew in a general way that golf was now big business with new courses being built all over the world and that television had brought the great players before a vast public. To me there were three big questions:

"Would the land earmarked be suitable for golf at all?

"Could a top course if made, be properly run and maintained?

"Who was going to pay for it? "

Aneas McNally who worked on Lord Sligo's estate since the age of 13 years also tells of the Lord's moment of epiphany,

"In the late 1960's Lord Altamont approached me and told me of his plans to have an 18-hole

Past captains, Liam Friel and Val Murray.

Brothers in golf: Brother D. Murphy, Brother P.K. Maher, and Brother L.K. Walsh.

Three wise men sharing a joke in the locker room in 2004 : Bertie Farrell, Des Mahon, and Seamus Walsh.

A family affair: Colm, Liam, Ben, and Sean Walsh.

championship course built on the land he owned in Carrowholly. My first reaction was that anyone who put the best of farmland into a golf course should be put to jail. But Lord Altamont was a visionary. He saw the benefit for tourism in the town and the Westport area."

Walter J.P. Curley, Rossyvera House, tells the following story,

"The late Denis Browne, Marquess of Sligo, was a good friend of my father's and of mine. Lord Sligo who was not a golfer and knew that I was, asked me to tramp over some acreage he had and then to tell him if I believed it could be made into a golf course. We walked over the land for several hours and at the end I told him my own impression was that it could be excellent. We then discussed the next step. I had been (still am) a member of Portmarnock for many years and that I knew everyone admired Hawtree. Sligo in due time contacted him."

In 1964 the officers and members of Old Carrowholly were not privy to Lord Sligo's thoughts on golf in the town. Neither is there evidence that he was aware of their pursuit of Belclare.

On January 18th 1964 Tom Wallace proposed at the AGM:

"That we stay in Carrowholly"

A counter proposal was made by M. Staunton, seconded by Lorcan Gill:

" That we pursue Belclare and write to Lane."

In the background other movements were being made. It was stated at a meeting in the Central Hotel on Friday May 8th 1964,

"Bord Fáilte are to inspect possible sites
for a Golf Course. They are to send an
architect from G.X. Batton and Co. to
inspect possible sites."

On the 24th July 1964 a telegram was received from John Harris, golf architect,

"Mr.Harris will review suitable sites
around Westport with a view to
constructing an 18-hole golf course."

It was decided to show him the 80 acres at Belclare plus Mr. O'Malley's adjacent field. Mr. Lorcan Gill was to accompany Mr. Harris on the land.

Bord Fáilte obviously were not privy at this stage to Lord Sligo's thinking either. It appears that independently Bord Fáilte was thinking of a golf course for Westport but they had no idea where in Westport. It is significant that it was Westport Golf Club Bord Fáilte contacted. Did Bord Fáilte think of a golf course for Westport without any Westport input or had the Westport Tourism Development Co. put the idea to them?

On the 20th of August 1964 a plan for the proposed golf course at Belclare was received from Mr. Harris.

"It was agreed to show it to the
Development Committee."

By November 1964 Belclare appeared to be off the agenda once again and Lord Sligo was back on. On the 24th of November 1964 it was stated,

"Lord Sligo might be willing to sell or
rent land for a golf course. Mr. Gill would
see Mr. Kennedy (estate secretary) to
arrange an interview."

Mr. Gill saw Mr. Kennedy and he suggested that the golf club inspect Lord Sligo's land and if a suitable area was found to approach Lord Sligo. According to Lord Sligo he had already found the suitable area on his estate. Was he now looking for the Golf Club's opinion?

In January 1965 a delegation was formed to view the land comprising of A. Malone, M. Staunton, A. de Fleury, M. Mulloy.

They were to report back to the committee.

At the same time a delegation was also formed to see Mr. G. Ingham regarding the renewal of the lease. This delegation comprised M. McMahon, J. Kelly, G. Hall. They were also to report back to the Committee.

So by January 1965 the following movement had taken place and was ongoing in some repects.

■ Bord Fáilte had sent an architect to Westport to look at possible sites but not on Lord Sligo's estate. A John Harris, golf architect, had produced a plan for a golf course at Belclare.
■ The Club delegation were inspecting Lord Sligo's land.
■ Whilst doing this they were trying at the same time to negotiate with George Ingham for a renewal of the lease to Old Carrowholly.
■ Lord Sligo, since 1964, had come to the conclusion that a Championship Golf Course could be built on the estate but he had not told Bord Fáilte yet.

At the AGM in 1965 it was decided to get in touch with Lord Sligo through Mr. Gill. He was to enquire about the possibility of renting land, the rate of same and the question of an entrance. At the same time it was decided to write to Mr. Lane to see what rent he might be interested in re. letting Belclare. The situation in regard to Old Carrowholly and the interview with George Ingham was also discussed.

In February a letter was received from Mr. Lane stating that he may be willing to lease 50 acres of his land to the club at Belclare. The committee decided that they would offer him £300 a year for the lease of the land and a maximum of £350. On the 4th of March Mr. Lane rejected the rent offer.

On the 12th of March 1965 there was a dramatic new entrant into the ongoing options available. Mr. Tommie Brennan of the Westport Tourism Development Co. said if they bought the land at Belclare they would be able to get a grant from Bord Fáilte to build a course and a clubhouse.

If this were done he wished to know what the golf club would pay for the lease of the course. The matter was discussed and it was decided to offer £500 a year for the lease. A delegation was formed to meet officers of the W.T.D. to make the offer and to discuss the matter generally.

On the 26th March Mr.Lane decided to put the land at Belclare on the market. It was decided to write to the different organisations in the town stating the fact and telling them of the Club's position generally.

In April it was decided to write to the W.T.D. requesting a meeting with a view to making a proposal to Bord Fáilte regarding the land at Belclare.

In June 1965 at a meeting in the Central Hotel it was decided to write to the Westport Tourism Development Committee thanking them for their help in "dealing with Bord Fáilte regarding Belclare."

While this was going on Lord Sligo was writing to the Hon. Secretary, Portmarnock Golf Club asking him if he could recommend a golf architect.

> "This was Dr. Eustace. I would like to thank him for making it all possible. In his reply dated May 1965 he stated that they were re-designing some holes at Portmarnock and proposed approaching a Mr. Hawtree who was at the time laying out a revised links at St. Andrews. "We calculate," wrote Dr.Eustace, "that if the Royal and Ancient considered Hawtree to be good enough to allow him to alter the sacred ground at St. Andrews he should be good enough for us." If Fred Hawtree was good enough for St. Andrews and Portmarnock he should be good enough for Westport."
>
> (interview 1970)

While the W.T.D. were smoothing the path for Golf Club access to Bord Fáilte re a golf course in Belclare, unbeknownst to all parties, Lord Sligo had found his architect for a championship course.

By September 1965 the lease to Old Carrowholly was once more the main focus.

"A delegation of T. Wallace, M. Staunton, M. King will see Mr. Ingham to find out what his minimum price would be for the renewal of the lease with the cattle on the course as at present."

It was then decided to send out a questionnaire to all members and some non-members to find out their views with regard to the future of the club. 160

circulars were sent out but only 26 were received in reply. These indicated 21 in favour of staying in Old Carrowholly and increasing the sub to £10 for men and £5 for Ladies in view of the demand of the Landlord for £300 for renewal of lease with cattle off the course west of the road and £200 with cattle on as at present, for a lease of 10 years. It was proposed that an independent committee be formed to investigate alternative sites.

On the 12th of November 1965 the meeting discussed the prospect of acquiring alternative lands for a golf course. With this in mind it was decided to see Lord Sligo,

> "and to inspect a possible site on the
> Louisburgh Road at Killadangan."

A mood of desperation was creeping in. In December John Kelly proposed that contact should be made with influential people such as Michael Moran T.D. and Bord Fáilte to place the position of the club before them with a view to obtaining assistance. He also suggested that Michael Heverin, Bord Fáiltes local man be invited to come to Westport to discuss the position of the Club.

A meeting on the 4th of January 1966 considered the matter of advising Bord Fáilte that the Club was to be terminated on the 31/3/ 1967.

At the AGM on Friday 4th of February 1966, P. Cox proposed to renew the lease at Old Carrowholly. This was seconded by G. McAleer. It was stated that the landlord in Belclare did not seem interested. John Kelly said he had contacted W. Reilly but his land was not available.

Then M. Staunton gave the most dramatic good news. He said he had met Lord Sligo and he was very keen to develop an 18-holes links but he has to have Bord Fáilte's assistance. He would also need hoteliers, Westport Golf Club, and other interested parties as shareholders. He would be the largest shareholder. He would lease to the Club on a graded basis. The entrance would be by Carrowholly as it is a public road. His Lordship suggested that the club should approach Bord Fáilte again. It was Lord Sligo's opinion that the project would take two to three years.

This information does not appear to have been acted upon because in March, "the decision regarding land at Carrabawn was deferred pending the return of the Captain, Mr. McAleer."

On the 10th of March the possibility of getting land for a golf course was discussed and it was decided to investigate further the site at Carrabawn and to:

> "Ask Lord Sligo what land if any he
> would have available for £150 a year."

On the 23rd of March 1966 the *Mayo News* broke a dramatic story:

"NEW WESTPORT GOLF COURSE"

The report detailed Hawtrees findings and his enthusiasm for the project. In his plan Ballyknock Farm, formerly the residence of the O'Reilly family and later the Carolan family, would be the location of the clubhouse.

"Mr. Hawtree was asked to inspect the land purposely in mid-winter when probably the weather would be at its worst. To my delighted surprise within a few hours I was told we would have a Championship Course. Within a forthnight his report and plan had arrived.

"The nature of the terrain, part inland and part seaside, the panorama which it commands and its considerable golfing virtues will combine to make it worthy of any of the major tournaments.
(Lord Sligo Interview 1970)

At the club meetings in April, May and June which followed this report there was no reference made to Hawtree or the new course.

On the 19th of August the officers made a new offer to George Ingham of £150 for a five-year lease with an option to renew the lease for another five years at £200 per year.

During all the discussions on this offer no reference was made to Bord Fáilte, Belclare, Lord Sligo, or Hawtree.

George Ingham ignored the offer. On the 3rd of September the *Mayo News* reported "Westport Golf Club closed" and that only the ladies waked

WESTPORT Moments

Enjoying the 19th hole: J. McAleer and J. McCormack

On a golf outing in Ballybunion:
J. Bredin, Bro. P.K. Maher, P. Murphy, O. Underwood.

1999 Austin O'Malley carpets sponsorship. Front - B. Burns (captain), A. O'Malley, S. Hyland. Back - D. O'Sullivan, H. Hoban, D.O' Connor.

St. Patricks Day is always special. Left to right – R. McCreave, M. Cavanaugh, H. Murphy, G. McAleer, G. Reilly

Grand marshal M. Cavanaugh with B. Bolster.

the old club on the Sunday evening and hopefully toasted the new one. The last competitive game played on the Links was won by Mrs. J. McGreal." On Monday the fences around the greens were to be removed. In this report the *Mayo News* made no reference to Lord Sligo's plan or Hawtree.

On the 23rd September 1966 while the groundsman was removing the wire from around the greens he was stopped by George Ingham the landlord. Contact was made with club officers and the outcome was Mr. Ingham was prepared to accept a new lease of £150 per annum. One would have expected the officers to be delighted with this news but now the discussion focused on whether it was financially possible to renew the lease. Members now differed on whether to return to Carrowholly or not. Mr. B O'Malley argued that there was no option to returning since alternate lands had not been found and it would be the end of Golf in Westport if the links were closed.

Mr. Lorcan Gill disagreed with Mr. O'Malley. He said he was always in favour of leaving Old Carrowholly as it would never be a good links and also it would never benefit the town as a tourist amenity since the condition and location was bad. But under present circumstances he felt it was necessary to keep Carrowholly for a year on a shoe-string basis.

> " The Old Course In Carrowholly was simply no longer suitable for WGC'S needs. It was too small and there were many boggy patches in it. The out-of-bounds were marked with white-washed rocks. I brought Major Deacon (A Director in Ranks and a scratch golfer in Lahinch for 30 years before) down and standing on the 1st tee, he asked me where the fairway was. When I pointed straight ahead he told me he had never seen the like of it before!!"
>
> (John Kelly/Capt.1958

Now the discussion moved on to whether to go back for good or on a shoe string basis. The vote on going back was 6 to 5 with two abstentions. Now a vote was called on going back to spend money on improving the links or going back on a shoe-string basis. After three hours of discussion and further differences the vote was unanimous in favour of going back to Old Carrowholly. The following clauses were to be stipulated in the lease:

- Fairways to be defined and cut as the club saw fit.
- No horse on course.
- Option to get out within a year.
- No feeding of stock on fairways or near greens or tees.

Those present at this meeting were: H. J. Staunton, John Kelly, M. Mulloy, T. Wallace, G. Hall, M. King, B. O'Malley, N. Ashe, M. Staunton, A. Malone, G. McAleer, H. Murphy, P. Cox.

So after all the searching for land for a New Course it was back to Old Carrowholly. Some were obviously glad. Others were different. They were aware something else was needed. Something better than Old Carrowholly.

Belclare was now a distant memory. Lord Sligo, Hawtree and the *Mayo News* story were forgotten. Did they consider the search to be over? Was the future of golf in Westport to be dependent on the renewal or non-renewal of a lease?

But for now it was back to Old Carrowholly and the old golfing life. There was now an enthusiastic burst of activity.

It was decided to consider the possibility of lengthening the third hole by placing a new green beyond the present green, near the precipice.

It was decided to approach the bank for £500 to finance this burst of enthusiasm. A letter was received from the bank stating they would require the names of ten guarantors before considering the sum required.

The ten guarantors were: G. McAleer, B. O'Malley, M. Henehan, P. Cox, M. Staunton, M. King, J. Kelly, L. Golden plus three Hoteliers, P. D. Rees, J. Jeffers, B. Ruddy.

Work parties were organised to get the greens in shape:

Malone, Hope, Murphy at 10.00a.m.Sat.;
McLaughlin, Adams, King at 2pm.

Work-parties were formed to improve drains and Charles Cannon was appointed Greenkeeper at £9 minus cost of his stamp. The official re-opening of the Club was fixed for 21st or 28th of May 1967.

In the background the Westport and District Tourism Development Co. Ltd had been working hard on an Amenity and Tourism Development Plan. On the 6th of May 1967 the *Mayo News* boasted a banner headline,

"MAJOR AMENITY DEVELOPMENT
PLAN FOR WESTPORT!"

Details of the 25-page plan, the first by any Development Company in Ireland, were released at a press conference in Jeffers Hotel. It was stated that the company would look " for full government aid and local co-operative effort to carry the plan through. Included in the plan are proposals for the erection of an 18-hole golf course."

On the 13th of May the *Mayo News* elaborated further on this plan. The report stated that an 18-hole course was essential for tourism in this area. The report went on to say that the Marquess of Sligo has made available a site on his estate. That said site had already been examined by a firm of golf architects, Hawtree and Son, Addington Court Golf Club, England and that preliminary site plans and reports had been prepared. It further stated that many organisations and Bord Fáilte were already aware of the plans. The Club also favoured outside capital being invested in it.

The report ended calling on Bord Fáilte to waste no time in putting their weight behind the venture because of the land available now.

This report does not appear to have caused any ripple of excitement in Old Carrowholly. No committee meeting from 13th of May 1967 up to and including the AGM of the 26th January 1968 made any reference whatsoever to the 18-hole course. These meetings were concerned with finance, investigating ways of raising cash from Bord Fáilte, seeking extension of lease, annual dinner dance, a golf film, a rugby film and the ladies wanting a guarantee of numbers for teas in future but no discussion ever on the *Mayo News* story.

REFLECTIONS FROM JOHN KELLY, CAPTAIN 1958

‘The breakthrough came with the Marquess of Sligo. I used to meet him coming down from the Central Hotel where he would go for his regular beer.

He was a prolific letter-writer to the Times – articulate and knowledgeable pieces and he would ask me did I read the latest letter and I would say I thought it was good or it was rubbish or whatever and we would have those kinds of little chats.

During one of those exchanges he said to me: "You're connected with the golf club in town, isn't that right?" I said I am. "Well," he said, " I've been in contact with the golf architect , Fred Hawtree and Bord Fáilte. I have plans for the development of a championship golf course in the Demesne, would the club be interested?"

I said we would be very interested. So, we arranged a meeting for the next week and I got in contact with the committee and told them about this and of course they were staggered. We all went down (myself, Maurice Mulloy, Brendan O'Malley, Pat Cox and maybe one or two others, I cannot recall now) to Westport House. Lord Sligo invited us in and offered us drinks. He then spread out the maps on a big mahogany table and we all looked at it with our mouths open. The whole thing was drawn out – a championship course covering maybe 130 acres of the Demesne. He said the estimated cost will be £20,000 to purchase the land, £20,000 to build a clubhouse and £20,000 to develop the course itself. So we looked at it all and then we asked him what the next step might be, and he said Bord Fáilte would be in touch with us and duly we were invited up to their offices on Earlsfort Terrace.’

REFLECTIONS FROM JOHN KELLY, CAPTAIN 1958

'A delegation of us (armed with two packs of cards with which we played many a game of "Solo") went up on the train – Fr. Tobin, Mickey Hastings, Philip McLaughlin, Gerry McAleer and the rest of us went up. We went for a little browse around Cleary's sports department (Philomena Garvey, the famous Irish Champion golfer was in charge of it) – but we didn't buy anything. We popped into the Royal Hibernian Hotel on Dawson Street for a memorable lunch in the "Lafeyette Room"- probably the best dining room in Ireland at the time. Following the gateux dripping with Grand Marnier the waiter brought the cream for the coffee saying , " from our own Jersey herd, Sir!"

Duly fortified, we went to the Bord Fáilte offices and met a Mr. Barry. He said, "the reason you are here is that we must have local involvement in this proposed golf course. We have the classic failure of a West of Ireland Championship Golf Course in Bundoran. There is a Great Northern Hotel up there and they have a championship course but it is inactive because there is no local involvement. The proposal for Westport is fundamentally a tourism venture but it is still absolutely necessary that we have local involvement."

I asked him what kind of a subscription did he envisage for the members and he said that we would be paying no more than £15 per annum. So Bord Fáilte were to be the landlords and they came to Westport soon after to meet the local committee- principally Dr. Sean Tobin, Philip McLaughlin, Mickey Hastings and others. I wasn't as active as those regarding the committee work; I found it very frustrating. You would ask a Bord Fáilte man a question and you'd invariably get a very vague reply.

The Club had to raise money and we went around to the various businesses in town. About £17,000 was raised but none of the Banks would subscribe to the fund.

I am sure of one thing in this story: without Lord Sligo there would be no golf course in the Demesne. It was nothing short of a miracle that things came out the way they did and it has always been my view that Sligo should have been made an honorary officer of the Club. There was a major land shortage in Carrowholly at that time. Many farmers were holding only ten or twelve acres each and here the Golf Club gets 150 or 170 acres of the prime land. One major field in the property was known as the fifty-acre field where Lord Sligo used to run horse races twice a year, approximately located where the present first to seventh holes are to-day.

So Hawtree came with a manager of his, Mr. Jiggens,who always wore jodhpurs. Bord Fáilte paid his fee. The course was about three or four years under construction. When it opened the subscription was about £10 or £15 p.a.

WGC has grown in so many ways since then. What we have now is a thriving club, we enjoy a premier golf course in a spectacular location. Long may it prosper.'

■ Dragged Into The Future.

On the 22nd February 1968 the President, Captain, Secretary and Treasurer of Westport G.C. were invited at very short notice to meet with Mr. Michael Heverin at his Bord Fáilte office in Westport. The future development of golf for Westport had arrived and they were to be invited to partake. Club members who were used to a relaxing golfing lifestyle were to be propelled into a major undertaking. Mr. Heverin outlined some tentative proposals in connection with the purchase of land for a new golf course in Westport which would be an 18-hole Championship Course. Local interests would be protected in any development. He requested information about the number of members in the club, green fees for the past five years and club rules.

At a Bord Fáilte Press conference in Galway Mr.Ceannt had said a new golf course was envisaged for Westport. In future golf in Westport would be an amenity for tourists.

Golf as a business had arrived.

Movement was now rapid.

On the 12th of March 1968 Myles Staunton received a telephone call from Bord Fáilte requesting the attendance of representatives from Westport G.C. at a meeting in Dublin on the 20th or 22nd of March, 3.30-4.00 p.m. in connection with a proposed new golf course in Westport. (meeting took place on 29th of March) It was agreed that the following members of the Committee would attend the meeting in Dublin: Fr. Tobin, Myles Staunton, B. O'Malley, J. Kelly, G. McAleer, M. Mulloy, P. McLaughlin.

The resignation of Vice-Captain, B. O'Malley for personal reasons was accepted with regret.

Bord Fáilte asked the Club to decide on its wish and ability to operate the new Golf Course .

On the 1st of April the Golf Club Committee was informed of the details of the meeting. A lengthy discussion followed.

In attendance were:

H. J. Staunton, Fr. Tobin, P. McLaughlin, J. Kelly, M. Mulloy, M. King, G. McAleer, A. Clarke, L. Golden, B. O'Malley, H. Murphy.

This Club meeting considered the following points:

■ Who would be responsible for building new course?
■ The entrance to the course as planned and suitability of?
■ The local contribution by loan and grant.
■ The involvement of other local bodies in fund raising and in the operation of the new course?
■ Could the new course be operated at a profit?
■ Are we willing to operate it?

It was decided to hold a meeting with other organisations in town to discuss the new course and to get their views on the raising of local contribution and the operation of the course.

In the meantime the *Mayo News* waxed lyrical about the asset the new course would be to the town:

"The project is one from which the entire community will reap the fruits of.
It is one of the most important developments in Westport's history."

On the 17th of April there was full support for the new course from other organisations in Westport. It was decided to form a committee to do all in its power to promote the new Westport golf course. Each club and organisation was to nominate two members to represent their organisation on the Committee.

Westport Dev. Co.: J.F.O'Malley / M.O'Donnell
Sea Angling Club:
Michael McLoughlin / P.J.Clarke
St. Patrick's Club: Chris Lavelle / T.P. Brennan
Boat Club: M. Crowley / T. Durcan

Horse Show Society: M.King / T.J.Nolan
Hotel Federation : D.Rees / J. Jeffers / B. Ruddy.
Chamber of Commerce:
Marc Trimmer / M. L. Browne
G.A.A.: P. Muldoon / Jackie Gibbons
Order of Malta: Dr. H. Farrell / P. O'Flanagan
Westport United: Niall Halpin / P. Glavey
Rugby Club: Stephen Walsh / D. McKeown
Boxing Club: L. Hingerton / John McGreal.

Bord Fáilte did not come to town until the 10th of October 1968. The organisation was represented by Mr. K. Barry, Mr. D. Cassidy, Mr. Reddy and Mr. Joe Lally.

They announced that the purchase of the land from Lord Sligo was almost completed except for some legal details.

The cost of developing the course would be £30,000. A clubhouse would cost £30,000.

Bord Fáilte would pay £16,000 for the land and would make 50% grant towards developing the course and building the clubhouse.

The Local contribution would be £30,000 (present value-circa €1.5. million).

The deeds of the property could be used to raise a £15,000 bank loan and this would leave a further £15,000 to be raised locally.

Mr. Cassidy B.F. said they were promoting golfing holidays and when facilities were provided there was no doubt but the tourists would come. He said they were now trying to bring the tourists further North from Kerry and Galway and if the facilities were put in Westport they would come this way.

Mr. Cassidy said he recognised the entrance as a problem but that it should be left to Bord Fáilte at the moment.

Mr. Barry said the title deeds would be held by the Regional Tourist Organisation.

They would make an acceptable arrangement with Westport Golf Club for management/operation and control of the new course.

It was necessary that the people who knew about golf, an existing golf club, should take charge. One condition was that green fees would not be increased by a greater percentage than subscriptions.

The long search for suitable land was finally over.

The *Mayo News* now reported a huge increase in membership in Westport Golf Club. The problem of raising the local contribution was now tackled in the form of a special Finance Committee.

The Chairman of this Finance Committee was Liam Golden, along with a committee of ten which included Stephen Walsh, J. F. O'Malley, and Michael Kennedy as secretary.

It was generally agreed that the Golf Club Committee would be responsible for dealing with Bord Fáilte re. the new course and not the Committee for raising funds.

On the 12th of December 1968 Liam Golden informed the meeting that the Finance Committee would ask members of the Golf Club to act as collectors in a fund-raising scheme.

At the AGM 17th January 1969 Mr.Gerry McAleer proposed, seconded by Ailbhe Malone that the Secretary write to Bord Fáilte and formally accept responsibility for the management and operation of the Westport Championship Golf Course and for the raising of the local contribution.

The long search for suitable land was finally over. The Officers in Old Carrowholly could only ever visualise renting land at a reasonable sum.

They, as it were, were waiting in the wings for some outside catalyst to change their golfing experience.

Lord Sligo had found his golf course on his estate and his architect but he needed a risk-taker to come on board.

In his interview in 1970 he said: "I approached the Tourist Board and put the case that a Championship Course was just what Westport and Mayo needed."

What better risk-taker to find than a state agency in Bord Fáilte!

But who pushed the idea at Bord Fáilte long before anyone else?

Here tribute must be paid to the Westport Tourism Development Co. and their vital part in this story. Bord Fáilte was the catalyst that brought all parties together for the first time and now a Championship Golf Course was about to be built.

■ **Keeping The Pressure On Bord Fáilte:1969-1970.**
The land had been purchased. The Architect's plan was ready. The organisation of the local contribution had begun. Those with the knowledge of golf would take charge. The unity of purpose in Westport for the project was astonishing and a great tribute to the generous nature of the many organisations in the town.

The family of Westport Golf Club was not found wanting at this critical time and with their long engrafted knowledge of golf they soon realised Bord Fáilte would need constant heckling if the project was to come to fruition..

In January 1969 Westport people were anxious to know when would the architect arrive and the date for the commencement of the work. They decided to write to Bord Fáilte for this information.

In February 1969 Mr. Michael Kennedy, Secretary of the Finance Committee, applied to Westport District Court for a lottery licence to run "Home Bingo". He explained to the judge that a committee of 10 had the task of collecting £30,000 (c. €1.5. million presently) within two years. It was a vast sum of money and worked out at £10 per head of the entire population of the town.

Supt. Sean Murray said he had no objection as the new Westport International Golf Course would be a huge benefit to the community. The licence was granted and alongside Home Bingo local firms and individuals were asked to make contributions by bankers order. Guinness were asked to make a contribution to the cost of the bar in the new clubhouse. National subscriptions and life membership would be dealt with at a later date.

On the 28th of March it was emphasised at a club meeting that pressure would have to be kept on Bord Fáilte to proceed with the development of the new course.

On the 31st March Fred Hawtree wrote to Michael Kennedy, Secretary/ Agent, Marquess of Sligo's Estate office,

"We have now received instruction from Mr.Cassidy of Bord Fáilte to go ahead. Mr. A. H. F. Jiggens, F.R.I.C.S., M.I.C.E., A.M.T.P.I. is to come over on Tuesday 8th of April. He will peg out

Driving in the first stake: Hugh Murphy (Captain), A. H. Jiggens, the golf architect with Fred Hawtree. Supporting are (back left to right: Pat Cox, Gerry McAleer, Philip McLaughlin (vice-captain), Brendan O'Malley, and Reginald Blackstock.

the greens and tees and take details for our bill of quantities. Would it be possible for you to arrange for someone to accompany him to help with the pegging out and also to provide approx. 50 pegs.

If we can get tenders in by the middle of May it should be possible to start work later that month."

■ Driving In The First Stake 1969.

On the 19th of April the *Mayo News* reported that, "The ceremony of the Captain of a Golf Club driving into office had a unique twist when Westport Golf Club Captain, Mr. Hugh Murphy assisted Mr. A. H. Jiggens to drive in the first stake at the new Westport International Championship Golf Course."

Now the question of the entrance began to emerge as a major problem. The question of some concerns having a private entrance was raised. The Finance Committee were finding the question of the entrance hindering the raising of the local

contribution. At this stage the main entrance was to be through Carrowholly but at the meeting of the 21st April it emerged that alternative entrances were under review by someone as estimated costs of construction were given at the meeting:

> Entrance at A. McMahons
> (Jarlath/ Anne Duffy's): £4,000
> Entrance at the Quay: £12,000
> Entrance at the Town: £15,000

Another request was made to Bord Fáilte to come to Westport or if not Westport delegates would travel to Dublin.

On the 1st of May 1969 Mr.Cassidy, Bord Fáilte, agreed that the question of entrance was urgent. A serious rumour had emerged that Jury's Hotel in Westport would have a private entrance. Mr. Cassidy was questioned about this. He said he would check this but he was left in no doubt that a private entrance by Jury's and the main entrance by Carrowholly would have a very grave effect on the local contribution.

At this meeting he announced that Mr. Simon Kelly had been appointed clubhouse architect by Bord Fáilte. He said anything to do with the clubhouse and site for same could be discussed with Mr. Kelly.

He said Bord Fáilte would discuss the watering of greens with Fred Hawtree and they would check on the necessity and requirements of same for a championship golf course.

On the 23rd of May a golf club committee was formed to deal with the new course on a day to day basis. The people selected for this were B. O'Malley, P. McLaughlin and J. Kelly.

In the background Home Bingo was running into difficulty as more promoters were needed and these were not volunteering. Only 12 promoters emerged from 80 members in the golf club.

By June it appeared to B. O'Malley that Bord Fáilte were using delaying tactics.

On the 3rd of July a progress report meeting was held in Dublin. Here the re-siting of the clubhouse was discussed. Bord Fáilte stated that it would be a clubhouse on modest lines. Bord Fáilte asked the delegation to trust them on the matter of the entrance. Bord Fáilte would like to see an alternative entrance other than Carrowholly. Bord Fáilte gave an assurance that money was available for the project and that there would be no stinting on expense. They hoped work on the course would commence early in September.

By August the Committee had selected Barretts Hill as the site for the new Clubhouse. They decided to write to Bord Fáilte stating this.

Friction was now beginning to emerge between the Golf Club Committee and the Finance Committee. Mr. Vincent Roughan, Hon. Secretary, in a letter stated that:

"the liaison between the Finance Committee and Westport Golf Club is unsatisfactory."

In November more urgent matters emerged to

> *The lowest tender was £56,000 or roughly £3000 per hole, a figure far in excess of which Bord Fáilte would wish to pay*

focus minds once more. Two members of the Finance Committee, J. F. O'Malley and Stephen Walsh, attended a golf club meeting and stated that Hoteliers in town were not going to put up any money until they knew where the entrance was going to be. They wanted this position to be forwarded to Mr. Barry

In January 1970 at a meeting in Dublin Mr. Barry could not tell if there was going to be any other entrance other than the Carrowholly way.

At a club meeting Gerry McAleer said it was essential to get work started this Spring otherwise "we would have to wait until October or November next".

"Home Bingo" was abolished on Jan 12th 1970. The overall effort showed a profit of £800.

By February 1970 there was a degree of hostility at the Westport end towards Bord Fáilte. The Westport Officers were fed up of oral dialogue with Bord Fáilte. They wanted Bord Fáilte to commit themselves to the project in writing. Something Bord Fáilte had been reluctant to do so far. The Westport Officers now demanded a meeting in Westport with Bord Fáilte under certain conditions.

■ Bord Fáilte to forward a specification /bill of quantities for scrutiny by a select sub-committee, the members of which would have expertise in these matters.
■ That Niall P. Reddy along with Bord Fáiltes Quantity Surveyor come to Westport to discuss Bill of Quantities with select sub-committee.
■ That Mr. Barry come at the earliest time to meet the Golf Club Committee subsequent to this meeting.
■ That a stenographer be present at the latter meeting to put an end to the oral dialogue.

Westport Golf Club Officers and Committee were now driving the project.

But on the 12th. of March 1970 Mr. Niall Reddy's letter delivered bad news. His letter informed the meeting that the lowest tender was

SEARCHING FOR A GOLF COURSE

£56,000 or roughly £3000 per hole, a figure far in excess of which Bord Fáilte would wish to pay.

Bord Fáilte now wanted to discuss extensive local involvement in drainage, earth moving, water supply to greens, and planting in order to effect economies.

The select sub-committee consisting of A. O'Mhaoileoin, B.E. and John Farrell, were puzzled by these figures. Their pricing of the Bill of Quantities performed as a contractor would normally do so, protecting himself where he saw the need for such, resulted in a figure of approx. £90,000. They now re-visited the bill of quantities and repriced the document at rock bottom charges, making no provision this time for unseen eventualities. Their pricing now came to £54,161 which was as near as made no difference to the price of the lowest tender. The opinion the select sub-committee now expressed was that if Bord Fáilte required a Championship Golf Course, then it was going to cost money.

No one could produce a formula for effecting economies, even with extensive local involvement, except by means of a pruning down of the whole operation.

It was now felt once again that the access road was vital to the whole project. Mr. Rory Daly of Jury's Hotel scotched the unfounded rumour about a private entrance for his hotel. He said he was authorised to state that Jury's only requirement was an access road from the town and common to all. They were not seeking preferential treatment in any way.

In the background golf tourism was continuing to develop. In April 1970 the *Mayo News* reported that members of 500 clubs had played Westport in 1969. The visitors book revealed that over 70% of these tourists were from England, Scotland and Wales. Others came from Holland, Germany, Italy, Canada, Israel, South Africa, Australia and America. The report went on to say that this tourist traffic in this area made it possible to envisage the establishment of a Championship Course at Westport.

On the 4th of May a club meeting discussed a strategy for a meeting with Bord Fáilte. Here a long discussion took place on the access road and it was felt that the air would have to be cleared with Mr. Barry and Mr. Cassidy on this subject.

Finally on the 5th of May 1970 a key meeting took place with Bord Fáilte in Westport. This meeting was characterised by tough talking from Sean Tobin. Present at the meeting were:

Hugh Murphy, past Captain, chairman.
Bord Fáilte: Kevin Barry, Technical Manager,
D.Cassidy, Development Officer.
Westport Finance Committee; J. F. O'Malley,
Stephen Walsh.
Regional Tourism Org.: Michael Heverin, Michael
Kennedy.
Westport Golf Club: Cormac Hughes, L. Gill, G.
McAleer, Gar Golden, J. P. Campbell, H. Murphy,
M. Henehan jr., J. Farrell, L. Golden, J. Kelly,
M. Mulloy, B. Ruddy, M. King, H. J. Staunton,
M. Cavanaugh, E. McCrea, B. O'Malley, Dr. S.Tobin.
Apologies received from the Captain
P. McLaughlin, A. O'Mhaoileoin, P. D. F. Rees.

Bord Fáilte admitted there had been delay and the reason was money. But Mr. Barry said Bord Fáilte were committed to the project and they were going ahead with it.

He said that when Bord Fáilte became interested the budget was £75,000/£80,000 – £30,000 for Course, £30,000 for clubhouse, and £17,000 for purchase of lands.

It now appeared that the project would cost a staggering £125,000. He wanted to know if assistance to cut cost could be forthcoming from Westport end. Instead he was told that the select sub – committee findings suggested that the total cost might be greater.

Mr. Barry said in Westport they were starting from scratch. He admitted under questioning that Bord Fáiltes original estimate was too low. He was bluntly told that Westport could not contribute in excess of £30,000. That in

It now appeared that the project would cost a staggering £125,000.

fact the Finance Committee would do well to reach £20,000. Gouldings had submitted the lowest tender and maybe economies could be discussed with them and Mr. Jiggens when he came in May.

Questioned about the access road Mr. Barry said he was able to predict a favourable outcome.

He said he was interested in the Quay area as a major tourist amenity area with water, boats, fishing and in addition the Golf Club.

He said he foresaw the development of the Quay area as running into a number of years and that it seemed logical to him that the entrance to the Golf Course should be in this area.

He was a state employeee entrusted with the expenditure of public money as a boost to tourist development.

Dr. Tobin pressed Mr. Barry for an assurance that the access road question would be a subject for discussion with the Golf Club Committee before the details are finalised.

On the 26th of May a meeting was held in Westport between representatives of Bord Fáilte, Hawtree, Gouldings and Westport Golf Club to discuss Hawtree's specification, Bill of Quantities, and Gouldings tender price.

The Golf Club was represented by Liam Golden, Gerry McAleer, John Kelly, Maurice Mulloy, John Farrell, Ailbhe Mhaoileoin and Dr. Sean Tobin.

On the 6th of June the *Mayo News* announced that construction work would begin on Monday June 15th, 1970.

Course construction would be carried out by an Irish firm, Gouldings Ltd. Consultants as to soil improvements, fertilisers and seed mixtures would be the Sports Turf Research Institute, Bingley, Yorkshire.

In July the *Mayo News* reported that the contract was signed and that the price was £59,293 . The work would be completed in 16 months. The contract did not include a new clubhouse but it was expected that the course and clubhouse would open simultaneously.

> *"This development is not provided merely for the benefit of visitors; the tourist trade has made it possible; but it is primarily a social development for the people of Westport and Mayo. The West of Ireland has a great need to provide leisure amenities, both to make it a desirable place to live in, a desirable place to come back to and for industrialists contemplating setting up factories, a desirable place to settle in."*
>
> JOE LALLY,
> REGIONAL TOURIST MANAGER

Speaking at the signing of the contract, Mr. Joe Lally, Regional Tourist Manager, said,

"This development is not provided merely for the benefit of visitors; the tourist trade has made it possible; but it is primarily a social development for the people of Westport and Mayo.

"The West of Ireland has a great need to provide leisure amenities, both to make it a desirable place to live in, a desirable place to come back to and for industrialists contemplating setting up factories, a desirable place to settle in."

By the end of July the Finance Committee was having grave difficulty in raising funds.

They requested a meeting with the Golf Club Committee. Liam Golden, Stephen Walsh, Tommie Brennan, J.F. O'Malley reported distressing news.

The amount collected and committed locally was only £8,000. Money would have to be raised from new sources.

Tommie Brennan outlined a proposal for sponsorship of holes by national firms. This was passed without objection.

It now also emerged that tree planting originally included in Hawtree's plans at a cost of £3000 was not included in the contract with Gouldings. Hawtree wanted the trees to be planted this winter. Plans for a water source were also absent.

Despite everything by September 1970 work on the course was progressing steadily. Gouldings would be moving off the site in October for the winter break. They would not be returning to the site until March 1971.

There were no developments in relation to the clubhouse.

In October the Secretary wrote to Mr. Barry deploring the inactivity in the matter of planning of the clubhouse. Bord Fáilte sanctioned the demolition of "O'Malleys House".

In January 1971 it was announced that the estimated cost of the clubhouse would be £42,500.

Westport and District Tourist Development Co.
Seated: left to right: John Hastings, Frank Gill, Eamon Hynes, Liam Golden, Benny McAleer, John Kelly,
Verdon Clarke, David Reece.
Standing: left to right: John Mulloy, Lorcan Gill, Stephen Walsh, Pascal Burke, Pat McEvilly, Bertie Staunton,
Tommie Brennan, Ann O'Donnell, Jeff O'Malley, John Jeffer, Michael McLoughlin, Michael Gibbons.

■ Building A Championship Golf Course
   1971-1973.

When Lord Sligo sold the land and Hawtree's plan to Bord Fáilte his input was over for the time being. Now the building of the golf course was between Westport Golf Club and Bord Fáilte.

The state body had never built a golf course from scratch before. It is true to say that Westport Golf Club now drove the project to fruition.

The club kept the pressure on Bord Fáilte to deliver. The golf club raised the important issues and demanded answers and action to same.

The members of Westport Golf Club had extensive knowledge concerning golf.

They had a lifetime's experience of fairways and greens. They knew what was required and they prodded a sometimes reluctant Bord Fáilte in the right direction.

Westport members were aware the lease on Old Carrowholly was up on the 31st October 1971. Time was now of the essence so efforts were redoubled.

In May 1971 the Finance Committee released money for the purchase of machinery. By June the Club realised that steps would have to be taken to renew the present lease on Old Carrowholly.

An applicant of considerable merit, Mr. Paul Cook, applied for the position of Head Greenkeeper. He had been recommended by Mr. Hawtree.

Bad news came re the cost of E.S.B. supply to the Clubhouse.

> " The costs were staggering but we had little option but to go along with them."

In July they discovered in the draft plan for the car park there was no reference to a machinery shed to house the club's equipment. There was also no provision in the specification for a practice putting green.

Another key meeting took place on the 16th of August in Cavanaugh's Hotel.

Bord Fáilte: Mr. Niall Reddy, Technical Department.
Western Tourism: Mr. Brian Flynn.
Mr. Hawtree; Mr. Jiggens.
Bingley Sports Turf Research: Mr. Ryan.
Westport G.C. : President, H. J. Staunton;
Captain, Rev. E. O'Malley; Vice-Captain, Mickey
Hastings. Messrs. G. McAleer, V. Roughan,
M. Mulloy, C. Hughes, J. Kelly, M. Moran,
D. O'Regan, Dr. S. Tobin. Apologies: L. Golden,
M. Henehan, Simon Kelly, clubhouse architect.

July 1, 1970: The making of a golf course on the 13th fairway during construction. Left to right: Dr S. Tobin, L. Gill, Fr E. O'Malley, J.P. Campbell, J. Farrell, Mr Kelly, B. O'Malley, E. McCrea, B. Ruddy, A. Malone, J. Lally, M. Heverin, H. Staunton, R. Blackstock. Inset: The 13th today.

A view of the 2nd hole (index 8) with a putting surface which slopes from back to front.

This meeting proceeded under three headings:

(1) Bord Fáilte/ Westport G.C. problems.
(2) The Championship G.C.
(3) The Clubhouse.

Mr. Reddy said matters relating to the leasing of the Championship Course to Westport G.C. were well advanced. The "hot potato" of the access road was raised by Sean Tobin.

It was still hindering fund-raising efforts. Mr. Reddy said it would be a matter between Bord Fáilte and the Estate. He said the financing of the road would come from several sources, possibly the County Council, the Urban Council, Bord Fáilte, the Estate and Westport G.C.

Mr. Jiggens was asked by Sean Tobin about the practice putting green and yardages for the holes. Mr. Jiggens replied that the practice putting green was vital but could not be shown on drawings until the exact location of the clubhouse was known.

As regards yardages, Mr. Jiggens said a hole is measured from two yards from the back of the tee to the centre of the green in one plane and he would do this.

The construction contract ended when Mr. Hawtree and Son were satisfied that the work was completed to their satisfaction and they would issue a certificate to that effect. There was a defects clause and Hawtree would make periodic inspection during this 12-month period from the issuing of the certificate.

■ Whole Project Dependent On Head Greenkeeper.

Mr. Ryan of the Bingley Institute said it would be April 1973 before the course would be playable. He said the first five years of maintenance were the important years. Construction was the easy part. One would not have Championship greens for five years and then only with a high standard of maintenance.

Mr. Ryan said that the whole programme was dependent on the appointment of a proper head greenkeeper. Mr. Ryan was also of the opinion that a shed of 1600 square feet would be required to house machinery, store fertilisers, prepare

compost indoors in winter months and a tea room for ground staff.

On the 30th of August Mr. Simon Kelly displayed his plans for the clubhouse. His drawings showed a machinery shed of only 800 square feet. He said along with this the existing buildings would be retained.

In the meantime George Ingham had agreed to a rent of £175 for the coming year. This figure would cover Golf in Old Carrowholly until cessation in Spring 1973. The Clubhouse would become the property of Mr. Ingham on cessation of Golf. The removal of posts and wires, flattening of tees, rebuilding walls and removal of stones and posts would be Mr. Inghams responsibility.

In October 1971 it emerged that single phase E.S.B. supply would be sufficient despite it being agreed that three phase supply was essential for clubhouse and ancillary requirements. People were becoming unhappy with many areas.

The clubhouse plans were not popular with some members. Mr. A. Malone produced a list of some 20 or more criticisms of the clubhouse plan the most radical of which was that the clubhouse was entirely unsuitable and should be redesigned. Hawtrees were not happy with some of Gouldings work on the course. Hawtrees were suggesting that the remaining work be taken out of their hands and put in charge of the Head Greenkeeper, Mr. Cook. They wanted a sum of money, £2,000, withheld from Gouldings which would be paid into the Golf Club account.

Mr. Ryan of the Bingley Institute was not satisfied either. He was very unhappy with the execution of the maintenance contract under the headings, mowing, cutting, fertilising and dressing. In his opinion Gouldings had failed. Mr. Cook said he would need four men in addition to himself to finish the Goulding maintenance contract. He submitted a list of machinery he would require costing £5,650 and he gave an estimated figure of £13,000 for the maintenance of the course for one year.

These figures led to Mr. Reddy wanting to know the Westport position before going any further. Mr. Liam Golden said £8,000 had been collected with a further £2,000 committed in bankers orders. He said £3,000 of this had already gone to provide machinery, leaving a balance of £5,000. He again pointed out the problem caused by the access road in the matter of raising finance.

Mr. Reddy then put it to Mr. Golden that if the access road was sorted out did he think the target of £30,000 would be reached. Mr. Golden replied in the negative. Mr. Reddy was very perturbed by this and said it would weaken his hand in looking for money from Bord Fáilte.

He was anxious to know if Westport was backing out of the £30,000 contribution which had always been agreed. He was assured this was not so but the amount would not be speedily to hand. He asked that he be sent in writing Westport's commitment to £30,000 and that the question of using the deeds as collateral for a loan be incorporated in same.

While this anxiety was troubling minds the Secretary, Dr. Tobin, informed the meeting that after the lease was signed a draft constitution for the Championship Course would have to be drawn up in order to apply to the G.U.I. for affiliation.

In this regard he had written to various big clubs for copies of their constitution.

He had received replies from Royal Dublin, Woodbrook, The Hermitage, Killarney, Ballybunion, Lahinch – but none from Portmarnock or Co. Sligo.

In November Gouldings agreed to leave the site and to the withholding of £5000 by Bord Fáilte. The Committee now decided to press ahead with the recruitment of staff and the purchase of further machinery. Mr. A. Malone and Mr. Simon Kelly disagreed on the clubhouse.

Bord Fáilte had given him a brief to design a multi-purpose clubhouse with the cost not exceeding £60,000 and with the front aspect affording views of the 9th and 18th greens. He said there would be no possibility of obtaining a new brief for a more expensive clubhouse.

The clubhouse was now becoming a priority if it was to be erected by the time the course was ready for play.

On the 23rd of Nov. 1971 a discussion took place on the financing of the maintenance of the golf course. Bord Fáilte would be prepared to provide £15,000 in the year with another £5,000

coming out of the local fund. Bord Fáilte said this figure could not be exceeded and would only be issued on the foot of certified accounts.

Mr. John Kelly suggested that it might be possible to go ahead with the building of the permanent machinery shed independently of the clubhouse and this was agreed by all as a very sensible suggestion.

By February 1972 difficulties were emerging in relation to the E.S.B. supply and the telephone link. It now appeared from the E.S.B. that an underground supply would be the only one feasible. The provision of the telephone link would probably cause the same difficulty and an underground supply would probably be necessary in this instance also.

The 6th hole:
A beautiful par 4 –
index 4 – rising to an
elevated green.

The draft of a new constitution and a scale of fees for the new course was becoming a priority due to a request from hoteliers as to a weekly green fee charge which they might have published in brochures for 1973.

Another problem arose in relation to the road from the 4th Tee to the 17th Green. A complaint received from Austin Browne had been referred to the Tourist Board.

An announcement on the access road was now expected within a matter of weeks and this would pave the way for the release of the clubhouse for tender.

Because of the many issues to be dealt with sub-committees were established on February 28th to compile a constitution and a set of rules for the Championship Course and to deal with current affairs.

The Constitution committee comprised, Mickey Hastings (Captain), Dr. S. Tobin, G. McAleer, John Kelly, Fr. Eamon O'Malley, E. McCrea.

The Steering Committee appointed to deal with current affairs in relation to the Championship Course comprised, Messrs. Michael Moran, Gerry McAleer, Dr. S. Tobin.

A vacancy for Assistant Greenkeeper had arisen and nine replies were received. A long discussion led to the following guidelines for future appointments,

(1) That successful applicants should have a background connected with agriculture.

A view of the 8th hole – index 2 – with the
lake on the right-hand entry to the green.

(2) That permanent appointees be drawn from a young age group, preferably in the twenties and

(3) That everything else being equal preference be given to married men on the assumption that these might be reasonably expected to have let their roots down in the area. Mr. John Garavan was appointed to the vacancy.

The Head Greenkeeper now had a problem. He had nowhere to prepare compost. Progress in the matter of the machinery shed was slow. Mr. E. McCrea volunteered to approach Lord Sligo for the use of one of his sheds in the farmyard for this purpose.

By the 21st of March work on erecting the machinery shed had not begun. The E.S.B. were looking for an annual service charge of £78. The supply and maintenance of machinery was also causing headaches. A second-hand tractor had been supplied without a safety cab.

On the 12th of April 1972 a key meeting took place in Cavanaugh's Hotel. Lord Sligo's input was to prove vital once more. There was no set agenda. All aspects of the golf course would be discussed under appropriate headings.

Bord Fáilte: Niall P. Reddy, Tom McLoughlin.
Finance Committee: Liam Golden (Chairman),
Stephen Walsh (Vice-Chairman)
Westport Golf Club: President , H. J. Staunton,
Eddie McCrea, Dr. S. Tobin, John Farrell,
John Kelly, Gerry McAleer.
The Right Hon. The Marquess of Sligo was also
in attendance.
Apologies were received from Captain, Mr.
Mickey Hastings and Rev. Fr. Eamon O'Malley.

Leenareevagh was causing concern as were the flap valves in the Churns. Lord Sligo said the drainage at Leenareevagh had always presented problems.

It was now the feeling that the drainage scheme designed by Hawtree and as executed by Gouldings had not solved the problem. It was agreed that a close eye would have to be kept on this area.

Lord Sligo then displayed maps of the proposed access road. It was emphasised that a through public road to Carrowholly rather than a road to the clubhouse was envisaged. The road outlined was agreeable to all but information as regards financing the road was not forthcoming.

The Golf Club Members then pressed for the release of the clubhouse to tender.

They pointed out that the course was practically completed and that a clubhouse would be a necessity for the intake of money. Mr. Reddy said his budget for 1972-73 would not leave him with enough money to complete the clubhouse without a contribution from Westport and he said he would not let the clubhouse to tender until he knew that the financial position was right.

It was then Mr. Stephen Walsh delivered bad news to Mr. Reddy.

The Finance Committee had been inactive for over a year and a half. He said initially when they started everything was fine but then they came up against a stone wall with the hoteliers on the question of the access road. But now that the access road was resolved they would start again. He could see the fund reaching £20,000 (€1m value presently) but the remaining £10,000 would be a different matter.

Mr. McLoughlin of Bord Fáilte then gave information on the lease as to Bord Fáilte's thinking. The lease would be between the Western Regional Tourism Organisation and Westport Golf Club. The lease would be short and the rental a few hundred pounds per annum.

The lease could be used as collateral for overdraft facilities. However he was adamant that Westport's contribution of £30,000 would have to be reached.

The Golf Club members protested about the figure mentioned for rental. Mr. McLoughlin demanded a letter stating the amount of money raised locally so far, the amount which could be confidently expected to be raised in the next three months and the amount expected to be raised in the next year.

Lord Sligo went on to say that the local hoteliers had been slow to show their enthusiasm

> *The Draft Lease and Deed of Covenant now raised hackles in the Golf Club.*

for the project for fear Jury's Hotel would gain any advantage in the way of access to the course.

Now however, the access road question had been solved and as things turned out Jury's Hotel was the hotel situated farthest away from the start of the access road.! Nevertheless in order to show their confidence in the project he proposed to hand over a cheque for £1,100 on their behalf to the Finance Committee. This gesture was applauded by the meeting.

■ The Passing Of A Valued Friend.

On the 21st of April 1972 golf in Westport lost a great and valued friend when Mr. Lorcan Gill passed away. It was hoped he would have steered the Golf Club through a legal maze into the new golf course but the Lord ordained otherwise.

Mr. Gill was a Club Trustee, Club Solicitor and long time advocate for the development of Golf in Westport. The club now found itself without a solicitor at a time when quite a number of legal problems were likely to arise.

By May 1972 the machinery shed was erected. The E.S.B. had received the go-ahead from Bord Fáilte for an underground supply. Leenareevagh was causing problems as the herring bone system was not taking the water away.

The clubhouse had been let out on tender. The four assistant greenkeepers were looking for a pay-rise which was refused. Pressure was mounting as regards compiling a constitution, set of rules, local rules, subscription table and such matters. A copy of the revised Portmarnock Constitution had been received.

By June it had been ascertained that the firm of Kelly, Byrne and Gill were to remain in business and that legal problems would be dealt with by Mr. Paddy Durcan and Mr. Tom Durcan, solicitors.

The question of Leenareevagh had continued to play on Michael Moran's mind. Mr. Jiggens had visited the site but Mr. Moran thought his reasons for the problem were simplistic. Michael Moran believed the answer was far more complex. He asked Mr. Jiggens if there was a map of the levels of Lennareevagh in existence but he received an evasive answer. Mr. Moran knew no soil testing or any scientific data had been obtained prior to designing the drainage system. The system had been designed following a visual inspection. He suggested that the golf club seek the services of a soil chemist, a drainage expert from An Foras Taluntais and a research officer from Wavin Ltd. Balbriggan. His opinions were vindicated and Leenareevagh was not a simple problem.

The tenders for the clubhouse were opened in the Tourist Office and the lowest tender was from Conlon Brothers. The bill of quantities was being checked and the appointment of the firm of contractors was expected within the week.

In August a series of problems emerged.

Mr. Reddy of Bord Fáilte had been transferred and his successor would be Mr. Tom McLoughlin. Before Bord Fáilte would sign the contract for the clubhouse they decided to play hardball. They required a letter stating the amount of the Westport financial effort to date and giving a guarantee that they would raise and be responsible for the remainder up to a total of £30,000.

It then transpired that the telephone and E.S.B. cables could not be laid in the same trench because if this were done the telephone would never be satisfactory.

The draft lease and Deed of Covenant now raised hackles in the golf club.

The Committee members agreed they were too restrictive. Ireland West intended to have all the power and let the local Golf Club Committee do all the work without having any real say in the development of the club.

There was no clause in the draft lease to protect Westport's contribution to the project. There were clauses that would bind their hand in the future development of the club. The lessors gave themselves the right to fix green fees. The tone of the Deed of Covenant was excessively restrictive. One clause opened the door to a manager-type situation which the Golf Club Committee would not buy.

In the meantime Michael Moran's concerns about Leenareevagh led to a site meeting between

Mr. Jiggens, Dr. John Mulqueen, B.Agr. Sc. P.Hd of An Foras Taluntais and Mr. Ryan of the Sports Turf Research Institute, Bingley.

A soil chemist and a representative from Wavin Pipes were also present. Dr. Mulqueens findings were diametrically opposed to the opinions of Mr. Jiggens and Mr. Ryan. The drainage of Leenareevagh was now in the court of Bord Fáilte, Hawtree and Bingley.

On the 30th of August 1972 a special meeting took place at Cavanaugh's Hotel.

The Captain, Mr. Mickey Hastings was in the chair. Golf Club: President, H.J. Staunton, Dr. S. Tobin, John Farrell, Fr. Eamon O'Malley, David O'Regan, Liam Golden, John Kelly, Brendan O'Malley. Bord Fáilte: Mr. Niall Reddy, Mr. Tom McLoughlin Finance Committee: Stephen Walsh, J. F. O'Malley. Western Regional Tourism Org.: Joe Lally, Dan O'Neill, Mr. Michael Browne sol. Kelly, Byrne, Gill, sol.: Mr. Tom Durcan.

The discussion started with the Golf Club's objections to the draft Lease and Deed of Covenant. Nowhere in the Deed of Covenant was there any mention of Westport's contribution. Mr. Joe Lally proposed that a provision should be made in the deed to the effect that, " if at any time the club was wound up and assets realised, both parties, that is Bord Fáilte and Westport Golf Club should be paid off in proportion to the original investment."

Why was there no renewal clause in the lease? What happens after 49 years? This was to protect Bord Fáiltes interest and to preclude Westport Golf Club from acquiring the fee simple of the course. Mr. McLoughlin said there was no renewal clause which might confer rights on the golf club.

This did not mean there would be no renewal as Bord Fáiltes interest was in the continuity of the golf club. As regards the review of Rents every seven years, Mr. McLoughlin said this was to protect Bord Fáiltes investment in the event of the club making large profits. No increase would be sought if the club was doing badly.

Mr. Liam Golden then dealt with the local

contribution. He said to date £12,000 had been collected in hard cash and £7,600 was already spent on machinery. Bankers Orders would yield another £3,000 by late 1973 making a total of £15,000 in all. Mr. McLaughlin said this information was disquieting because as far as he was concerned the project only went ahead on the understanding that Westport would contribute £30.000. Mr. McLoughlin then tried to get a financial response.

He said there was no possibility of signing the clubhouse contract without a commitment from Westport for £30,000.

It was pointed out to him that the course was already in existence, that the Golf Club was in no position to finance maintenance of it without a clubhouse which would be their means to earn income. It was also pointed out to him that Trustees could not be appointed or overdraft procured without the authority of an E.G.M. The draft lease and Deed of Covenant would have to be agreed in final form before an approach could be made to the bank as the lease and Deed of Covenant would be needed for collateral.

On the 7th of September 1972 an Extraordinary General Meeting was held in Cavanaugh's Hotel.

Here it was stated that Bord Fáiltes only interest was that a properly organised and well run golf club be present in Westport for all time. The fact that the lease might be 200, 49, 21 or any other number of years did not mean that at the end of the term golf would cease.

Bord Fáilte were offering a lease as long as is possible under the Landlord and Tenant Act but not of such length as to confer on the golf club the right of acquisition of the fee simple. Bord Fáilte were not prepared to write some form of guarantee in respect of Westport's contribution into the lease. If the club ceased to exist Bord Fáilte would only seek their original investment in the project. The

> Another major problem had emerged. The Head Greenkeeper had departed without Notice.
> What would they do?
> The Financial constraints were suffocating.

surplus would return to the original Westport contributors.

A discussion took place on Bord Fáiltes demand for the £30,000 contribution. The Finance Committee had obtained £12,000 in cash.

Now Mr. McLoughlin was demanding a written guarantee from the Bank for the other £18000 and also that the cash balance held by the Finance Committee be lodged to the account of Ireland West to meet bills coming in at present. Mr. Liam Golden said the Finance Committee would not be prepared to release any further monies from their funds until the clubhouse contract was signed and work on the clubhouse had started.

The following proposal to be put to Bord Fáilte was agreed. That the balance of £18000 be provided by way of:

(1) A bridging loan of £8000 for one year. This loan only to be negotiated on condition that the clubhouse be started without further delay.
(2) Defer action on the final £10,000 until the Clubhouse is built and the golf course is in operation and earning income.

In the background another major problem had emerged. The head greenkeeper had departed without notice. What would they do? The financial constraints were suffocating. Should they advertise for another head greenkeeper or carry on with the staff they already had under Michael Moran's supervision? Or would they nominate one of the four remaining staff to a position of authority over the other three?

Mr. Moran thought it was possible the remaining four were capable of doing the job under his supervision. The guidelines in relation to the cutting of greens, mowing of fairways, maintenance of rough, mixing and spreading of compost were rigidly laid down and the men were

**A view of the
5th green (index 12)
with the gorse in
full bloom in the
background.**

familiar with the routine. In the event of an outbreak of disease he would call on experts from An Foras Taluntais.

It was agreed to proceed on these lines.

A charge hand, Mr.Tony Joyce, was nominated to check the men in in the mornings and check them out in the evenings. He would also apportion work under Mr. Moran's directions. It was also agreed that the four men, Mr. Joyce, Mr. Chas Cannon, Mr. Willie Hopkins and Mr. John Garavan, be offered an increase in wages.

On the 22nd September Bord Fáilte accepted the financial arrangements. The cash balance held by the Finance Committee would be lodged with Ireland West along with the bridging loan of £8,000 plus a letter of intent from the bank saying that £10,000 would be forthcoming by way of a loan next year if required.

These figures had a sobering effect. Everyone was agreed that to go into the new course with an overdraft of £10,000, which would have to be serviced as well as providing funds for maintenance and operation of the Club, would be madness. The Secretary came up with a scheme for Overseas

Life Membership but this would demand further thought as there was a danger of selling away a part of the club forever.

On the 26th of October 1972 a major storm arrived in connection with the access road. Opposition had emerged to the Bog Road entrance. Instead other sources wanted the old road by the textile factory which links up with the Quay to be developed instead. Bord Fáilte, Kilmeena residents and the golf club saw the Bog Road as practical and impartial in the matter of local interests. Bord Fáilte would give a grant of £35,000 for this road provided that Mayo County Council would give £12,000. Bord Fáilte believed this road would provide better access to the golf club but also it would provide easier access to Westport and open up new areas.

Unfortunately, the Co.Engineer saw this road as a private development proposal for Westport House Estate. As a result of his report Mayo County Council voted by sixteen votes to seven not to join with Bord Fáilte in developing the proposed access road. This vote was a major disappointment as Lord Sligo had agreed to make the land available free of charge and the road would result in a saving of two and a half miles in travel between Westport and the new golf course.

The heated Council debate resulted in some startling accusations. Bord Fáilte was accused of spending £170,000 on a golf course to which there was no access. They were accused of using public funds to construct a road serving private, internal development. In defence of the Bord Fáilte proposal, Mr. Myles Staunton described the Co.Engineers technical report as "the most biased and misleading" he had ever seen. He said Bord Fáilte are providing funds for the building of a road to a golf course because it is considered necessary to provide a major tourist amenity. He pointed out that the road would be of benefit to the people in Carrowholly. That the road enters at a point where there is land which if developed would be in the interests of Westport Town. That the land for the road, some 50 acres, is being offered free and the land for the Golf Course was sold at a reasonable price. He praised Westport House Estate for their liberal attitude.

Mr. Sean O'Malley also said the report was biased. He said it was irresponsible to suggest the route via the Old Demesne Road from St. Marys Crescent since it started at one of the most congested points in the town where there were three schools, a hotel, a factory and a housing estate. Mr. Miko Browne was critical of some nationalist speeches being made. He said the issue was of grave importance to Westport people and was really a parochial one.

Mr. Padraic Flynn mocked the proposal. He said, " could anyone imagine a semi-state body building a golf course and not giving people a way into it. I would hate to think we would give a "bob" to any round into this golf course. I don't see why we should have to give money at all."

The County Manager, Mr. Gerry Ward, quietly pointed out that if they did not spend the money on the Westport development there was no other development in the county which the money could be put to.

On the 18th November Westport U.D.C. adopted a resolution supporting the Bord Fáilte proposal. Many of the Urban Councillors believed that such a road by the Bog Gate entrance would open up a huge area of land, several hundred acres within the urban boundary, for vast development over the next thirty years.

■ Massive Westport Deputation.

On the 25th of November a 30 strong deputation from Westport attended a Mayo County Council meeting.

The deputation was the biggest and most representative ever received and consisted of Urban Councillors, Chamber of Commerce, Junior Chamber, Westport and District Tourism, the Golf Club, and Carrowholly Ratepayers Assoc.

They were granted one hour to make their case. Mr. Michael Browne said they were getting the land free, the work could start straight away, the road would open up a large area of the town for development, Westport

DISTANCE CHART

From Holy Trinity Church	Distance to Golf Club	Distance to Newport Rd. Mc Mahon's.
(1) via Bog Gate,N/port Rd	2 miles/177 yds	3miles/257yds
(2)via Textile factory:	2 miles/80 yds	3 miles/160 yds.
(3)via existing Carrowholly Rd.	4 miles/1,313 yds.	3 miles/1,233yds.

Distances saved:
Between (1) and (3) above 2 miles/1,136 yds   976 yds.
Between (1) and (2) is only 97 yds

Individual Road stretches distances were also pointed out.
(1) Mc Mahons Cross(Duffys) to Golf Club: 1 mile and 80 yds.
(2) Golf Club to point on existing estate road where New road will start: 980 yds.
(3) Point as at (2) to estate gate near Textile Factory via existing road : 1 mile/320 yds
(4)Gate near Textile factory to Holy Trinity Church: 540 yds.
(5) Point where New Road joins existing road as mentioned at (2) to Newport Rd. junction with Bog Gate R: I mile / 90 yds.
(6)Newport Rd. Junction with Bog Gate to Holy Trinity church : 867 yds.

Estate would benefit but so too would the people of Carrowholly and Westport and the Council had the powers to recoup the actual cost from the developers of the land.

Comparative distances were produced to support their case. (See table, opposite).

However, this professional presentation did not have the desired effect. By 15 votes to 11 the Council had reaffirmed their previous decision to turn down the Bord Fáilte proposal.

The *Mayo News* went on to say that this meant the Championship Golf Course due to be opened for competition in summer 1973 had no proper means of access.

Mr. Owen Hughes and the Fianna Fail members of the Council had remained steadfast in their view that it was not proper to put their hands in the pockets of the ratepayers to fund a private development.

The County Manager had pointed out that in almost every road works undertaken and where water and sewerage facilities were provided the Council could be said to be helping private individuals and that while Lord Sligo would benefit there could be no doubt but that the benefits would also come for the town of Westport and as a result to the county at large.

Bord Fáilte was now soured by the County Council rejection. Mr. Tom McLoughlin in January 1973 said there were now two alternative proposals.

(1) An access road from Alf McMahons (Duffys) to the clubhouse costing £7,500 and Bord Fáilte would bear the entire cost.
(2) A lesser road than formerly envisaged from the Bog Gate to the Clubhouse, the total cost of which would be £30,000.(original costing £50,000) Bord Fáilte would contribute £21,000 and £9,000 would have to be funded locally.

He said Bord Fáilte never expected Mayo County Council to build the road to the golf club but seeing the road as planned was one of public utility as well as servicing the golf club Bord Fáilte had expected a token contribution and that was all the County Council was asked for towards a £240,000 project.

Mr. McLoughlin said that if the road from Alf McMahon's was built the chances of finishing this road to the Bog Gate at a later date were nil .

Mr. Joe Lally insisted that the £30,000 road was the one to go for and this was agreed. It was agreed that a sum of £6000 should be sought from Westport House Estate and the balance of £3000 from Westport Urban Council.

On the 10th of February 1973 the *Mayo News* reported on a Westport Urban Council meeting. The Council unanimously agreed to make the £3000 contribution and to enter into negotiations with Westport House Estate for the purchase of suitable land for housing developments. (Michael Davitt Park/ Berrys Printing, Industrial Park, Waste Water Treatment Plant, Gaeilscoil))

On the 22nd of March 1973 the 47th and final AGM of Old Carrowholly was held and then the First AGM of the Championship Golf Course. Tributes were paid to the outgoing Captain, Mr. Mickey Hastings, the last Captain of Old Carrowholly.

Mr. Hastings in his address proposed a vote of congratulations to President, Mr. H. J. Staunton on the election of his son Myles Staunton to Dail Eireann. He went on to recall the helpful attitude of Mr. Myles Staunton in the matter of the access road. Prophet like, he said the sense of informality and leisurely approach to golf, which was the hallmark of Old Carrowholly, might not be possible in the Championship Golf Course. He said the future would tell whether this was to be regretted or otherwise.

Mr. H. J. Staunton felt that he should step down as President and be replaced by a younger man. It was agreed however that in the new constitution the office of life President may be replaced by President on a rotational basis but that until the constitution is drawn up Mr. Staunton should remain as President. He accepted office again.

The incoming Captain, Mr. Eddie McCrea, thanked the members for the honour accorded him in being the first Captain of the championship course. He reminded members of the awesome responsibility of running the new course.

It was agreed that play would start on the new course on May 1st 1973.

But problems continued to emerge.

On 21st May water leakages were discovered. The watering system pipes in several parts of the course were less than seven inches underground and were punctured by fairway spikes.

A caravan was parked in front of the 18th tee and this matter was for the Western Regional Tourism Org. as no lease had been signed yet.

Competitive golf began on the 6th of May. The opening competition was won by Tony Joyce(8) and Rev. Paul Fitzgerald (17) with a score of 77 nett. The runners-up were Perry O'Reilly (9) and Dr. S. Tobin (16) with 78 nett.

By the 19th of June it was felt that frequent meetings were necessary to get the infant course on its feet and to solve teething problems. Approval from Ireland West was awaited for drainage to begin on the 7th, 8th and 10th fairways. Volunteers were needed to water the greens in the summer months.

By the 3rd of July disappointment was emerging with Bord Fáilte. Valuable time was being lost by their failure to make a decision re. drainage. It was proving impossible to contact Ireland West officers in Galway or Dublin..

The stop-cocks were found to be totally inadequate for the job and if retained would lead to trouble in the watering system. The rota of members in watering greens had failed due to leakages in the system. It was decided to replace the 18 stop cocks.

The tenders for the new road were opened on the 26th of June but no word had been given to the Club Officers as to when the work would begin.

On the 21st August 1973 a letter was read from Bord Fáilte inviting three members of the Committee to attend a meeting in Dublin on the 28th of August to dicuss the whole matter of the access road.

The meeting felt Bord Fáilte had failed to honour commitments re drainage and the road and that further delays would be disastrous to the development of the course and the clubhouse.

It was decided not to send a delegation to Dublin.

Dr Sean Tobin: elected as an honorary member of Westport Golf Club.

■ Dr. Sean Tobin.

The meeting ended on a sad note with the resignation of Dr. Sean Tobin, Hon. Sec. as he was taking up an appointment in Castlebar. This resignation was observed as a disaster blow as Dr. Sean had carried the whole negotiations and running of the club. It was proposed by the Captain, seconded by Liam Golden and passed unanimously that Dr. Sean Tobin be elected an Honorary Member of Westport Golf Club.

On the 24th of September 1973 the *Mayo News* reported that Westport U.D.C. had granted planning permission to the Western Regional Tourism Org. to construct an access road to the new Westport Golf Course.

In October Westport U.D.C. was asked to contribute a further £2,500 to the road as it would now cost £37,000. Bord Fáilte had granted a further £2,500 and a local consortium consisting of Westport Golf Club, Lord Altamount and Jury's Hotel were providing another £2,500. Joe Lally pointed out that the golf course and overall development when completed will have been subsidised by Bord Fáilte in the sum of £230,000 and it would never realise its real potential without a proper road. Westport U.D.C. unanimously donated the required amount.

In the meantime the road had been subject to a planning appeal but in November following representations from Mr Myles Staunton the Parliamentary Secretary, Michael Begley made Orders granting permission for the proposed road.

In November, Michael Moran, who had attended Bingley Seminars, and Fergal Hope discovered that the pipes on many fairways were very close to the surface of the ground and the whole system would have to be unearthed and replaced to a depth of 18 inches. The sods to be cut by hand and replaced. Bord Fáilte and Lenihans were to foot the bill.

Also in November a major discussion took place on the old buildings. The Architect wanted to hold on to some of them. The Committee wanted them cleared and car-parks laid out.

On the 19th of December 1973 the New Constitution of Westport Golf Club came into force following an EGM.

At the AGM on the 23rd January 1974 the Deed of Covenant and lease were signed. The contract for the infamous road was signed. The clubhouse bar would be ready in February and the Club would apply for a licence then.

John Farrell revealed the paid-up membership of the club:

Full Male 68, Family 11; Country 34; Lady Associates 46 ; Juniors 8 ; Juveniles 4

The outgoing Captain expressed thanks to Bord Fáilte for providing such a wonderful course and clubhouse. He went on, "I don't think the members really realise the great gift which was handed to them at a very small cost. The best thanks we can tender to Messrs. Lally, McLoughlin and Heverin is to keep the course and clubhouse in top-class condition."

On the 2nd of February it was revealed that the contractors for the road would be Corcoran Bros, Westport.

On the 8th of April 1974 the first meeting was held in the new clubhouse. The Three Rs were discussed – rake bunkers, replace divots, repair plugmarks.

■ **Golf Course Boosting Hotel Trade.**

On the 18th of May the *Mayo News* reported that the new golf course was boosting the hotel trade in Westport.

> **"The Championship Golf Course is proving a major attraction and economic boon to the town."**

In June Simon Kelly and Bord Fáilte expressed unhappiness with the pro shop.

They suggested it might be located in the old building which they were in favour of retaining but any cost arising from repairs to the old building would have to be borne by the golf club. The Committee decided not to retain the old building.

On the 16th of October 1974 the telephone poles had arrived. Bord Fáilte insured the road on Saturday 19th of October and the road was opened on that date in time for the Connacht Alliance Day on Sunday the 20th of October.

In the financial year 1973-1974 the running costs amounted to £20,000 and Income was £13,000. Membership amounted to 228 consisting of Full 96; Associate 65; County 40; Juvenile/Students 15; Family 12.

On the 9th of June 1975 the new course was officially opened by the Taoiseach, Mr. Liam Cosgrave.

A gathering of past captains at their annual function in September, 2000.

Seated left to right: N. Connell (1982), C. Hughes (1985), L. Walsh (1984), P. Hopkins (1986), N. Halpin (2000), D. Blythe (1981), G. Golden (1975), P. Murphy (1987).

Middle row: Left to right: C. O'Neill (1990), H. Murphy (1969), D.O. Regan (1974), M . Staunton (1964), M. King (1967), J. Kelly (1958), G. McAleer (1966), D. McDermott (1998), V. Coakley (1977), M. Mulloy (1963), A. Redmond (1989), B. Burns (1999).

Back row: Left to right – R. McCreave (1988), Dr. H. Farrell (1976), P. Duffy (1996), M. Hastings (1972), F. Hope (1980), L. Friel (1997), P. McLaughlin (1970), S. Walsh (president 92/94), P. Bree (1979), V. Farrell (1992).

The Land:

" All that and those" the hereditaments and premises described in FOLIO 51135 of the register, County Mayo comprising firstly that part of the lands of Westport Demesne containing 38 acres – 2 roods – 12 perches and secondly that part of the lands of Westport Demesne containing 172 acres – 0 roods – 6 perches."

Chapter 5

NEW Carrowholly

The Racecourse:

The land which makes up the present course was involved in hosting sport of a completely different kind many years ago. In 1809 the Marquess of Sligo built a racecourse on the present site of the 1st, 2nd, 3rd, 4th, 5th,6th and 18th holes of Westport Golf Club. It was known as the Ballyknock Racecourse and its reputation spread as the best horses in Ireland raced on this great piece of land. The first race on this course was recorded in 1809 and the last race was in 1900. During the intervening 91 years the Lords, Earls and gentry raced against each other in the Sport of Kings.

Such was the wealth and enthusiasm of the Marquess of Sligo, that in 1811 he bought the 1809 English Derby winner, Waxy Pope, and brought him to stand at the Westport House Estate stud. This was the first and only Derby winner to reside and stand at stud West of the Shannon.

The power of the Westport House racing establishment started to grow and in the *Sweeney Guide to the Irish Turf 1501-2001*, it can be seen how the Westport House Stud expanded. The following is a listing of famous stallions in these days who stood at the Westport Estate:

    1809/10 Woodcock
    1812/13 Recordon (won £3,071)
    1813/14 Waxy Pope (Derby winner)
    1817/21 Oiseau
    1820   Navigator
    1824   Langer
    1830/32 Picton

As the bloodstock breeding flourished and racing continued, the racing establishment of the Marquess of Sligo became known throughout the land. In the years 1822, 1823, 1824 and 1825, the Marquess of Sligo was Ireland's leading racehorse owner with winnings of over £8,000, which in today's money was a huge amount of winnings.

Towards the end of the 19th century racing in Westport

was on the wane. Bigger racecourses in better locations were attracting the public and so it was decided in 1900 to close the course. The land reverted back to agricultural but one historic memento of bygone days still stands on our course – The Judges Tower. This is located beside the 4th tee and while no Judge, Steward or Starter stands on top of this structure now with raised flag in hand, it is a constant reminder of what went before.

■ Ballyknock House.

Ballyknock House and stables were built in the early 1800s. One can see the remains of the walled garden today and a gable piece of the house. The racecourse is clearly illustrated in ordinance survey maps of the 1830s with the winning post and distance post clearly marked. All the fields, woods and waterways around the course have individual names – Fergusons Park, Byrn's Park, Bridgers Park, Cannons Park.

■ First aeroplane.

In July 1918 the *Mayo News* reported on the arrival of the first aeroplane to Westport.

"The first aeroplane to visit Westport arrived here on Wednesday morning and attracted considerable attention. A clear sky admitted of a very fine view of the machine. It landed at Ballyknock, Westport Demesne, and after a few hours stay left in an easterly direction, flying again over the town en route."

William Reilly, artist, grew up in Ballyknock House. "I spent all my youth and teens there and know every stream and fox lair. I think back and know that is where I got my love of trees. "

■ Tillage And Ploughing

In 1942 at the age of 13 years Eaneas McNally starting working on the estate owned by Lord Sligo. The estate covered a massive area including the ground where Westport Golf Club now stands. For 35 years Eaneas ploughed and tilled this ground. This was rich land that was reclaimed and developed by the Browne family. Carefully constructed French drains drained the land and highly engineered sluice gates controlled the effect

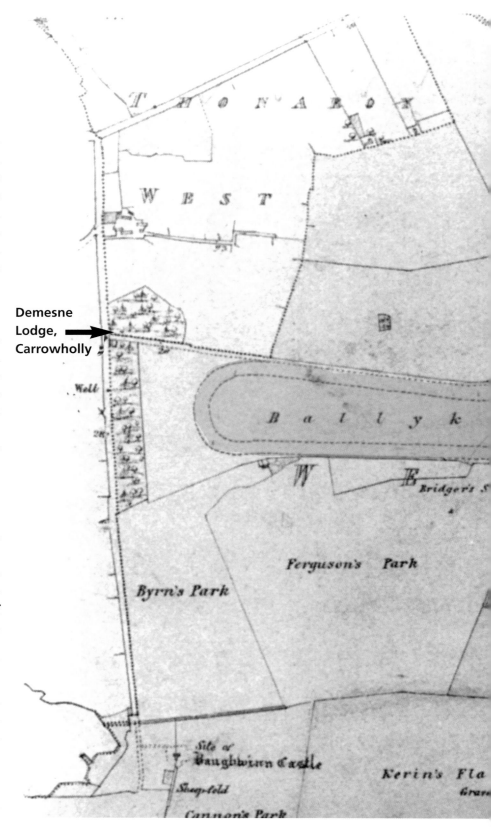

Demesne Lodge, Carrowholly

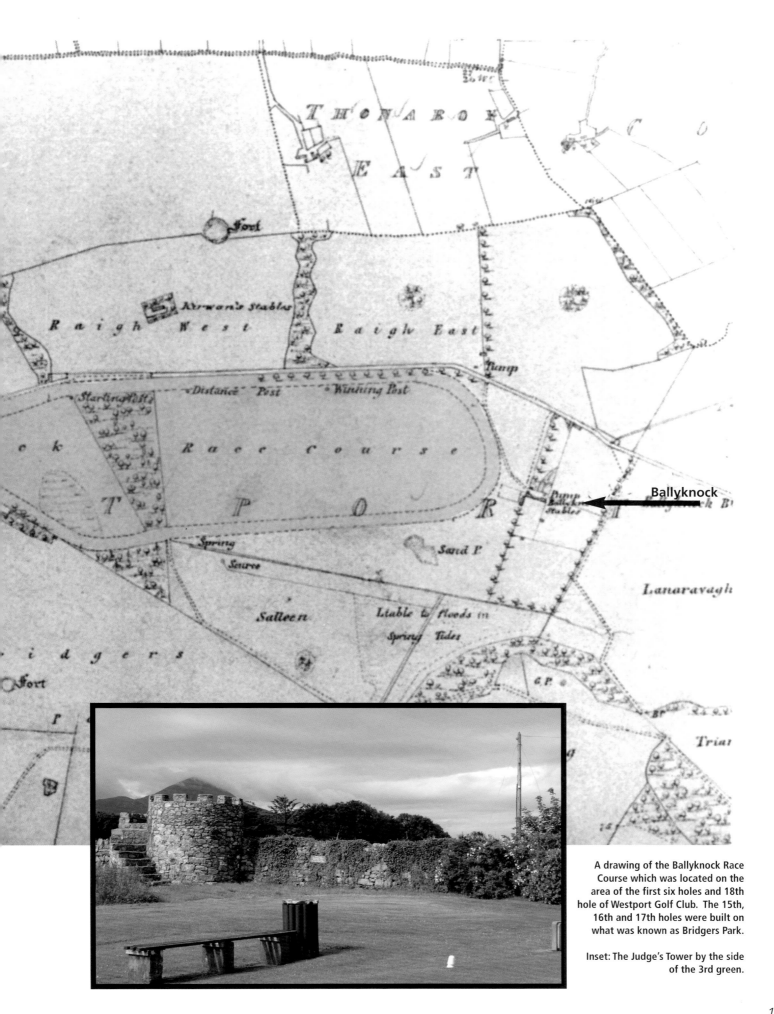

Ballyknock

A drawing of the Ballyknock Race Course which was located on the area of the first six holes and 18th hole of Westport Golf Club. The 15th, 16th and 17th holes were built on what was known as Bridgers Park.

Inset: The Judge's Tower by the side of the 3rd green.

of high tides at the Churns. Gifted craftsmen built the gothic designed buildings to detailed plans. There were two stone built wells at the farmhouse that were operated by big pumps. The area included a look-out tower for the racecourse that ran all the way up the 4th fairway. The ground was divided by natural rivers, stonewalls and surrounded by massive old trees.

Three families lived on the estate. The O'Malleys lived at the 17th. (Lord Sligo bought this land back). The Reilly's and Carolan's lived in the farmyard. "They were the most decent people you could meet. You would never leave any of these homes hungry or thirsty."

The fields known as Gibleen, Rusheen, Lenareevagh, the racecourse field, Cleevelough, Johnsies field and Ballinlough are now part of Westport Golf Club. These fields produced wheat, oats and corn. These crops were exported from Westport quay to distilleries in Carlow and other locations.

Seed potatoes were grown and sold in 5 tonne lots. These certified seed potatoes were exported to Spain and Portugal.

The area chosen for the golf course was selected because of the quality of the land, the natural and French drainage, the natural contour of the ground and the original old stone buildings that were there. It was especially selected because of the natural woods, streams and most of all for its picturesque location. The course would have Clew Bay as a backdrop and sit proud under the shadow of Croagh Patrick.

On a recent visit to the course Eaneas expressed his disappointment that the stone buildings in the farm yard were demolished. These stone buildings and the unique old wells were part of our history.

■ The House At The 17th

John O'Malley and his family did a deal with the Land Commission around 1929 to move in from their land in Louisburgh to the Demesne, Carrowholly. A house had to be constructed around where the 17th tee is now. It took two years to build because at that time all the building materials had to be transported by horse and cart. The holding of land consisted of 71 acres of very good land. 25 acres of it was out in Roslea (now owned by Joe Mortimer) and they were controlled by the tides because their access to Roslea was behind the 16th tee. Lord Sligo bought the land back for £1,800.

■ The Mobile Milking Parlour

Jim Browne's first memory of Lord Sligo's estate was a ploughing competition circa 1949 around the area where the 3rd and 4th holes are now. Jim remembers this because his late father Josie won a slash hook as a prize.

"In 1952 my father went to work for Lord Sligo and in 1954 we all moved to one of the estate houses. Around that time I used to help the Ketterick brothers, Sean R.I.P. and Patsy to milk the estate herd of milch cows. They had a mobile milking parlour and the cows grazed in the area where the first six holes are now. The area where the 7th, 8th and 10th holes are now was all under tillage. The crops produced were potatoes, carrots, turnips etc. During the summer holidays up to twenty boys from Westport would be employed weeding, thinning and picking potatoes. The ganger on that job was John "The Bomber" Browne R.I.P. from Carrowholly. He was a very good golfer and renowned for long hitting. Ballyknock house, now demolished for the car park, was lived in by Tommie Reilly R.I.P. and his family. And after he left by Hubert Carolan R.I.P. and his family. They were herdsmen on the estate.

■ Fred Hawtree And The Hawtree Philosophy

Fred Hawtree, the renowned golf course architect, arrived in Westport in 1970. He had been recommended to Lord Sligo by Dr. Eustace, Hon. Secretary, Portmarnock.

The name of Hawtree has been associated with golf and golf course development since 1912. After the First World War Frederick George Hawtree had set up a company with J. H. Taylor (British golf professional) to design and build golf courses. In 1932 he built and set up Addington Court, the first privately run golf course to be opened to the general public. His son Frederick William joined the practice in 1938. He designed new courses in France, Belgium, Spain and back in the United

Kingdom in the 70s. He was assisted by his partner A.H.F. Jiggens. Martin Hawtree joined his father in 1972. and the firm is now one of the largest golf architectural practices in Europe.

The Hawtree Philosophy of golf course design is based on the integrity of the site and the original fun and enjoyment of the game.

The golf course must be inspired by the site and not be an academic solution imposed upon the site because of a passing fashion. A careful approach to layout will save money, preserve the existing character of the site and ensure that a wide variety of golfers leave the course contented.

Once the layout is established the design is then directed towards the site, the enhancement of natural features, the strategy and fairness of play, the detailed elements of the course and the broader fields of landscaping and maintenance. Concern for the future greenkeeper and the machinery at his disposal is uppermost.

Within a few hours of his inspection of the site Mr. Hawtree announced that Westport would have a Championship Course.

He pointed out that the site lends itself admirably to development without exhorbitant expense.

He said it provided both hazard and interest with two-thirds of the course benefiting from the spectacular scenery of the coast line along Clew Bay and the shoreside woods. With bursting enthusiasm he continued:

" There will only be one hole with any noticeable ascent.
The course will in no sense be fatiguing. The land lends itself to the construction of spectacular short holes and to providing the variety of shots demanded in a round. It is unnecessary to multiply the number of bunkers where the intrinsic character of the ground already provides both hazard and interest. The total length will just exceed 6,800 yds. This is a championship length and gives a standard scratch score of 73 equal to the best courses in Ireland and indeed anywhere. To achieve 6,800 yds a number of very long Par 5s will have to be included."

Mr. Hawtree proposed Ballyknock Farm as the location for the clubhouse as it would be in a location convenient to all parts of the vast 145 acres.

■ Lord Sligo

Lord Sligo (Denis Browne) was thrilled and excited by the Hawtree report. Although not a golfer he articulated a vision reflecting a knowledge of the game and its big names.

" I have visions later of tycoons in aeroplanes, family golfers in minis, the West of Ireland Championship occasionally and sponsored competitions, the emergence of our own Christy O'Connor – a huge cash prize from big business to the first to do the long shore hole (15th) in three – Tony Jacklin, Arnold Palmer, in fact, the lot. We offer in return a warm welcome, great golf, unsurpassed scenery and from the clubhouse window a grandstand view of half the course and a miniature wild duck sanctuary thrown in for good measure. What more can a golfer ask for? "

STEPHEN WALSH, A FORMER PRESIDENT OF WESTPORT GOLF CLUB, HAD THIS TO SAY ABOUT LORD SLIGO.

"Lord Sligo was a man of the town following his father's footsteps. His father provided the first Fire Brigade in Westport. Lord Sligo bought his paper in McGreeveys, talked to the people of the town and dined in the Grand Central Hotel.

Around 1966/7 it transpired that Lord Sligo was trying to entice a large hotel to Westport. This idea was to attract a large motel, then all the rage in England at that time as motorways were being constructed.

Shell and Esso were to the forefront in building these developments but they did not show interest in Lord Sligo's proposal because Westport was a terminal town and also on account of poor access road structure.

A meeting between Lord Sligo and the Westport Tourism Development Company representatives Bertie Staunton, Lorcan Gill and Liam Golden took place.

They heard from Lord Sligo that Jury's Hotel (now Westport Woods Hotel) would come to Westport if a first class Golf Club would be made available. When Bord Fáilte came on board the Golf Course became a reality."

THE CARD OF

Blue Tee measurements

| Hole 1 | Ballyknock | Par 4 | Index 14 | 348 yds |

A large green to aim at with fairway sloping to the left.
The green is reachable in one for the big hitters.

| Hole 2 | Bridgers Stable | Par 4 | Index 8 | 342 yds. |

Keeping slightly left is the key to cutting this dog-leg. The right edge of the bunker on the left can be used as a guide. The approach is narrowed by bunkers left and right. The green slopes up from front to back

| Hole 3 | Judges Tower | Par 3 | Index 16 | 164 yds. |

A big green protected by 4 bunkers. Easy par if green is found in one. OB on left should not come into play .

| Hole 4 | Road Hole | Par 5 | Index 18 | 496 yds. |

OB on left should not cause problems.
The green is reachable in two on this short Par 5. Approach needs to be well-judged to hit narrow front part of the green.

| Hole 5 | Clare Island | Par 4 | Index 12 | 356 yds. |

A big drive is required straight down the middle. This will leave a wedge shot to this green.
Uphill green from the front and downhill either side underlines the need for a well placed second shot to the centre of the green.

| Hole 6 | Wheatpark | Par 4 | Index 4 | 455 yds. |

Tight fairway and two deep bunkers at the green to catch the inaccurate.

| Hole 7 | Old Canal | Par 5 | Index 10 | 520 yds. |

Driving to the left eliminates OB (practice area) on the right.
Second shot best left short and again to the left to avoid the lake on the right side guarding an undulating green. Par or better essential here.

| Hole 8 | Saleen | Par 4 | Index 2 | 472 yds. |

A tough and demanding par 4. Don't be right off the tee.
Anywhere else is fine.The approach to the green needs to be from the left. It must be accurate.It is a risk and reward hole for low handicappers

| Hole 9 | The Churns | Par 3 | Index 6 | 204 yds. |

OB left, right and centre (rear of green). Select a club that will get to the back of the green. Short shots may find bunkers.

| Hole 10 | Leenarevagh | Par 5 | Index 13 | 500 yds. |

Drive needs to find the fairway here. Water on the left the whole way to the green. Bunkers guard the green to the front and left.

BLUE: Par 73   SS 74   6,980 yds.
WHITE: Par 73   **SSS 72**   **6,720 yds.**
GREEN: Par 73   SSS 70   6,289 yds.
RED: Par 74   SSS 73   5,616 yds.

The distance from greens to next tees is an additional 1,700 yds. Total distance from 1st tee to 18th green is over 5 miles. The original design had 5 par 3's-the 17th was a Par 3. The Par 4 and Par 5 holes had to be made longer to qualify as a Championship course. The course was originally designed with 60 bunkers.The character of the course lies in length, boldness,openness, grandeur and a certain ruggedness.

THE COURSE

| Hole 11 | Barrets Hill | Par 4 | Index 3 | 434 yds. |

A large sloping fairway awaits the drive. Aiming right will avoid a blind approach shot. A bogey is not a bad score on this hole. Low handicappers will find a par hard earned.

| Hole 12 | Roman Island | Par 3 | Index 5 | 231 yds. |

If the wind blows this is not an ordinary par 3. The drive is from an elevated teeing area. If the green is missed there is no shame in a four!

| Hole 13 | Cleavelagh | Par 4 | Index 1 | 449 yds. |

A long, uphill dog-leg left par 4. Taking on the trees with the drive will make the hole easier. The approach needs to avoid the right side of the green as there is any amount of trouble to be found there.
Par is an excellent score here.

| Hole 14 | Green Island | Par 3 | Index 11 | 191 yds |

Avoid being right or big. From the tee hidden in the woods the golfer takes his line from the Church on the summit of Croagh Patrick. He must hit and hold an elevated green to be sure of par. The putting surface is difficult. Three putting is a possibility.

| Hole 15 | The Reek | Par 5 | Index 9 | 560 yds. |

The Atlantic rolls up on the leftside. Be right with the drive. The tee shot is crucial and must travel 200 yds across an inlet of Clew Bay to reach the fairway.
The second shot becomes tough with OB on the left. The second shot if taken from the left will open up the green which slopes away to the left. Take care of OB in left rough and bunkers left of the green.

| Hole 16 | Winters Hill | Par 4 | Index 15 | 363 yds. |

A dog-leg right which can be shortened by cutting the corner and avoiding the trees on the right.
An uphill putt is the preference so the approach should be planned carefully whilst considering the pin position.

| Hole 17 | Old Carrowholly | Par 4 | Index 17 | 335 yds |

A long, accurate drive is demanded. Too far left or right will cause trouble. Note the house to the rear of this green!

| Hole 18 | Gibleen | Par 5 | Index 7 | 560 yds. |

The drive needs to be long and straight. There is trouble on the right with water. The green in elevated in the middle and can lead to three putts. If laying up with the second stay to the left side of the fairway.

The Courage To Progress.

Play began on the new championship course on the 1st of May 1973.

The Captains were Mr. Eddie McCrea and Ms. Nuala Moran.

Vice. Captain: Capt. Dave O'Regan.

Hon. Sec: Dr. Sean Tobin and Recording Sec Bro. P.K. Maher.

Hon. Treas: Michael Henehan jr. and John Farrell ("the old reliable firm").

Committee: Michael Moran, Gerry McAleer, Fergal Hope, Dermot Blythe, Liam Golden, Niall Halpin, Mick King, Hugh Murphy, Mattie Reidy, Gar Golden, Padraic Higgins, Gerry Hughes, Perry O'Reilly.

Membership Fees were as follows:
Men: £15
Ladies: £7.50
Family: £25
Juniors (14-21yrs): £5
Juveniles: £1

Green Fees:
Daily: £1
Weekly: £4.

"The magnitude of the new complex was vast in terms of revenue even in its embryonic stage."

This was the phrase used by the treasurer, John Farrell, in his report to the 1974 AGM. The reality of financing the new course was beginning to strike home. The new course devoured money. Lack of finance would hamper course and clubhouse projects by anything up to ten years.

The paid-up membership of the Club in 1974 was:
Full Male: 68,
Family:11,
Country: 34,
Lady Associates: 46,
Juniors: 8,
Juveniles: 4.

It was agreed there was nothing in these figures to be complacent about and that a determined effort would have to be made to increase membership. Fees had to be increased.

Men £30; Lady Associates £18; Family £50; Junior £8; Juvenile £2; Pavilion £12.

Green Fees remained at £1 daily.

The Year The Mindset Changed .

1974 was the year a dramatic mindset change was demanded. The new course had character, subtlety and breathtaking scenery but it was going to cost large amounts of money to finance. Thus raising the required finance was going to be the supreme test of every Golf Club Committee in the future. Old Carrowholly was a club for the members but now visitors and the wider golfing fraternity had to be attracted if the new course was to survive financially.

"Committee members were asked if and when they would be available to meet visiting societies to the club in the absence of the captain or vice-captain. All agreed to do so and to give a *Cead Mile Fáilte* to visitors and the golfing fraternity." (1974)

There was an active move to increase membership.

A term loan needed to be raised. There seemed to be a fear initially in revealing the accounts to the general membership.

"After a long discussion it was decided to publish the accounts."

Hay money was used to buy bar fittings and a piano.

"£250 hay money was sanctioned to buy a piano."

In 1975 green fees had increased from £1,800 to £2,861 but still the excess of expenditure over income came to £7,181. The major focus now was to increase golf activity in the club and to make sure that the course became a major tourist attraction. The highlight of the year was the official opening. This cost £175 and the installation of a telephone cost £161.

There were also a number of "firsts". The first W.J. Walsh competition, the first Connacht Shield Final for the club, the first Open Week,

Comments of Noel and Fiona Barr.

Westport to us is a must each year.
1. Hospitality is no.1 – staff on and off the course.
2. Golf is no.2 – Alex and Aidan and ground staff.
3. 19th Hole is no. 3 – Catering staff.
4. Entertainment is no.4.
5. Characters over the years: Mr. Ed – Musician

The official openng of the golf course in 1975: Harry Bradshaw (Portmarnock) accompanies Fred Daly (Balmoral), the only Irishman to win the British Open (in 1947) until Padriag Harrington's famous win at Carnoustie in 2007.

Course Records

From the beginning the course presented a tough challenge. In 1973 in an Open Fourball , Michael Halpin (12) and Niall Halpin (9) won with a score of 1 down. The runners-up were Gerry McAleer (7) and Hugh Murphy (16) with 2 down. The Championship Course was defeated for the first time when Gar Golden (12) and Dr. Sean Tobin (16) returned a score of 2 up in winning the Fourball v Par in aid of the blind. In 1976 gruelling winds ruled the course for the Club Foursomes and that was confirmed by the winners card. Bro. P.K. Maher and Fergal Hope finished 8 down and claimed first prize! Liam Gibbons and Tony Joyce were awarded second prize with 9 down!

1973: The first holder of the Amateur Course Record was Padraic Higgins (8) when he had 83 gross in the Gill Cup.
Niall Halpin (9) became the new holder when he had 82 gross in a Singles competition.
Gerry McAleer (7) then held the mantle when he had 77 gross in the Guinness Masters.

1974: Perry O'Reilly (5) 76 gross.

1975: Tony Joyce (5) Club Steward, 73 gross in W.J.Walsh competition.

1976: Vinnie Freyne (3) Ballyhaunis gross 72. He was gross 36 for the front nine, two over after 12, but birdied 14, 17 and 18.

1983: Perry O'Reilly 70 gross (42 points in Guinness Masters)

1984: Liam Gibbons (3) during a Garda outing. 68 gross. Liam was level par for the front nine and scored 6 birdies on the back at 10,12,13,15,16,17.

1987: Perry O'Reilly equalled the course record with a gross 68 in Open Week.

1996: Ms. Kay O'Briain (8) Ladies Course Record-75 gross.

1998: Liam Halpin (2) – 67 gross in Open Week with birdies at 1, 3,5,7,16th and eagle at the 10th. Liam had 25 putts for the round.

2005: Sean Mc Ternan, Co. Sligo during Irish Close – 61 gross compiled with 10 birdies and 1 eagle.

Professional Course Record: Paul McGinley – 65 during P.G.A. Tournament.

Ladies Course Record: Lillian O'Brien (4) 73 gross.

extraordinaire. Old Conna – Pat, Chad and Mick. Stackstown – Tom and Nuala. Dr. Whyte – remember "Under the Boardwalk". Michael John McDonnell R.I.P. – comedian, dancer and great craic. Freddie Molloy – "workaholic" on and off the course. George Reilly – ex-bar manager and good friend. Liam and Niall Halpin – such talent as singers as well as golf. Donie O'Connor R.I.P. Perry O'Reilly – always great golf stories to be told. Brendan Bolster R.I.P. – minister for everything. Joe Gibbons – storyteller and singer. Padraic and Marion Duffy – without them there would never be a sing-song after a meal and a few jars!!! Brendan Burns and pal, Pat. Liam Gibbons – "the mobile photographer".

6. We have great memories of the barbecue and showband held down in the big work sheds in the car park. I think it was 1986. Rosaleen and her husband – ex catering staff prepared and supplied all the food for about 300 people. What a night! Maybe another one would be a great idea?

7. Maureen Flynn, Bridie and Gerry Hughes, Assumpta and Pat Bree (Lay the Blanket on the Ground), Ned Fitzpatrick R.I.P. , Anne Duffy and Sal O'Connor. Frank and Mary Dolan. All great friends over the past 22 years. To all connected with Open Week we thank you for 22 great golfing holidaying years in Westport."

The first Scratch Cup presented by his Grace, the Archbishop of Tuam, Dr. Joseph Cunnane, the first juvenile competition for the Cavanaugh Trophy. Bridge and 25 drives were also a regular feature throughout the year.

In 1979 Pope John Paul 11 visited Ireland and Knock. There was great excitement and enthusiasm created by his visit.

However in Westport Golf Club enthusiasm was being sorely tested. Golfing tourism had not developed as envisaged. Outside forces were creating serious financial difficulties. 1979 had been a most difficult year due to a petrol shortage, postal dispute and one of the wettest Springs on record. Green fees, the life-blood of the club, had decreased. Tourism grew but not in a way beneficial to golf. The English tourism market did not expand as expected. A small, local golfing population had now in the main to finance the club.

By 1980 Westport Golf Club had become a large

1974: The new clubhouse under construction. View from the 18th green.

Inset: A gathering of ladies at the annual party in 1973.
Left to right:
E. Hughes, M Mulloy, L. O'Malley, B. Blythe.

enterprise. The financial costs of an expanding club were increasing. Generating finance demanded imaginative and active involvement. Every activity that could possibly increase the financial well being of the club was instigated. These activities ranged from 200/300 draws, financial inducements for a hole-in-one during Open Week,

"£75 for the first person to have a hole-in-one at the 9th, £50 for the first person to have a hole-in-one at the 3rd and £40 to the first person to par the four Par 3s in regulation." (latter won by Fr. Michael Golden, the Mall)

Candlelight suppers, Saturday social nights and the Open Day were all utilised to attract membership.

"For the past two years Westport Golf Club has been thrown open to the public on one particular day. The reasons for this were two-fold, to quell any idea that Westport Golf Club, or golf in general had a snobbish element or that the game was just for the select few and to entice the rest of the "ordinary" people to take up the game. "

A free subscription was also offered during Open Day and in 1979 it was won by Fonsie Cannon, Westport.

By 1980 fees had more than doubled reflecting a sobering reality of the financial costs the course demanded.

Men £72; Lady Associates £43; Family £120; Junior £16.50; Juvenile £5.
Senior Citizen(over 65): Men £15; Ladies £10
Green Fees: Daily £3; Weekly £12.

It was now becoming evident that the voluntary ethos was not going to be enough to maintain the club in the future. A professional approach was going to be needed.The appointment of a Secretary/ Manager was mooted.

"The out-going Captain, Dr. H. Farrell, stated

Hole in One Club

1974: Perry O'Reilly – 5 iron at 12th.

1975: Fergal Hope at 9th.
Perry O'Reilly at 12th.
John Kelly at 14th.

1976: Michael Crowley at 3rd.
Mrs. Beda Tobin, Castlebar, at the 9th.

1982: Christy O'Malley at 12th with a 2-wood.

1984: Padraic Higgins at 3rd.

1985: Tony Browne at 3rd.
Perry O'Reilly at 3rd.
Jean McAleer at 9th.

1989: Tony Fitzpatrick at 9th with 5-wood.
Sheelagh Ryan at 9th with 4-iron.

1991: Mick King at 3rd with 4-iron.

1992: Pat Bree at 9th.
Vincent Farrell at 3rd.

1993: Sean Hyland at 9th.

1995: Liam Friel at 3rd.

1996: Haulie Hoban at 3rd.

1997: Ms.K.O'Briain at 9th-March 23rd.

1998: Albert Gallagher (15) at 12th in G.O.Y.
Tommie Reilly (13) at 12th in G.O.Y.
Jim Lyons (19) at 14th in G.O.Y.

1999: Freddie Molloy at 3rd.

2001: Niall Halpin at 14th.

2006: Jim Fergus at 12th during Captains Prize
Tony Browne at 12th during Captains Prize.

2007: Tommie Reilly – 7 iron at the 3rd

Albatross Club

1989: Keith Mongan , Club Professional, at 18th, par 5.
After a 280yd drive Keith holed a 3-wood.

1989: Tony Browne at 18th. Tony holed a three wood.

1990: Padraic Walsh (7) a 5-wood on the 17th , par 4 – 310 yds.

that the time was fast approaching when a secretary/manager must be employed to promote and manage the affairs of the club.

He said: "The club is expanding each year and its management by a voluntary body is becoming more difficult." (AGM 1977).

The Captain read a letter from Liam Walsh proposing the appointment of a secretary-manager on a trial basis. (1987)

But there were dramatic successes.

The staging of the Irish Close in 1977 was a vote of confidence in Westport by the G.U.I. and a vote of confidence in the organisational ability within the club. Winning the Junior Cup Green Pennant gave a tremendous lift to the club at a time when the financial situation was tight.

At the end of 1980 the financial situation had improved and some optimism had returned.

This optimism did not last for long. A major problem affecting finances had emerged. This was the flooding along the 7th, 8th, 9th and 10th fairways.

In his address, Mr. Dermot Blythe stated that:

"Westport Golf Course would never be a truly viable project until we had a course dry enough to attract and capitalise on society outings during the Autumn and Spring seasons. The flooding in the Leenarevagh area had to be alleviated." (1982)

Then, in 1983: "Outgoing Captain, Mr. Noel Connell was high in his praise of club engineers, Seamus Walsh, Ailbhe Mhaoileoin, Denis Egan and John Staunton. They successfully completed the work on the outlet at the barrier.

"After the success of this job open drains were made in the lower area of the course. He stated it was highly satisfactory that we were able to utilise the full 18 holes."

From 1981-1989 the cost of upkeeping a parkland course to a high standard was increasing yearly.

In 1984 the upkeep of grounds had increased by 86%.

In 1987 the accumulated losses amounted to £35,000.

In 1988 overall income had increased by 28% but expenditure on the upkeep of grounds had increased by 6.8%.

Increasing membership, attracting societies, developing green fees and cultivating sponsorship were all vital areas if the financial health of the club was to be maintained. In 1988 the suggestion of introducing a levy was made but the members were not ready for this yet.

"A notice of motion to introduce a levy of £25 for "A" members was defeated. A notice of motion to introduce an entrance fee for all new "A" members of £50 and £25 for new "B" members was defeated."

The financial pressure was so great the introduction of gambling machines as a source of income was actively considered but eventually defeated.

"The Captain confirmed that gambling machines were legal outside the Westport Urban area but there would be a limit to the amount they would pay out and they were a major source of finance in other clubs. The Captain proposed that gambling machines be accepted and was seconded by Aiden Redmond. There was a counter proposal by Brendan Bolster, seconded by Noel Connell not to accept gambling machines in the clubhouse. The Captain's proposal was defeated." (1988)

Poker classics were held regularly.

"The profit from the poker classic amounted to £1400 nett and takings in the bar amounted to £1200. It was very unsatisfactory that IOUs were left in the till in the bar. It was proposed that this practice be discontinued and no further IOUs be cashed."(1983)

During this period Captains were under severe pressure in trying to accommodate members and societies.

Many members were upset when finding it difficult to make the first tee on Saturdays and Sundays due to Society bookings.

Tolerance was asked for by Captains and they pointed out regularly that reasonable membership fees and the financial well-being of the club depended on society bookings.

Members did not like hearing this factual message but eventually an agreeable accommodation was secured.

The necessity to attract new members was also the focus during these years.

The development of a pitch and putt course on the site (1982) helped in no small way to introduce future members.

In 1987 one large pitch and putt competition attracted 100 players most of whom had never played golf before. Martin Keane and Westport Youth Activities held a regular mini-golf tournament.

Marketing the Club became a live issue also during this period. In 1981 a fairly successful initiative by Sean O'Malley, the then Hon. Sec. of the Club, was undertaken.

He obtained the names and addresses of all the registered Golf Societies in Ireland and he sent out about 100 letters to those societies he thought might be interested in visiting Westport depending on their location and society numbers. The small playing membership in those days meant the first tee could be sold for a few hours on a Sunday morning.

This initiative helped put Westport on the map and strong links were developed with golfing societies. Mr. O'Malley had the following to say at the 1983 AGM: "I was disappointed that I was not successful in having a suitable brochure made available."

In the early eighties golf writers from the national press including Northern Ireland were invited to the club.

But by 1985 the club still lacked a brochure.

"Mr. Michael Cavanaugh expressed disappointment that the club still did not have a colour brochure." (1985)

This was felt to be a major drawback to attracting new business.

In 1986 Paddy Hopkins attended the Barbican Golf Conference in London and there he discovered the absolute necessity for a club to have a brochure to properly promote the club. In 1989 a major development was the decision to set up a marketing company in conjunction with Connemara, Enniscrone and Rosses Point. A large selling point was the amount of practice area in

Westport and operators from Sweden were impressed by this.

Despite financial worries the Club continued to be very progressive. The drainage programme in the Leenarevagh area was set in motion. A driving range and putting green was actively discussed in 1983.

"This was being actively pursued. It would be down through the practice area. Spotlights would be provided and there would be a permanent driving range, going as far as the first drain on right of the 7th Fairway. It is also hoped we would have a putting green possibly near 1st Tee."

Later......

"Mr.Liam Walsh said he had investigated the question of a driving range and the costs would be extremely high. Big items of expense would be installation and maintenance of lighting. In addition golf balls would be very expensive. The question of having some form of driving range available with members using their own golf balls to be considered."

■ A Wild Life Sanctuary.

The Course and Gibleen became a wild life sanctuary.

"Mr. Paddy Hopkins had contacted the
Forestry and Wildlife Federation and
they advised him they would do a report
and survey for a fee of £25."(1983)

While waiting for official sanction some cruel deeds were taking place.

"While playing a round of golf at Westport on Saturday last (Dec. 17th,1983) Liam Walsh (vice-capt.), Cathal Hughes (Treas.) and Martin Phillips came on a very cruel scene. In heavy grass off the 16th fairway they found a young fox trapped in a snare. The unfortunate animal had been trapped for 24 hours and in trying to escape had trashed the ground all around it, resulting in the snare cutting into its neck. Despite the risk to themselves the three golfers managed to free the fox."

A new constitution was introduced in 1984.

"Concern was expressed that the new constitution and bye-laws were not in a proper booklet form. The cost of doing this would be £400. It was suggested that a charge of £1 be imposed on members for a copy of the constitution."

■ Trees.

The question of trees became a controversial one. By 1977 some 4000 trees had been planted throughout the course. In 1985 Sean O'Malley pointed out that 2,500 trees had been planted in 1983, 3000 trees in 1984 .

In 1986 Joe Gibbons outlined a very ambitious programme with regard to the planting of trees. Many members emphasised that they considered it undesirable to make the course more difficult. It was considered undesirable that we would have tree-lined fairways.

In 1989 a map outlining where trees would be planted was on display. Many members spoke on the issue and the position of trustees re major changes was quoted from the constitution. Mr. Cathal Hughes proposed the following amendment:

"Under no circumstances could any trees
be planted which would interfere with or
obstruct a view of the course."

The amendment was seconded by Paddy Hopkins and carried on a vote of 36 to 18.

■ The Hawtree View Of Trees.

In January 1989 Martin Hawtree reported on a visit to the course:

"Our own view would be that Westport should most certainly not be transferred into a woodland course. Its character lies in length and openness. It should not be tamed. You had the idea of putting down the spare land to forestry planting for which you could receive a substantial grant. Our view is that mass planting of species likely to be approved would change the character of the course quite significantly and weaken the present splendidly bold, open, wild character of the landscape. Forestry tames as well as darkens the landscape and we feel that would not be a change for the better."

■ Planting The Gibleen.

In 1997, 19,500 trees were planted in the Gibleen area. Coillte chose the following varieties of trees – sycamore, beech, birch and alder. Many saw this venture as a way of improving the view from the clubhouse. Its real value was an investment in the future. The club was able to plant trees at a minimal cost as opposed to buying trees from a nursery costing thousands of pounds. The hope was a cash boost to the club when the trees matured. The trees could be sold and the area re-planted again.

In 2003 the Captain read a letter from Coillte outlining the cost to the club to take 0.75 hectares of trees from the Gibleen. The club would have to repay E2,247.43. It was agreed to go ahead and purchase the area. It was noted that a number of trees could be sold later on.

■ A New 9 Holes?

The Hawtree firm was also asked to consider the possibility of a new 9 holes.

"You have considered two extremes of topography for this purpose-the low marshland of Gibleen and two hill summits of Clevelagh and to the left of the 16th and 17th holes. This is the only remaining land owned by the course and it was land deliberately avoided in the first 18 hole course. We do not see the end product justifying the means and the expense. We do not believe that holes 11,12,13,14,15,16 should be changed. They are among the finest at Westport. If there is to be an additional course at Westport it should be given reasonable land and acreage. We would have thought it worthwhile making enquiries for adjacent land."

■ Up-Skilling The Grounds Staff.

A seminar for greenkeepers was held at the Club in 1985. The initiative for the seminar came from Mr. Sean O'Malley, chairman of grounds and Mr. John Garavan, head greenkeeper at the club. Nine local clubs were represented at the seminar which was organised with the help of Dr. Tom Kavanagh, Agricultural Institute, Kinsealy, Dublin. Lectures were conducted on drainage, construction and establishment of greens, tees and fairways, main-tenance and renovation, machinery and equipment. A practical session was held out of doors on spraying, chemicals and machinery.

In 1986 it was proposed by Cathal Hughes, seconded by Noel Connell that:
"We join the Sports Turf Research Institute at Bingley as comprehensive members."
In 1988 the Bingley report on ground staff indicated that the normal requirement for the upkeep of a course of Westport's size was four groundstaff and one greenkeeper.

Other progressive developments were the hosting of the Irish Close in 1985, the appointment of a professional, Mr. Keith Mongan, in 1988, a proposal by Gar Golden in 1989 for a future development plan for the course, the suggestion by Mr. Michael Browne that the course be purchased from Bord Fáilte and active consideration for a McGregor Golf Academy,

"Jack Nicklaus would open the Academy. It would provide all year round teaching. An indoor facility would be required especially in winter. It would be situated near the practice area and as we had plenty of grounds a few par 4 practice holes could be built. "

From 1990 club and course development continued to be progressive and varied. Mr. C. Hughes mentioned the necessity for a sprinkling system at the earliest possible opportunity. He also felt that the idea of having strokesavers for the course should be examined.

The cost of installing a sprinkler system from Vesta would be £42,000. This would include two valves for tees and four for greens. It was decided to go ahead with the work straight away.

In 1991 the Grounds Committee felt that to long-finger the sprinkler system would be detrimental to greens development:

"Our green fee prices must reflect our ability to ensure good greens all the time." All agreed that a sprinkler system was desirable but a majority felt that it could not be afforded in 1991.

A motion from C. Hughes that permission be sought from an EGM to install same was not carried. In 1992 the new green sprinkling system was officially turned on by the Minister for Justice, Mr. Padraig Flynn. It cost the club in the region of £56,000 and was installed by Vesta Irrigation Ltd, Belfast. It enabled the club to have direct control over the watering and fertilising of the greens. Heretofore they had to rely on the weather forecast to gauge when was the best time to fertilise the greens.

In 1997 Mr. Cathal Hughes asked that costing be obtained for the provision of sprinklers on tees. To date this very necessary development remains to be tackled.

In 1992 a new course adviser, Mr. Eddie Connaughton, was appointed. His brief was to set out a programme for each green separately after carrying out various soil tests.

In 1993 a Strokesaver containing the names of the holes was produced.

In 1999 Mr. Peter McEvoy of McEvoy and Cook, Golf Partnership Limited, surveyed the course. In his findings he intimated that in his opinion Westport has the potential to house a genuinely magnificent course. However, he considered it was too long due to the nature of the soil coupled with the windy coastal conditions. In order to move to a position of outright excellence he believed that the following steps were necessary:

■ Greens and tees to be rebuilt to U.S. P.G.A. specifications and greens reshaped to include much more character.
■ The fairways and green-side bunkering to be reviewed with less length in the middle section of the course and more subtlety required in the test presented by the course.

He indicated it would cost £73,000 plus VAT to develop two tees and two greens.

In 1990 Mr. C. Hughes asked the committee

> *The Gibleen covers a triangular area in the centre of the Golf Course. In the 19th century it was an inlet of Clew Bay with a direct tidal connection to the sea between two low hills.*

and their member friends to consider the idea of adding a bit of colour to the course by the planting of furze and rhododendron. It was also decided to build two hump-back bridges at the 7th and 10th and to lower the brow on the 1st fairway.

In 1994 an ecological report on the Gibleen area at the request of Mr. Paddy Hopkins, President, was carried out.

The area was considered to be visually unattractive. The object of the report was to consider options for the development of the Gibleen in order to make it both a visually attractive landscape feature and to enhance the nature conservation value of the site.

The Gibleen covers a triangular area of approx. 26 acres (10.5 hectares) in the centre of the golf course. In the 19th century it was an inlet of Clew Bay with a direct tidal connection to the sea between two low hills.

At that time the vegetation was all saltmarsh which was covered by spring tides on a few days each month.

The building of the embankment between the two hills allowed the marsh to be drained and converted to wet grassland which could then be grazed. This also meant that the area was liable to flooding by freshwater entering the marsh from both east and west.

To counteract this occasional flooding several main drainage channels were excavated in the marsh and a pair of tidal flaps were installed in a chamber built on the inside of the embankment. The flaps are located between high and low water marks. They open at low tide to release water from the marsh and close with the pressure of the rising tide.

The channels in the Gibleen are supplied with water from three main sources; a stream which flows under the road near the main entrance to the club; a spring which rises near the western perimeter of the course and flows directly into the

main east-west channel; the tidal valves in the embankment which permit some seawater to enter the marsh at high tide.

Seawater had been coming through the tidal valves for some time and there was regular tidal inundation. This happened because the more modern tidal valve with an external flap on the seaward wall was heavily encrusted with seaweed and barnacles which prevented it from closing completely at high tide.

The ecological report underlined an option for this area that would have major visual benefits and major conservation benefits. This was to create a reedbed.

The visual benefits would be an annual variation in colour from fresh green growth in spring and summer to light brown in autumn and winter. Reedbeds are also a valuable habitat for wildlife. They provide both breeding and feeding opportunities for wildfowl including swans, mallard, teal, moorhen and little grebe as well as a major habitat for songbirds such as sedge warbler and reed bunting.

The reeds would also provide cover for larger mammals such as the otter.

The reeds would also make a major contribution to absorbing the excess nutrients. The capital works involved for this option would be install new sluices , excavate berm along the channels and plant reeds.

The maintenance involved would be the manual adjustment of sluices and the digging out of the reed litter every five years.

In 2000 it was decided to cultivate a flowerbed illustrating the name "Westport G.C." on the hillside across from the first tee.

It was also decided to rebuild the Judges viewing Tower at the back of the 4th tee.

This re-furbishment led to the decision that the policy of not crediting sponsors for improvements on the course should continue.

It was also decided to plant more coloured shrubbery. The old tree to the right of the 9th green was also considered. It was deemed to be a major feature to this hole. It was agreed that a mature tree should be planted by way of replacement. A quotation was sought for a Sycamore tree approx. 25 feet high and 10 feet wide.

In 2001 an EGM on course development was held to discuss the proposed development of the 7th , 8th and 18th holes in line with architectural drawings as drafted by Eddie Connaughton.

Three new greens involving a striking water feature would be built.

In 2000 it was decided to cultivate a flowerbed illustrating the name "Westport G.C." on the hillside across from the first Tee.

The feelings expressed were that stagnation of club and course must be avoided. The course must climb the grading ladder. The motion was carried by a huge majority.

In 2003 a general discussion took place on the first season's play on the three newly developed holes; the 7th, 8th and 18th.

It was stated that both Des Smyth and Paul McGinley had criticised the 18th. Both players felt that the entrance to the 18th was poor and that the middle section of the green was almost unplayable.

They felt that the traditional green structure predominant in the West of Ireland was flat and that undulating surfaces would not be helped by the prevailing winds.

An observation was made that in business or sport the hardest thing to view is when something is wrong. The general consensus emerging was that the development should be revisited.

In 2005 a motion was presented to the AGM. that " the surface of the 8th and 18th greens be removed and resodded as was the 7th green when it was reconstructed." An amendment that the 8th would be revisited was put to a vote and carried.

The Irish Close Championships were held in 1997 and 2005 and in 2002 the Irish P.G.A. became the first professional tournament to be played at Westport.

The hosting of these major championships underlined the perception of Westport golf course as a true championship course.

The holding and running of these major championships demanded organising ability of the highest standard and this quality was forthcoming time and time again from the officers, committees and membership of Westport Golf Club.

■ Purchasing Our Club

The major highlight of 1999 was the purchase of the club and course outright from Bord Fáilte.

Westport Golf Club now belongs to its members. (See Chapter 6).

Off course developments were also progressive.

In 1990 Gar Golden, longstanding Westport member, was elected President of the Golfing Union of Ireland.

In 1991 a new deal with McGregor Golf was negotiated and Alex Mealia arrived as the golf professional. It was also agreed in 1991 that the committee would present the incoming Captain with a blazer and that a motion would go forward to the AGM to the effect that the Officers of the day in the club should be Honorary members.

In 1992 an AGM decision offered full membership to women. There was unanimous endorsement of the proposal after it was explained to members that "grant assistance for future developments at the club would be conditional on women having equal rights with men."

This decision led to the re-drafting of the existing constitution and the setting up of a Joint Club consisting of men and ladies. The inaugural general meeting of the joint club convened in December 1994.

The new Committee of Management formed comprised the Lady Captain, Mrs. G. Murphy; Ladies Hon. Sec, Ms . M. Grimes; Ms. C. McMyler; Ms. S.Ryan; Ms. B. Walsh; Ms. B. Ruddy; Messrs, J. Moran; D. McDermott; J.Cox; G. Golden.

Ms. G. Murphy, Lady Captain, stated that on behalf of the ladies they were very pleased to be full members.

Mr. James McNamara was appointed the new manager of the club in 1992.

The inaugural Past Captains dinner was held in Ardmore Restaurant, Westport in 1992. It was attended by 27 Past Captains.

■ The Club Brochure And Marketing

In 1993 Paddy Hopkins was given approval for the production of a club brochure. In 1995 the Marketing Committee requested that the club image be improved to enable a marketing strategy to bear real results.

It was felt that the locker rooms, showers and toilets should be improved and that the entrance hall, stairs and upstairs needed upgrading. In 1996 the Captain said he felt the state of our locker rooms let us down.

Tourists must be looked after and acceptable standards were expected. He felt we had three choices: stay as we are; build a new clubhouse; or renovate the downstairs area.

It was felt the first two choices would be too costly and after much discussion it was decided to redevelop the downstairs area at a maximum cost of £400,000. This decision led to the introduction of an entrance fee in 1997. The feeling was that the club was now in a position to accommodate more members and thus spread the cost of development over a greater divide.

In 1997, the Captain Liam Friel suggested that consideration be given by Westport Golf Club to the establishment of a competition to cater for members aged 55 years and over. Thus the Mayo Seniors Competition eventually became a reality.

■ The website

In 2001 Captains Anne Duffy and Pat Kearns launched the Clubs official web-site.

It is a six-page site designed by general manager Paul O'Neill with the help of club secretary, Margaret Walsh and club professional Alex Mealia.

The site offers a wide range of information including graphics of all 18 holes. The site is an essential marketing tool allowing consumers to visit Westport Golf Club from the comfort of their living rooms.

■ The Driving Range

The most significant development off course was the erection of a quality driving range.

A large majority passed the motion in 2004 that " a driving range be developed on the current practice area."

This was first mentioned in 1983.

In 1990 it was felt to be too ambitious.

In 1992 a three-bay indoor facility was mooted.

In 1993 a full development was suggested rather than a temporary one as it appeared that Leader grants of up to 50% were available then. In 1993 the Rugby Club had sought assurance that the club would not build a driving range.

In response the club reserved the right to apply for planning permission in order to qualify for grants. Finally under Captain Liam Walsh jr. a driving range became reality. This facility has become a wonderful amenity for the Club as well as a financial booster to the club's income.

Hon. Secretary & Hon. Treasurer

1973: Hon. Sec. Dr. S. Tobin/ Bro. P. K. Maher. Hon. Treas. Michael Henehan jr. / John Farrell.	1990; Hon. Sec. Pascal Quinn Hon. Treas. Terry Sheridan.
1974: Hon. Sec. M. Moran. Hon. Treas. J. Farrell.	1991: Hon. Sec. Pascal Quinn Hon. Treas. Terry Sheridan.
1975: Hon. Sec. M. Moran Hon. Treas. Mr. J. G. Colbert.	1992: Hon. Sec. Frank Fitzgerald Hon. Treas. Jimmy Kearns.
1976: Hon. Sec. M. Moran. Hon. Treas. G. Colbert.	1993: Hon. Sec. Padraic Duffy Hon. Treas. Jimmy Kearns.
1977: Hon. Sec. Denis Egan Hon. Treas. G. Colbert.	1994: Hon. Sec. Padraic Duffy Hon. Treas. Dermot Blythe.
1978: Hon. Sec. Denis Egan. Hon. Treas. Mr. Peter Daly.	1995: Hon. Sec. Pat Murphy Hon. Treas. Dermot Blythe.
1979: Hon. Sec. Denis Egan Hon. Treas. John Hanlon.	1996: Hon. Sec. Dermot Ruddy Hon. Treas. David Mc Dermott.
1980; Hon Sec. Sean O'Malley Hon. Treas. John Hanlon	1997: Hon. Sec. Noel Connell Hon. Treas. Tom Walsh.
1981: Hon. Sec. Sean O'Malley Hon. Treas. Cathal Hughes.	1998: Hon. Sec. Noel Connell Hon. Treas. Tom Walsh.
1982; Hon Sec. Sean O'Malley Hon. Treas. Cathal Hughes.	1999: Hon. Sec. Noel Connell Hon. Treas. Tom Walsh
1983: Hon. Sec. Pat Murphy Hon. Treas. Cathal Hughes.	2000: Hon. Sec. Noel Connell Hon. Treas : John Keavney.
1984: Hon. Sec. Pat Murphy Hon. Treas. Dermot Blythe.	2001: Hon. Sec. Noel Connell Hon. Treas. John Keavney.
1985: Hon. Sec. Pat Murphy Hon. Treas. Dermot Blythe.	2002: Hon. Sec. John Collins Hon. Treas. John Keavney
1986: Hon. Sec. Dermot Blythe Hon. Treas. B. King.	2003: Hon. Sec. John Collins Hon. Treas. David Mc Dermott.
1987: Hon. Sec. Stephen Goggins Hon. Treas. B. King	2004: Hon. Sec. JohnCollins. Hon. Treas. David Mc Dermott.
1988: Hon. Sec. Stephen Goggins Hon. Treas. Denis O'Sullivan	2005: Hon. Sec. John Collins Hon. Treas. David Mc Dermott.
1989: Hon. Sec. Brendan Bolster Hon. Treas. Denis O'Sullivan	2006: Hon. Sec. John Collins Hon. Treas. David Mc Dermott.
	2007: Hon. Sec. John Collins Hon. Treas. Sean Durkan.

In 2004 it was agreed to twin Westport Golf Club with the Bytkowo Golf Club, located in Poznan, Poland.

In 2005 a Social Supplement of €100 was applied to the membership on payment of their annual subscription.

Westport Golf Club from the air: April 2006.

Liam Cosgrave, Taoiseach.
Bertie Ahern, Taoiseach
Christy O'Connor Sr.
Christy O'Connor Jr.
Ms. Margaret Heckler, U.S. Ambassador
to Ireland.
Peter Alliss
Ms. Jean Kennedy Smith.
Des Smyth.
Mary McKenna,
Dick Severino, golf photographer.
Sydney Chaplin son of Charlie Chaplin.
Hal Linden – T.V. fame
Tony Manzoni.
Alex Ferguson.
Robert Shaw – actor, "Jaws"/
club member.

Michael Smurfit,
" I enjoyed every moment of my trip
to Westport where I have not been for
some time. It was a revelation to see
the great changes that had taken
place in the community and yet
Westport still retained its friendliness
and sense of uniqueness which the
West of Ireland holds for anybody who
is an urbanite, like myself.

"The highlight of the Smurfit P.G.A.
2002 Championship for me was our
inimitable Paul McGinley, who also was
at that time a Pro attached to the
"KClub", winning the tournament, which
was a great outcome for the event and a
great satisfaction for me personally.

"I take this occasion to wish all the
members of Westport Golf Club lots of
happy playing days ahead and I
congratulate you as a Club on
achieving the Centenary. One of the
great things we have in Ireland is
traditional golf clubs, long may they
prosper and continue with their
improving facilities. Ireland has come
a long way golf-wise in the last 15
years. We still have some way to go
but we are well on the way to
becoming the Number One golf
attraction country in the world."

Christy O'Connor junior with P. Murphy.

U.S Ambassador to Ireland, Mrs. M. Heckler with
Mr. J. Kiely, celebrating the 10th year of Allergan
Pharmaceuticals in Westport.

1985: Peter Alliss visits Westport Golf Club.
Also in the photo left to right: M. Heverin, G. Golden, P. Hopkins, C. Hughes, S. O'Malley.

Gar Golden (chipping) with
Robert Shaw on the 17th.

2002: Des Smyth with left to right:
L. Halpin, N. Halpin, D. Ruddy.

CLUB TEAMS

Connaught Shield Winner 1988 v Ballyhaunis.
Front: left to right: T. Fitzpatrick, T. Browne, O. Whyte (captain), P. Bree (team captain), L. Halpin.
Middle: left to right: L. Walsh, T. Joyce, T. McHale, L. Gibbons, G. Reilly.
Back: left to right: D. Joyce, D. O'Connor, P. O'Reilly.

1975: Connacht Shield Final

This was the first time in the history of the Club that a team had reached the final. The team who defeated Castlerea in the semi-final was :
Tony Joyce(5) / Gar Golden (8);
Perry O'Reilly (5) / Gerry Hughes(14);
Gerry McAleer(7) / Michael Moran(12);
Michael Henehan(12) / John Farrell(10);
Jackie Morris(14) / John O'Hanlon(17).
Westport lost to Strandhill in the final.

1979: Connacht Shield Final

For the second time in the history of the club Westport reached the final. Westport had a fine win over Athenry in the semi-final.

This victory was achieved by winning their three home matches:
Gar Golden/ Donie O'Connor;
Perry O'Reilly/ Liam Gibbons;
Gerry McAleer/ Michael Moran.
Away: Tony Joyce/ Hugh Murphy;
Niall Halpin/ Gerry Hughes suffered

defeats. In the first leg of the final Westport defeated Co.Sligo 3/2 at home. However in Sligo Westport lost 4/1 thus giving overall victory to Co. Sligo. Westport lost on the last green in three of the five matches.

Perry O'Reilly / Liam Gibbons won 2/1; David Joyce / Tom McHale lost by 1 hole; Tony Joyce / Hugh Murphy lost by 1 hole; Gar Golden / Donie O'Connor lost by 1 hole; J. O'Meara / M. Moran lost 5/4.

1980: All-Ireland Junior Cup. (see Ch.7) Winning the Green Pennant

1983: County Cup Winning Team

M. Cavanaugh, J. Foley, P. Hopkins, G. Hughes, D.Kendricks, P. Kennedy, J. Kelly, M. Kearns, C. O'Malley, P. O'Reilly.

1985: All-Ireland Finals- Junior Cup/ Mixed Foursomes.

Junior Cup Team in Kilkenny: Gar

THROUGH THE YEARS

Connaught mixed foursomes winners 1985
Front: left to right: K. O'Mara, M. Murphy, M. Flynn, J. Bolster (lady captain), K. O'Briain, B. Hughes, L.O'Malley.
Back: left to right   L. Halpin, L. Walsh, P.O'Reilly, C. Hughes (captain), D. O'Connor, D. Joyce, L. Gibbons, M. Halpin.

Golden, Tony Joyce, Liam Walsh, David Joyce, Tom Mc Hale, Martin McIntyre. Mixed Foursomes in Monkstown, Cork: Liam Halpin / Kate O'Meara; Donie O'Connor / Kay O'Brien; Perry O'Reilly / Maureen Flynn; Liam Walsh / Moirin Murphy; David Joyce / Bridie Hughes.

This team lost to Ennis with two matches decided on the 18th and one decided on the 19th.

1986: Connacht Shield Team in Final

T. Joyce / T. McHale;
D. Joyce /L. Gibbons;
L. Halpin /D. Carroll;
D. O'Connor / P. Walsh;
P. O'Reilly / M. Halpin.

Westport defeated Tuam by 3 matches to 2 in the first leg at Westport. In the second leg Tuam defeated Westport by 4 matches to 1.

1987: Westport win Senior Cup

Liam Gibbons, Shane Underwood;

Perry O'Reilly, Donie O'Connor and Liam Halpin made history when they recorded Westport's first ever win in the Irish Senior Cup , Connacht section. This team was defeated by Warrenpoint in the All-Ireland semi-final. Warrenpoint became All-Ireland Champions.

1987: Westport win Connacht Shield

This team defeated Tuam 7 - 3.
Liam Gibbons / Donie O'Connor;
Stephen Goggins / Tony Joyce;
Shane Underwood / Liam Halpin;
Perry O'Reilly / Tom McHale;
Joyce / B. Frost.

1988: Westport retain Connacht Shield

This team defeated Ballyhaunis.
L.Gibbons / Tony Joyce;
Perry O'Reilly / Tom McHale;
Donie O'Connor / George Reilly;
 Liam Walsh (N/port) / T. Browne;
L.Halpin / D.Joyce;
Reserves: P.Walsh / T. Fitzpatrick.

1989: All-Ireland Finals – Jimmy Bruen/ Mixed Foursomes

In the Jimmy Bruen All-Ireland Semi-final Bangor (eventual winners) defeated Westport 3 matches to 2 at Woodbrook G.C.
Tony Joyce / Denis Kendricks;
T. McHale / T. McHale jr.;
N. Connell / Denis Carroll;
T. Browne / L.Walsh(N/port);
T. Fitzpatrick / J.Cuddy;
G. Reilly / D.Joyce.
Team Captain; F. Hope

In the All-Ireland semi-final of the Irish Mixed Foursomes played at Castletroy Westport defeated Rossmore by 3.5 matches to 1.5. In the final Tralee defeated Westport by 3 matches to 2. Two matches went to the 20th and 21st holes.

Tony Joyce / Nuala Hopkins; Liam Gibbons / Bridie Moran; Donie O'Connor / Brigid Gibbons; Perry O'Reilly / Bridie Hughes; Liam Halpin /Maureen Flynn; Tom McHale sr. / Kay Browne.
Team Captain; Aiden Redmond.

2000: Connacht Shield winners.

Westport defeated Claremorris 7-3.

Sean Walsh; Pat Griffith; Neil McNulty; Michael Kearns; Sean Fitzgerald; Padraic Walsh; Perry O'Reilly; Tom McLoughlin; Liam Friel; Cathal O'Malley; Bill Hopkins; Peter Healy; Tony Bree.

2000: Jack O'Sullivan Trophy-Connacht Final.

Westport defeated by Tubbercurry 7.5 to 2.5.

Perry O'Reilly; Tony Joyce; Donie O'Connor; Gerry Hughes; Pat Griffith; Liam Friel; Padraic Walsh; Sean Fitzgerald; Bill Hopkins; David McDermott; Noel Connell; John Collins; Pat Kearns; Peter Healy; Noel Feeney; D. Joyce.

2002: Junior Cup Connacht Final at Galway. Cecil Ewing Connacht Final.

Westport were appearing in their first Junior Cup Connacht Final since 1985. The team was defeated by Portumna 3 matches to 2. All 5 matches were extremely close with the vital match going to the 20th hole where Michael McGreal jr. suffered defeat.

Tony Bree; Tom McLoughlin; Michael McGreal jr.; Gar Golden, Niall Halpin; Padraic Higgins; George Reilly; Liam Gibbons; David O'Regan. Team Captain: Liam Halpin.

In the Cecil Ewing Final Westport took a 3/2 lead into the home leg against Gort. Westport were bidding to win the title for the first time. Gort won the title.

R.Coakley/ J.Gillivan; K. Cusack/ M.Groden; J.F.O'Malley/ J.O'Donohue; N. O'Malley/ E.Canning; I. Carroll/ D. McLoughlin; P.McNally/ N. McHugh; J.Mulhern / P.Moran.

2005: Pierce Purcell Connacht Final.

Westport beat Swinford, Ballinrobe, Belmullet and Gort by 3 matches to 2 on each occasion to reach the final against Portumna.

Westport lost the final by 3 matches to 2 with one match decided on the 19th and a second match decided on the 20th.

Martin Brennan/ Ger Needham; John Collins/ Mickey Carney;

Liam Friel/ Eugene Patten; Ivan Carroll/

Eugene Cranley; Matt Murray/ Liam Campion.; Panel: Noel Connell, Paddy Donohue, Noel Feeney, Pat Fleming, Pat Gallagher, John Keavney, Vincent Rigney, Philip Cawley, Vincent Coakley.

2006: Westport win Connacht G.U.I. Junior Cup to reach All-Ireland Finals – Junior Cup.

Westport defeated Ballinasloe in the Connacht Final played at windy Enniscrone.

Team: Tony Bree; Michael McGreal jr, Anthony Browne; Colm Walsh; Ronan Mahon; Liam Gibbons; Enda Lonergan. Team Captain; Shane Larkin.

In the All-Ireland Semi-Final Westport lost to the Leinster Champions, The Castle, by 4 matches to 1.

Winning Pennants

1980: Junior Cup – Connacht
1980: Junior Cup – Golfing Union of Ireland.
1981: Ladies Foursomes – Connaught
1985: Junior Cup-G.U.I. Connacht.
1985: Irish Mixed Foursomes-G.U.I. Connacht.
1985: Lina Black – I.L.G.U.
1986: Huzzar Vodka – Ladies Foursomes Connacht.
1987 : Senior Cup – G.U.I. Connacht.
1987: Connacht Shield
1988: Connacht Shield.
1988: Lina Black – I.L.G.U.
1989: Huzzar Vodka – Ladies Foursomes Connacht.
1989 : Jimmy Bruen Shield – G.U.I. Connacht.
1989: Mixed Foursomes – G.U.I. Connacht.
1989: Lina Black – I.L.G.U.
1999: Junior Foursomes
1999: Junior-U-15 – Inaugural
1999: Junior Inter Club
1999: Connacht Cup – I.L.G.U.
2000: Junior Inter-Club
2000: Junior Foursomes
2000: Fred Daly Trophy
2000: Connacht Shield
2002: Connacht Schools
2006: Junior Cup – Connacht
2007: Connaught Junior Cup – I.L.G.U.

Connaught Cup: Front: left to right: L. O'Malley, M. Murphy, M. Ryan, H. McMahon. Back: M. Walsh, B. Blythe, J. McAleer, S. Malone.

1976: Chris Lavelle, Fergal Hope, Pat Hoban, Liam Walsh, Liam Gibbons, Tom McHale (snr), Tony Joyce, John Coughlan.
Front: Jean McAleer, Michael Ryan, Bro L.K. Walsh, Alan Hastings,.

Photo: Frank Dolan.

1978: Connaught Trophy: Back row, Moirin Murohy, Sheelagh Ryan, Bridie Hughes. Front, Maureen Walsh, Loretto O'Malley, Marine Ryan.

1985: Lina Black: back, Kay O'Briain, Maureen Flynn, Sheelagh Ryan. Front, Bridie Hughes, Jackie Bolster (lady captain), Loretto O'Malley,

The 14th hole, a beautiful par 3, index 11.

Controlling
OUR FUTURE

T he land for Westport Golf Club had been made available by Lord Sligo and was purchased by Bord Fáilte. The people of Westport made a financial contribution to the purchase price. The Golf Club and Course was vested in Ireland West to preserve the property for the benefit of Westport and with the long term aim of developing golf tourism. Bord Fáilte developed the course and Clubhouse and leased it to Westport Golf Club by way of a 49 year lease. The rent payable was fixed at 10% of the membership and green fee income generated by the club. This lease would expire in 2023.

The 1974 Lease Agreement
The Lease was signed on the 24th of January 1974 by the Trustees of the Club. They were Brendan O'Malley, Rosbeg;

Rev. Eamon O'Malley; Dr. Sean Tobin; Michael Moran, Kilmeena; Gerard D. Golden, Bridge St; Michael Hastings, Castlebar St; Joseph Lally, Arus Fáilte, Galway. The Western Regional Tourism Organisation were proposing to lease "all that and those" the hereditaments and premises described in Folio 51135 of the register, County Mayo, comprising firstly that part of the lands of Westport Demesne containing 38 acres ...2 roods...12 perches and secondly that part of the lands of Westport Demesne containing 172 acres...0 roods...6 perches.

> *Bord Fáilte expected a premier Golf Club to satisfy tourist demand while at the same time denying Westport Golf Club any financial grants to enable the Club to present a top clubhouse and course.*

■ The Lease Restrictions.
The Trustees were forbidden to alter or develop the premises in any way without the prior consent in writing of the company. Any development would have to be in strict accordance with any such consent.

The Trustees had to agree to maintain the Golf Course land in good playing order at all times.

They had to agree that green fees and visitor charges would not be increased without the prior consent of the Company.

Neither could the rules and regulations of the Club be changed without the consent of the company. The regional tourism manager would be appointed as a Trustee and as a member of all Committees of the Club.

Any non-performance or non-observance of the conditions could lead to the Company demanding repayment of monies paid.

■ Inheriting Bord Fáilte's Oversights.
The lease presumed that the course and clubhouse were in a state of perfection. However this was far from being the case. Officers and committees were to find themselves severely restrained by this lease in their efforts to develop the Clubhouse and Course.

On the 2nd of April 1975 the Captain Gar Golden wrote the following letter to Joe Lally, Regional Manager, Ireland West, regarding the condition of the clubhouse.

"I wish to inform you that there is a very serious deterioration in the clubhouse structure. Bord Fáilte cannot expect Westport Golf Club to take over this building without future financial assurances, especially when the supervision of this project was the responsibility of Bord Fáilte and their employed consultants."

This letter was to herald years of frustration with Bord Fáilte and the lease.

■ Financial Pressure On Officers.
The financial costs of maintaining the new facility were now becoming a serious burden for the Officers. The worry and stress is audible from the following letter signed by the officers on December 22nd 1977. This letter was forwarded to Bord Fáilte.

"In consideration of the payment to Westport Golf Club of a grant in the amount of £30,000, covering an agreed programme of capital works, we the Officers of Westport Golf Club do hereby agree that no further demands for financial assistance will be made by Westport Golf Club on Bord Fáilte and will undertake to enter into such formal Deed of Covenant and charge as may be required by the Board for the protection of its interests."

■ The Bord Fáilte Paradox.
No grants for development could now be expected from Bord Fáilte and at the same time money generated by the club which could have financed development had to go to Bord Fáilte as rent.

This payment of the rent to Bord Fáilte now

became a major issue. Sometimes rent payments fell into arrears due to the financial costs of running such a large enterprise.

Bord Fáilte appeared to have little understanding of the financial sums demanded for the upkeep of a Championship Course.

Bord Fáilte expected a premier golf club to satisfy tourist demand while at the same time denying Westport Golf Club any financial grants to enable the club to present a top clubhouse and course.

The relationship between the Club fraternity and Bord Fáilte soured and a process to purchase the club outright from Bord Fáilte was commenced.

■ The Call To Purchase The Club.

The theme of the AGM in 1989 was the future development of the club. It was here that Mr. Michael Browne, solicitor, suggested that the course be purchased from Bord Fáilte.

In 1990 the Captain, Mr. Colam O'Neill, presented a list of development items including ,

"purchase of Club property from Bord Fáilte."

In the meantime Bord Fáilte proposed amendments to the lease.

■ Bord Fáilte Amendments To The Lease.

On the 14th of May 1991, Captain Mr. Jack Bredin, received the following letter from Arus Fáilte, Galway.

This letter underlines the control Bord Fáilte demanded over Westport Golf Club. The club officers would be merely "penny-pot boys" labouring in the facility without any real control over its future development.

"Following our discussions in Westport on the 10th of April last where the various amendments Bord Fáilte and Ireland West proposed to the existing lease agreement, all the conditions were generally acceptable to the Golf Club with the exception of the amount of the annual rent to be paid to Ireland West.

"I advised Bord Fáilte that Westport Golf Club were prepared to pay 5% of revenue accruing from green fees and club membership for three years, rising to 10% in 1994 with a review pending in 1995. I outlined the reasons given by the club why

they felt they could not afford to pay the 10% levy as per the existing agreement.

Bord Fáilte recommended the following amendments to the existing agreement:

1. Rental agreement:
1991   5%;
1992   7%
1993   9%
1994   10%
1995   Revision.

2. Existing lease to run for further 49 years term dating from when current lease expires in year 2023.

In addition the following conditions to be added to the amended agreement if not already included.

3. Details of opening hours and green fees to be approved annually by Ireland West and under no circumstances be any differential between retail green fee charged to Irish residents and that charged to out of state visiting golfers.

4. Course and facilities to operate and be maintained to international standard and be of championship quality.

5. Equal opportunities to be available to male and female golfers to enjoy course and facilities.

6. The normal tee time hours available to visitors to be not less than 60% including weekends and peak season.

7. Ireland West to have the right to nominate at least 2 Trustees.

8. Local membership should not exceed present level without prior approval of Ireland West.

9. Club to facilitate RTO/ BFE with free golfing for journalists and VIPs on familarisation.

A discount of 20% be made available on green fees when incorporated in holiday package with approved accommodation.

10. No alterations or building to be allowed without written approval from Ireland West and Bord Fáilte.

In addition we feel that some improvements to clubhouse and course will be necessary to maximise attractiveness to overseas tourists and limited grant assistance towards this work, particularly clubhouse facilities, might be available within the terms of the ERDF regulations."

■ Hotel On Grounds.

In 1992 Bord Fáilte envisaged the construction of a hotel on the Club grounds.

A delegation of six people was proposed to meet Bord Fáilte: Stephen Walsh, Bert Farrell, Vincent Farrell, (Captain) Gar Golden, Terry Sheridan (vice-captain), Frank Fitzgerald.

On the 15th of January 1992 Mr. Vincent Farrell, Captain, received the following letter from Brian Quinn, Regional Tourism Manager.

" I am to advise you that Ireland West / Bord Fáilte do not agree to the proposed changes in the constitution of the Westport Golf Club. It is hoped to set up a meeting in early February to discuss in detail the whole situation including the implementation of the lease agreement and possible grant assistance towards club house improvements."

■ A Deluxe Clubhouse …Promises…Promises!

In 1993, under Captain Terry Sheridan, a plan for a new deluxe clubhouse costing 1 million pounds was developed. The hint of financial assistance from Bord Fáilte had kickstarted this development plan. The plans for this building were drawn up by John Cox Associates. Everyone was excited on viewing these de-luxe plans. However this excitement did not last long. No financial assistance emerged from Bord Fáilte and these plans were binned. Bord Fáilte rejected these plans and instead they suggested that a developer for hotel/ leisure complex/ clubhouse be sought. To this end they agreed on placing an advertisement in the National papers. A long discussion followed on this information and the feeling was that the future of the club appeared to lie with a new lease.

■ The New Lease.

The new lease would consist of a new lease for 49 years and agreed Articles of Association of a new company. Patrick Durcan, solicitor, felt that the new lease and the new company together with the existing constitution was a better deal than the old situation.

■ Bord Fáilte Refuse New Lease.

Bord Fáilte were not prepared to go ahead with the new lease because Westport Golf Club refused to give permission for a hotel.

■ The Way Forward 1993.

It was now felt that the way forward was for a small sub-committee to draft a submission and present it to the Minister for Tourism. As a result of Bord Fáiltes refusal two items had to be amended for the AGM…. the position of lady members and the setting up of a limited company. Later an EGM was cancelled due to the advice that the formation of a limited company could leave the club open to a heavy tax liability. It was stated and restated that the majority of Westport Golf Club's problems related to the unsatisfactory relationship that existed between the club and Bord Fáilte.

■ Final Offer From Bord Fáilte 1994.

The final offer from Bord Fáilte was 7% of green fees and subscriptions until the year 2000 with 10% from there on in and a further offer of a longer lease.

Bord Fáiltes annual rent for the course was £12,000, index linked. It was agreed to go ahead with a submission to Charlie McCreevey (government minister) with a view to either purchasing the course at a nominal sum or acquiring a longer lease at a nominal fee. As regards arrears it was agreed that further negotiations should be carried out with a view to having these cleared off. The Captain, Michael John McDonnell (R.I.P.) during 1994 led a number of deputations to Bord Fáilte to try and secure the future development of the course.

In 1995 efforts under Val Murray (Captain) came to nought as Bord Fáilte was not prepared to negotiate.

■ Dramatic Development 1996.

As the captaincy of Patrick Duffy began in 1996 "word" was that Bord Fáilte were considering selling Westport Golf Club for £1,000,000. Westport let it be known that they were interested but not at that price as the club were committed to a £300,000 refurbishment of the clubhouse. Subsequently a letter was received from Bord Fáilte offering to sell the club for £636,000. A condition laid down was that Westport Golf Club would continue to facilitate tourists and would promote the facility as a tourist amenity. Bord Fáilte also indicated that there would be no discussion re this figure.

They would expect a downpayment of 75% and the rest in installments over five years. Padraic Duffy said this figure was at variance with the club's valuation.

The paradox emerging was that the club was now substantially enhancing the asset owned by Bord Fáilte through ongoing course development and the major clubhouse development. This was adding to the value of Bord Fáiltes asset with the added problem that this development was now substantially increasing green fee income which would in turn determine the rent payable to Bord Fáilte. Under the lease the more the club developed and increased the green fee income from tourist activity in Westport the more it would have to pay in rent.

In February 1996 advice was sought and received from Mary Geraldine Miller.

She stated that from her reading of the Sporting Leases Act 1971 it "is possible that the lessees will not be entitled to a renewal thereof" (when the lease expired in 2023). The application for such a lease cannot be made earlier than 15 years before its expiration(not earlier than 2008). She urged the Club to seek advice form a competent valuer.

She also went on to state the following..." Life West of the Shannon has its own rules and knowing how the Sporting Leases Act applies to the 1974 lease, you may now be in a better position to strategically defend the greens."

■ Negotiation On Price Begins 1997.
In December 1996 Liam Friel (Captain) and Dermot Blythe [President] wrote to Brian Flynn,

Mary Geraldine Miller stated that from her reading of the Sporting Leases Act 1971 it "is possible that the lessees will not be entitled to a renewal thereof" (when the lease expired in 2023).

Regional Tourism Manager, Ireland West.

Mr. Flynn had attended a meeting in Westport Golf Club on Tuesday 17th December where he had discussions with Liam Friel, Tom Walshe, Noel Connell, Dermot Blythe, and David McDermott.

They informed Mr.Flynn that as the club was already committed to expenditure of £300,000 on upgrading works they could not possibly cope with the extra expenditure of £636,000. (The actual expenditure by WGC in 1997 was £450,000 on refurbishment and modernising on the clubhouse and car park.) They pointed out the membership was reluctant to fund the upgrading in a property we do not own.

They went on to point out that Bord Fáilte made the decision to build the golf complex themselves and that if it had been carried out by a third party (Westport Golf Club) it might be logical to assume that Bord Fáilte would have been disposed to grant aid this work.

It seemed illogical therefore that Bord Fáilte now sought to secure full recompense of gross monies invested.

They pointed out that the local contribution more than covered the purchase of the lands from the Sligo Estate.

They pointed out that the club had invested a minimum of £215k (excluding club labour) since 1982 in upgrading course and clubhouse. They felt this should also be considered in arriving at an equitable price.

They also asked for freehold tenure while stating that golf for tourists was and continues to be the "raison d'etre" of Westport Golf Club. In light of the above they suggested a reserve price of £294k.

In January 1997 Liam Friel received the following response to the letter from Brian Flynn:

"Bord Fáilte have now advised me that the reserve price of £636k must stand as it is based on the cost of state investment plus inflation only.

Calculations based on theoretical grants etc. are irrelevant. "

■ Letter To Enda Kenny.

In February 1997 Liam Friel sent the following letter to Minister Enda Kenny. The letter conveys the Westport viewpoint in relation to dealings with Bord Fáilte.

" Westport Golf Club has demonstrated its commitment to tourism by continually improving the quality of the course for the benefit of tourists, visitors and members.

The Club is committed to financing £400,000 for the upgrade of the clubhouse to attract tourists to Westport.

The Irish Close in 1997 will be a key focus in marketing Westport G.C. The Club is an important local employer. The Club has invested over and above the maintenance requirements of the agreement of 1974. Between grounds, house, marketing, management and golf professional the club has invested a total of £500,169. To date Westport has received no funding under the E.R.D.F. scheme.

The Club minutes of the 5th of May 1970 show that the course cost £57,000, the clubhouse £40,040, the car park £5,000, E.S.B. supply £7000 and greenkeeper's house £5,000. Mr. Brendan Tuohy and Co. estimated the open market value of Bord Fáiltes interest in the property, based on rental terms, at £150,000.

Westport Golf Club has not benefited from grants to the extent that a tourist asset owned by Bord Fáilte would have expected to receive."

This letter brought a swift reply. In March 1997 Brian Flynn once more reiterated Bord Fáiltes demand for £636,000 with no further discussion.

Bord Fáilte also wanted a say in the level of green fees to be charged. They wanted membership to be capped at an agreed figure claiming that they must protect the asset for the benefit of tourism in Westport as this was the basis on which it was originally transferred to Bord Fáilte by Lord Sligo.

Liam Friel replied demanding that the sale special conditions be withdrawn.

■ Tough Talking.

A deputation of Liam Friel (Captain,) David McDermott (Vice-Captain), Noel Connell (Sec) and Tom Walsh (Treas) travelled to Dublin to meet Matt McNulty, Director General, Bord Fáilte. They had a long wait to meet the official involved. He was not prepared to name a price and when the Westport delegation offered £300,000 he rose abruptly and effectively showed the delegation the door.

An angry but determined delegation returned home and set about developing a strategy to finally resolve the problem. Firstly Liam Friel wrote a letter of complaint to Bord Fáilte and copied to the Minister for Tourism.

"I am extremely annoyed and disappointed at the antagonistic and dismissive attitude of Mr. Jim McGuiggan. I feel that it is unacceptable for a public servant to insult the Captain, Vice-Captain, Hon Sec. and Hon .Treas. of Westport Golf Club by his abrupt conduct. We had travelled 160 miles to discuss matters of mutual interest and were taken aback by the discordial reception we received. His arrogant manner completely undermined the progress that was made prior to his arrival. I hope that future discussions can be conducted in a more professional and cordial manner. Our aim is to achieve an agreement that is mutually acceptable and that guarantees the future of Westport Golf Club for our members and tourists."

This letter heralded a change of attitude by the Club.

Noel Connell followed up this letter four days later with a conciliatory tone.

" We wish to compliment your representatives on their professional approach to the subject and we note there is room for negotiations especially in regard to the sum you are willing to accept in settlement. Our records show your investment amounted to £150,000. "

Bord Fáilte had appointed Mr. Richard Trehy, Chartered Accountant to negotiate on their behalf.

On the 7th of May 1997 Liam Friel received the following letter from Richard Trehy. This letter followed a meeting in the Sligo Park Hotel with Mr. Trehy.

The letter brought good news:

> "I feel I can recommend that an offer of £450,000 should be accepted. I have stressed that the desire is to pass on the freehold. Failing this the best that can be offered is a long leasehold of maximum 249 years with renewals of further 249 year periods."

■ 999-year Lease, 1998.

Further negotiation with Richard Trehy in January 1998 resulted in Bord Fáilte proposing a 999-year lease at £450,000. With a large loan already in place for clubhouse re-development serious consideration had to be given to the financial situation.

However this was an opportunity not to be missed as it would secure the future of Westport Golf Club. The Club President, Mr Liam Walsh snr. (R.I.P.) showed great determination and used his famed business acumen to good effect.

The proposal to agree a 999-year lease at an annual rent of £100 was put to the members at an EGM on the 13th of October 1999. and was passed unanimously. The total borrowing requirement would be £575,000.

On the 16th of November 1999 Ireland West signed the new agreement and the negotiating team along with trustees, Gar Golden, Dr. Bertie Farrell, Fergal Hope, Brendan O'Malley, Dermot Blythe and Colam O'Neill, met in Liam Walsh's office to sign the necessary legal documentation and agree the arrangements for payment.

It was a long and anxious wait before Brian Quinn of Mayo Naturally arrived with the necessary documentation.

The transaction was finally completed on the 13th December 1999.

Many people made a vast contribution to the effort and it is a testament to the officers, committees and trustees that they showed the determination and foresight to pursue the objective.

Westport Golf Club now controls its own destiny.

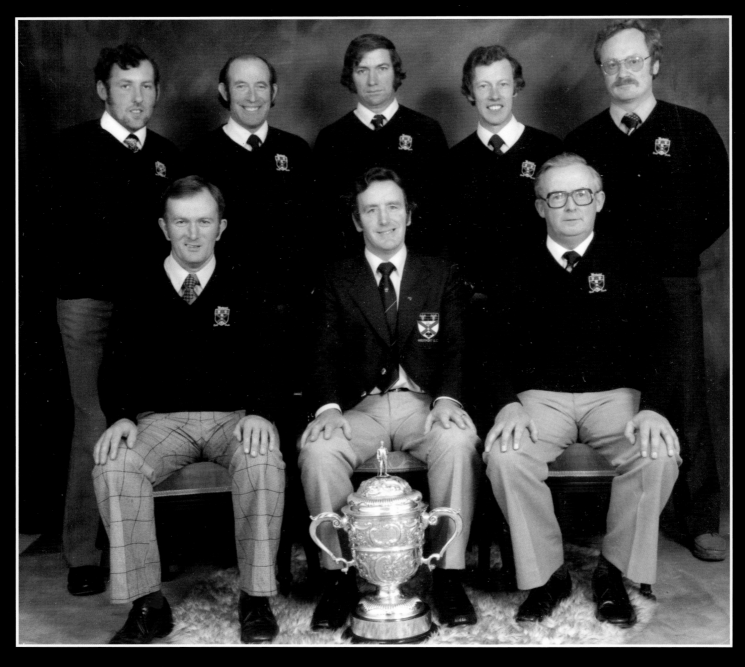

1980: Junior Cup All-Ireland Champions.

Front: left to right: P. O'Reilly, F. Hope (captain), G. Golden.

Back: L. Gibbons, G. McAleer, T. Joyce, M. Henehan, D. Joyce.

Chapter 7

WE ARE THE
Champions

T*he Irish Junior Cup was inaugurated in 1900. Cup teams are comprised of five players of five-handicap and over playing matchplay off scratch. John Ball jr., British Open Champion in 1890, is featured on the lid. He was a member of Royal Liverpool G.C. and he was British Amateur Champion in 1888 , 1890, 1892, 1894, 1899,1902, 1909 and 1912. He was Irish Amateur Champion in 1893, 1894,1899. The Junior Cup has been described as the most difficult amateur club competition to win in Ireland. When the Westport Junior Cup team won this trophy in 1980 it was the first time the trophy came to Mayo.*

■ Westport Golf Club 1980.

On the night Fergal Hope was elected Captain a senior member said to him, "you are inheriting a very sick financial scene!"

The financial reality of administering the new course had begun to diminish club confidence in the future. Serious financial difficulties were emerging due to external forces. Golfing tourism had not developed as envisaged. 1979 had been a most difficult year with petrol shortages, a postal dispute and a very wet Spring. Green fees, the financial life-blood of the Club, had decreased dramatically. Trading losses were increasing each

year. In 1978 the loss was £2,500. In 1979 the loss was £9000. This latter figure was a very considerable sum at the time. However the sickly gloom was about to be banished and by a most unlikely source, the Westport Junior Cup Team.

■ Westport Junior Cup Team.

In 1979 the Junior Cup Team comprising Perry O'Reilly, Tony Joyce, Gar Golden, Liam Gibbons and David Joyce had been defeated by Portumna 3/2 in Westport.

Now in 1980 they were embarking on a new campaign with Gerry McAleer and Michael Henehan joining the panel. They may have had some inkling regarding the Club's financial position but in their wildest dreams they could not have imagined how their heroics in 1980 would change the atmosphere in Westport Golf Club for ever.

The story of winning the Green Pennant is one of character-testing in the white heat of competitive golf. It is also a story of courage, commitment and personal sacrifice.

■ The Quest for All-Ireland Gold.

Westport received a bye in the first round. They would meet the winners of the Castlebar v Ballina match.

Castlebar won and with their established players were expected to proceed further. Westport would play "the auld enemy" (sporting-wise) with the five matches in Westport.

■ Westport v Castlebar.

Team: Perry O'Reilly, Liam Gibbons, Gar Golden, David Joyce, Tony Joyce.

Liam Gibbons had begun to take golf seriously circa 1975. He was working on the course and his starting handicap was 18. By 1980 his handicap was 5.

When the matches started the wind was gusting wildly around the course. The only consolation was that it was a dry evening. Playing the 6th hole Liam was 3 down to his Castlebar opponent, Jim Mc Govern.

Playing the 14th he was 1 up. The wind was really wild at this Par 3. Liam hit a wood to beat the wind but found the bunker and lost the hole.

Word was conveyed that Perry and Tony had won their matches but that Gar and David were losing. Liam's was the vital match. He won the 15th by chipping into the hole for birdie. One up and 3 to play. The 16th was halved. Due to the prevailing wind Liam hit a poor drive on the 17th. As he walked down the fairway, Perry who had defeated Brian Mc Donald on the 14th joined him.

" Put the ball on the green and it will make it difficult for Jim," was his advice.

Liam found the middle of the green. Perry was proved correct. Jim missed the green and failed to get up and down for par. Liam took his par and the match 2/1. Westport had defeated their rivals 3/2 and would meet Ballinrobe in the next round.

A view of the beautiful par 3 14th hole (index 11) in Westport.

PICTURE: GOLF IMAGE

■ Westport v Ballinrobe.
Team: Perry O'Reilly, Tony Joyce, Liam Gibbons, Gar Golden, David Joyce.

Westport had five home games which was a tremendous advantage. Liam's opponent was a young Des Maye jr. Playing the 14th Liam was 1 up. He put his tee ball on to the 14th green. His opponent missed the green on the right but chipped to 8 feet. Liam hit his putt to two feet and marked his ball.

What happened next was to be the turning point in a tense and exciting match. Des Maye lined up his putt and left it a foot short and proceeded to pick up his ball. Liam watching was astonished.

"Is my putt ok ?"

"No. You have to putt out." Des replied.

"I'm sorry," said Liam, "but I did not give you your putt."

Anger flashed across Des Maye's face for a few seconds before he reluctantly said,

"All right!"

As Liam walked away he said to his caddy, Pat Bree, "Two-foot putts are no gimmes on the 14th in Westport! He is after letting his concentration lapse."

Liam won on the 17th 2/1. Later when he reviewed the match he concluded he had learned a valuable lesson from the incident on the 14th. He now knew that concentration is the most important factor in a tight match or any match.

Perry and Tony had won their matches easily. Gar and David were beaten. Westport had won another round 3/2 and they were now in a zone final (Connaught semi-final) against Loughrea.

■ Westport v Loughrea:
Team; Perry O'Reilly, Tony Joyce, Liam Gibbons, Gar Golden, Michael Henehan.

Loughrea was a 9-hole course with very tight driving holes. It was a dry, calm, sunny Sunday evening. Michael Henehan was brought into the team as it was felt his accuracy off the tee and his short game would be an advantage on this tight course.

Liam Gibbons was beaten 3/2. He felt very disappointed. He had played badly. Perry and Tony won as usual but Michael Henehan was beaten 2/1 so it was up to Gar Golden to take Westport to a Connaught final.

As Gar Golden stood on the 19th tee he was annoyed with himself. He had just lost the 18th hole and a Connacht Final place for Westport. He felt enormous pressure .

He said to himself, " Gar, don't blow it. One more good drive, PLEASE God!!"

His drive was safe and sound. Before he realised it he was standing beside the green ready to chip. Both balls ended up six feet from the hole. Nobody could call who was first to putt.

Both putts were measured and found to be equidistant. Both had six footers for par.

A coin was tossed to see who had the right to go first. Gar won the toss but dramatically he decided to let his opponent go first. Perry watching the drama unfold thought, "Gar you are making a mistake!" The Loughrea player left his putt on the rim...SHORT!

Now it was Gar's turn. A host of whispers.

143

Can he sink it? He has to. He's a good putter. The air was pregnant with tension.

Amidst graveyard silence Gar putted.

The ball held the line but stopped on the rim. Gar began to walk towards it and then miraculously the ball revolved and fell in. The cry was, "Golden had delivered!"

Westport were in the Connacht Final of the Junior Cup.

■ Connacht Final: Westport V Strandhill.
Team: Perry O'Reilly, Tony Joyce, Liam Gibbons, Gar Golden, David Joyce.

Team Captain Fergal Hope had a problem. The teams involved had to agree a neutral venue between themselves for this provincial decider. Strandhill insisted that the matches be played in Enniscrone or Rosses Point, both links courses. Strandhill coming from a links course would have a decided advantage if this came about.

After a discussion with his selectors Dermot Blythe and Gar Golden, Fergal decided to dig in and refuse to play on a links course. This approach led to a prolonged "stand-off" and was referred to the Connacht Council.

The Council decided that the match be played in Athlone on the 20th of August. Athlone was a parkland course like Westport.

It was a cold, wet summer's evening. A few carloads travelled from Westport. Strandhill had a very strong team with Declan Rooney, Eddie Keane, Joe Dolan, Gerry Kilbride and Martin Nyland.

When Liam Gibbons had played practice rounds he had noticed a pile of grass cuttings beside the 14th green.

At the time he little thought that his awareness of the environment around a green would prove to be so vital.

He was square with his opponent, Gerry Kilbride, when they approached the 14th hole. Gerry played his second shot through the green into the pile of grass cuttings.

" I am claiming relief here."

"Hold on a minute," said Liam," when I played practice rounds those grass cuttings were there. The rule is if they are piled for removal then and only then can you have relief."

"Well, I want a ruling."

The ruling was in Liam's favour, no relief. Liam won the hole to go 1 up. Walking to the next tee he said to his caddy, Pat Bree,

"Thank God I have a good knowledge of the rules and I always play by the rules!"

Light was beginning to fade. The 17th is a short par 3 with a road behind the green which is out of bounds. Liam's opponent hit his tee shot through the green and it reached the road. The match was Liam's.

Perry had won as usual defeating Declan Rooney 2/1. Tony and Gar had lost. The score now was two matches each. The fifth match was pivotal.

David Joyce stood on the 16th green one down and facing a 35-foot putt for bogey. He could see his opponent's ball four feet from the pin.

Joe Dolan would have that for par and the probability of going 2 up with 2 to play.

David looked around at the sea of faces watching. He could see Perry. What was he thinking? Probably, "Ah well, we had a good run."

He stalked the putt once more. He would have to give it a chance. It was definitely right edge.

He stroked it. He could see it had a chance.

"My God!" he exclaimed, "it's in!"

Joe Dolan missed his four-footer.

As he followed the crowd to the 17th tee Perry said to himself, "Golf is a funny game!"

David won the 17th .

On the 18th he stroked a four-footer in semi-darkness into the centre of the cup sending delirious Westport into the All-Ireland Finals in Lahinch.

■ All-Ireland Finals, Lahinch, 25th/26th September 1980:
Lahinch is a beautiful but challenging links. It is a tight course with the fairways very bare and the rough very difficult to get out of. The greens are lightning fast. It is a course steeped in history and a magnificent venue. It is a completely different course from Westport. Only worthy winners will emerge from here.

■ Westport V Massereene GC (outskirts of Belfast)
11.30 a.m. Thursday 25th of September.

Team: Perry O'Reilly, Tony Joyce, Liam Gibbons, Gar Golden, David Joyce.

When Perry O'Reilly reached the first tee he discovered that the Westport team was not rated by the G.U.I. starter. George Reilly, his caddy, had just handed him his driver. Perry was practice swinging when he heard the voice loud and clear.

"That's the worst swing I have ever seen."

The official was smirking. A. Peoples, Perry's opponent, showed no reaction. Perry decided to let his swing do the talking. He defeated A. Peoples 6/5.

When Liam Gibbons arrived on the first tee his hands were sweating. His knees were trembling and he could feel every part of his body shake. His opponent, H. Mitchell, looked frightened of the occasion also. Liam had thought that the fear of losing, of letting your club, teammates, supporters down would have concentrated his mind. Now he was learning that singles matchplay is a really man or mouse time when it comes to an All-Ireland semi-final. His caddy, Pat Bree, did his best to calm him but Pat was not allowed to play any of the shots for him.

Liam won his match 2 up.

Out on the course Gar Golden knew something was amiss. He couldn't command his mind and body no matter how he tried. He couldn't putt to save his life. He was as helpless as the iceberged Titanic. He was in trouble against M. Arbuthnot. He struggled with all his might but to no avail. He lost 6/5.

The match stood at 2/1 to Westport. Could they get the vital third match and a place in the All-Ireland Final?

David Joyce was all square with B. Warwick. Tony Joyce was in a ding-dong battle with M. Warwick. They had just left the 19th all square. They were now playing the 20th. Perry, George, Liam, Pat, Gar, Fergal, Dermot and the Westport supporters were there to salute Tony Joyce when he won on the 20th.

Westport had won the first three matches. David Joyce was called in.

The G.U.I. starter would have Perry's swing to admire in the All-Ireland Final of the Junior Cup versus Limerick.

■ All-Ireland Junior Cup Final, Lahinch, Friday 26th September, 10.00 a.m.:

Team: Perry O'Reilly, Tony Joyce, Gerry McAleer, Liam Gibbons, David Joyce.

Limerick were going for their third All-Ireland title in four years. Limerick's proximity to Lahinch meant they knew every blade of grass, every bunker and the right lines on the fairway. They were overwhelming favourites to beat Westport.

Gar Golden had a decision to make. He would love to play in the final. He might never get another chance again to grace an All-Ireland final. But how could he ignore what happened to him against Arbuthnot? Beaten 6/5 ! If he had only brought the match to the 17th it would not be so bad? He went looking for Fergal and Dermot.

"I'm stepping down, lads. I've lost form."

Fergal attempted to reason with him.

"Gerry McAleer hasn't even played a practice round."

"He'll be fine."

Gerry McAleer was settling into a pint at the bar when he heard the news. He was on the team for the final. He hurried to the practice ground. He had been ill earlier in the year but now he was easily playing to his 7 handicap. His caddy was Commandant Dave O'Regan.

After Gerry lost the first hole and halved the second Dave felt he should have a word with him.

"You are reading the putts wrong."

"O.K. you give me the line on this one."

The third is a par three. Dave gave the line. The hole gobbled the ball. Birdie and a win!

By the 14th Gerry was 4 up. He won 4/3.

He felt a tremendous exhultation fuse through his body. The relief mixed with a mountain of joy was incredible. Caddy Dave just said,

"What a supersub!"

Liam Gibbons had not slept well during the night. But the funny thing is he thought I am not a bit nervous.

"Why am I so calm?" he asked himself.

Maybe because it is the last match and win or lose, the competition is over? He did not think about this philosophical question again.

He was playing Gerry Casey. Liam got a

Moment of triumph: Westport captain, Fergal Hope receives the Junior Cup from the president of the G.U.I., Mr. M. McAuley.

couple up on him and never let him back into the game. By the 15th Liam was 3 up.

The thought of winning the match on this hole had a dramatic effect on Liam.

His hands began to shake and sweat. Butterflies were having a ceilidh in his stomach. Gerry McAleer was the first to reach him on the 15th green.

"We need only one more match," he shouted enthusiastically. " God, Liam, I would have beaten Jack Nicklaus to-day!"

Word arrived that Tony had been beaten by a very good player called James Carew. David was all flat in his match and Perry was all flat playing the 18th. Everyone now rushed towards the dramatic 18th.

When Perry reached the first tee he smiled at the G.U.I. starter. George handed him his driver. Perry began to swing.

" It's still the worst swing I've ever seen, but it's effective!" said the grinning starter.

Perry was to play Juan Fitzgerald in the top match. Fergal Hope had decided not to watch Perry's match as he was confident Perry would win as usual.

Perry was unbeatable in Junior Cup competition.

Fergal couldn't believe it when word filtered through that Perry was one down with two to play. He hurried to the 17th. Perry had squared the match. He now stood on the 18th tee.

He was nervous. He said to Gar, "Where to? Where will I hit it?"

"Aim for the bunker on the right side of the fairway."

"I'll put it into it."

"No, you won't"

The ball zoomed for the bunker.

"He's done for now!" someone said loud enough to hear. "It's all over."

But then miraculously the Atlantic wind pushed the ball into the middle of the fairway.

Juan Fitzgerald hit his tee shot well left. A Westport supporter watching said ,

"I know where it is."

Someone's foot got in his way and suddenly he was on the ground.

At this tense closing stage Westport were leading by 2 matches to 1.

Gerry McAleer had won his match 4/3 against J. Gleeson, Tony Joyce had lost 3/2 to J. Carew, Liam Gibbons had just won 4/3 against Gerry Casey and David Joyce was all square at the end of the field against Eddie Tuite.

Perry did not let Westport down. He won on the 18th. During the entire championship Juan Fitzgerald was the only opponent to take Perry to the 18th.

As he raced to congratulate him Fergal thought it was somehow fitting that the golfing Gods ordained Perry to be the one to win the vital match.

Westport had won a Green Pennant at last!

■ The Aftermath.

Fergal Hope said: "The emphatic nature of this success is a tremendous tribute to the spirit and dedication, not to mention skill, of all the players involved in all the rounds of the competition. It helped draw attention to Westport Golf Course as a place to visit and play.

"The Massereene team and supporters proved to be the most friendly and sociable. They socialised with us – those not on our team, that is – until the small hours of the morning in the Aberdeen Arms Hotel on the night following their defeat. They turned out the following day and supported us in the final."

Gar Golden added: "Perry, Tony, Liam, Gar, and Dave all played off 5 and Gerry and Michael played off 7.

"Perry, Tony, Dave, and I were long off the tee and Liam whilst not as long, more than made up with a superb short game. The club gave us special exemption to practice pitch and run shots to our greens so as to be better acquainted with a Lahinch type shot.

"Perry was a tower of strength and consistency

A civic reception given by Westport UDC to the Junior Cup team in 1980:
Back, M. Ring, Gar Golden, Margaret Adams, D. Blythe, Mickey kelly, Pat Durcan, J.P. Campbell, Fr E. O'Malley, John Joe O'Malley, M. Cavanaugh.

Front: Gerry McAleer, David Joyce, Perry O'Reilly, Fergal Hope (Club Captain), Liam Gibbons, and Tony Joyce.

in every match he played. His tenacity, his awesome powers of concentration, his fabulous putting along with brilliant shot-making were a joy to watch and his record in the club as a match player will never be equalled."

Many telegrams were received and the victory climaxed when the team and officials were awarded a Civic Reception.

Good news was to follow on the financial situation in the Club. At the end of 1980 income exceeded expenditure for the first time ever by £1,500.

Fergal Hope said: "I was fortunate to have a very shrewd and hard-working committee with me that year.

"The running of a club draw, the baling of our own hay, the running of attractive house events, a push for new membership, green fees, aggressive marketing, competitive events, reducing the working hours of the groundstaff during the winter months, the great support of the Ladies committee, all of these helped our finances.

"The Junior Cup win and the improved financial position helped to make 1980 a very successful year in the annals of Westport Golf Club"

■ Overview.

The Junior Cup win was a tremendous confidence booster to the Club. It renewed belief in the voluntary ethos, so necessary to ensure the continued survival of the Club.

It re-energised future captains and committees. Westport had arrived on the national stage and this fact was to inspire the club in all its activities in the future.

Team quotes

LIAM GIBBONS
I have to pay tribute and thank George Reilly, Tom Mc Hale snr. and Pat Bree. They travelled and caddied in every match. Fergal Hope, Dermot Blythe and Gar did a terrific job as selectors. They were not afraid to make tough decisions. Without that courage and commitment to Westport Golf Club we might not have won anything.

"We had won the Junior Cup! Christ! I was over the moon with excitement. The honour for the club, the honour for ourselves, it was terrific!"

PERRY O'REILLY
"What gave us a tremendous boost and self-belief was when the 'name' golfer on the Gort Senior Cup team, Frank Cooney, a Connacht player told us 'ye'll win Connacht, no problem'.
"We had just lost to Gort in the Senior Cup and he said this on discovering we had the same team for the Junior Cup. In Lahinch the big attractions were at Senior Cup and Barton Shield level. A young Philip Walton and an even younger Ronan Rafferty

at 16 yrs old. I would like to give a mention to two fantastic supporters, Pat Bree and George Reilly. It meant a lot to have friendly faces and words of encouragement. People who never hit a golf ball would come up to you on the street and say ,'well done!'. I never saw Frank Cooney since that night in Gort but his words were positive and encouraging-so thanks Frank!"

GERRY McALEER
"It was a very proud moment when we were presented with the cup and gold medals. We had a great reception in Westport. I found it hard to sympathise with Limerick as they had offered 5 to 1 they would beat us."

PAT BREE
"They were a remarkable group of men, a "Band of Brothers". Perry with George caddying won every match. Every team member contributed with Gerry McAleer coming in cold for the final to win his match with aplomb.
The part that Fergal and Dermot played as selectors/ managers should not be forgotten.

A view of the 12th hole, a par 3 – index 5 – with Clew Bay in the background.

Chapter 8

The Ladies
OF WESTPORT GOLF CLUB

I n 1915 when golf in Westport moved from Trafalgar Park to Carrowholly the ladies of Westport played an active role in helping to establish golf as a sporting and social outlet for the "fair sex". The course was closed to the members between May and September so golf when played was done so during the months of unpredictable weather. They played golf in wet and cold March. They played in blustery April and when October dawned they were on the 1st tee as enthusiastic as ever.

"A ladies Stroke competition was played on Tuesday, 13th of April, 1915, and it resulted in a decided win for Miss May Ruttledge who from scratch returned an excellent score of 93 which, so far, has beaten any of the efforts of the men. Mrs. Yelverton was second with a good 97."

The reporter conveying this information felt that sex rivalry should surely stimulate the men to greater efforts. An Eclectic Stroke competition was held for the ladies on

Top: A view of the 7th (index 10) in the foreground, and 10 (index 13) in the background, with Croagh Patrick in the distance.

Bottom: The 7th fairway from the bridge just in front of the tee,

the 24th. April. The report states that several good scores were returned with Miss Barry and Mrs.Yelverton being a shade in front of the others with fine scores of 38 nett each.

In the play off by match play, Mrs Yelverton won by a very safe margin, Miss Barry thus getting second prize. Amongst other good scores sent in were those of Miss Irene Ruttledge and Miss Trixie Yelverton, 41 each nett, and Miss May Ruttledge and Miss Jeffers 43 each nett.

So these were some of the ladies of Westport Golf Club in 1915. Six days later and the Club closed until October 1st. Considering their enthusiasm in March and April one can only assume that these ladies must have suffered terribly the loss of golf in the high summer months. These scanty reports still reflect their qualities-a love of the game, knowledge of the game, ability for the game in all weathers. These ladies helped to lay a foundation for ladies golf in Westport.

What can be truthfully said is that in 1915 golf

What can be truthfully said is that in 1915 golf was played with gay abandon by ladies in Carrowholly. Foul weather did not diminish their enjoyment.

was played with gay abandon by ladies in Carrowholly. Foul weather did not diminish their enjoyment.

In January 1916 Miss Viola Yelverton won the ladies with a nett score of 40. Miss Irene Ruttledge made the best gross score of 41. The bad weather interfered with the entry. The handicaps applied were a special club handicap.

"Ms. Viola Yelverton 48-8=40; Ms. Irene Ruttledge 41-scr.=41; Ms. Trixie Yelverton 52-4=48; Ms. Dorothy Kelly 54-6=48; Ms. Barry 66-7=59. Miss L. Staunton and Miss Eileen Kelly also competed."

So we salute Mrs.Yelverton, Miss Trixie Yelverton, Miss Barry, Miss Jeffers, Miss Irene Ruttledge, Miss May Ruttledge, Ms. Dorothy Kelly, Miss Lena Staunton, Miss Eileen Kelly, Miss Viola Yelverton and Miss Barry.

In April 1917 the ladies interest in golf was recognised by Henry J. McTernan (Captain 1915,1916).

The 9th hole
(index 6):
a daunting finish
to the front 9.

> "A competition open to the ladies of the club will be held this month for a prize kindly presented by Mr. Henry J. McTernan. Members wishing to compete are asked to kindly send in their names with entry of 1s to the Hon. Secretary, Mr.H. Yelverton as soon as possible. The entry money is for the benefit of the club. The competition will be nine holes."

By 1928 their names no longer resonated from the membership list. However their legacy was a ladies club in 1928 numbering 35 ladies. The membership fee was one guinea (£1-1-0). These 35 ladies were: Mrs. Egan, May Walsh, May McGing, G.Hartley, Mrs. Rees, Mrs. Kenny, Miss Gibbons, Mrs. Joyce, Judith Garvey, Mrs. O'Brien, Miss Stack, Mrs. Duncan, Mrs. John Kelly, Mrs. Hughes, Mrs. Hadnett, Mrs. W.J. Walsh, Mrs. Whyte, Mrs. Tobin, Mrs. Murphy, Mrs. Mulloy, Mrs. P. Golden, A.Ryan, Mrs. Jas Kelly, May King, Mrs. A de Fleury, Miss E. Dineen, E. Hughes, F. Casey, Mrs. Waters, Miss Lynskey, Miss Connolly, Mrs. O'Gorman, Mrs. Coen, Mrs. Hartley, Mrs. F. Tue.

Despite this large membership the ladies sent no delegate to the I.L.G.U. Galway Executive meeting in Greally's Hotel, Roscommon on the 28th of January 1928. Castlebar, Ballina and Claremorris had delegates present. By 1933 the ladies membership had fallen dramatically to 12 members.

This sudden fall may have been due to economic forces worldwide and nationally.

By 1936 membership had risen to 17 ladies and reached 25 ladies in 1942.

The ladies loved the mixed foursomes format and this was a regular competition in the Club.

> " On Wednesday the 21st a mixed foursomes will be held. Draw for partners. Entries close on the 19th and should be sent to Mrs. P.Golden."

> "There will be a mixed foursomes competition on Sunday 24th of June 1945. Draw in the Club House at 3 p.m. sharp. Entrance fee 2s/6p. Intending competitors please give names to Miss G.Stack or to E.J. Timoney before the 23rd of June. Carrowholly always looks its best on the day of a mixed foursomes. There shall be a prize or two and there is a promise that nine holes shall not pass without a cup of tea"

L. O'Malley, A. McDonagh, K. O'Malley, M. Corcoran, M. Walsh, E. Moran, S. Lawlor, B. Tobin, H. McMahon, E. Hughes, S. Bn uí Mhaeoilóin, J. McAleer, A. Colgan, M. Mulloy, N. King.

A mixed foursomes draw in July 1950 at 6.45. p.m. produced the following pairings:

P. Dempsey / Mrs. Blennerhasset;
J.F. O'Malley / Mrs. J. McGreal;
W. O'Brien / Mrs. F.Gill;
P. Naughton / Mrs. L.Gill;
J.B. Maguire / Miss G. Stack;
L. Gill / Mrs. De Fleury;
P. Golden / Miss N O'Malley;
A. de Fleury / Mrs. S.Mulloy;
Rev. Blennerhasset / Mrs. W. O'Brien;
J. Mulloy / Mrs. J.Hughes;
P. O'Driscoll / Miss N. Murphy.

The mixed foursomes format was also used as a fundraiser for charity.

> "A mixed foursomes will be played at Carrowholly Links on Wednesday 26th of June at 6.30 p.m.. The proceeds will be in aid of the Rehabilitation Institution, Westport Branch." (1963)

In 1970 the first mixed foursomes of the season was won by Mrs. Jean McAleer and Mr. Gar Golden. The runners-up were Ms. Barbara Madigan and Mr. Michael Hastings. In 1971 sixteen men were required for the visit of Ballina ladies for a 9-hole mixed foursomes. However there appeared to

Below: Prize presentations by Helen McMahon (Lady Captain). Left to right, Sheelagh Ryan, Bertie Staunton (President), Rose Golden. In the background J. Foley.

be a shortage of men as Mrs. Breheny and Mrs. M. Tobin took the first prize with Mr. Liam Walsh and Miss A.Coyne runners-up.

By 1974 the enthusiasm of the men for the mixed foursomes format was waning.

The ladies loved this format and they were not about to let it go easily. They had the imagination to overcome the men's reluctance by inviting them to play and paying for them.

"The Secretary reported that mixed foursomes appear to be gaining in popularity. Long may it last! The ladies took a step forward this year by inviting the men to be their guests at the ladies expense and it was a great success. We should do more of this sort of thing in the future."

The ladies did not follow the Secretary's advice.

"It is with regret that I must report that we had only ONE mixed foursome for the year 1975 and only eight pairs played."

The arrival of the new course saw the demise of the men's interest in the mixed foursomes format.

In Old Carrowholly the men were as equally enthusiastic as the ladies but they may have had an ulterior motive as the ladies in Old Carrowholly provided the catering duties. The arrival of club caterers in New Carrowholly eroded the men's relationship with the ladies. The mixed foursomes format is no longer a regular event in the lifestyle of the Club.

Besides mixed foursomes there were many other enjoyable days in Old Carrowholly involving the ladies. Open Day was a major event in the club. It was the day when the Club was on display to golfers in the county. The ladies provided the catering.

The following report from the *Mayo News* in July 1941 captures the colourful atmosphere of such a day:

1964 U. Helion, B. Kelly, E. Rabbitte, F. Rees, S. Malone, B. Wallace, E. Maher, L. Hall.

"There were 80 competitors from Ballina, Castlebar, Claremorris and the local club out for the morning competitions in weather that rendered golf a delight and the Westport Links a paradise in its situation. To visitors from inland courses, sun-scorched by the prevailing drought, the greenest of greens with the coolest of sea breezes must have appeared magical.

A full tide during the afternoon lured many of the visitors to Rosminney where they added a swim to the comforts of the day. A large marquee, kindly lent by the Marchioness of Sligo, allowed the ladies committee room to display their ability in catering. If the general appreciation expressed be a guide, the ladies went far towards stealing the honours of making the day the success it undoubtedly was."

Another enjoyable day took place in August. This was organised for a Wednesday.

It combined a mixed foursomes and a putting competition.

"Miss Sheila McBride was the winner in the ladies putting and she also came out best in the ladies chipping contest. Mrs. W. Murphy and Mr. D.P. Landers came first in the mixed foursomes. A very enjoyable tea was served at the Pavilion by the ladies."

In September 1941 another wonderful golfing experience took place.

"Westport Golf Club celebrated Wednesday's delightful weather with a full programme lasting the entire evening. Sixteen pairs competed in the mixed foursomes for which the first prize, a lady's handbag and gentleman's cigarette case, was presented by Mr. D.Landers.

Mr. Landers figured prominently in an unusual incident during the afternoon when a weasel carried off his partner's ball and he gallantly retrieved it."

The Club Day was a major fun day for the ladies. It was the men's way of saying thank-you to the ladies for their contribution to the life of the club.

In July 1943 the weather conditions were ideal for the annual club day with a fresh breeze from the North West varying at times to the North. But it was not just the weather the reporter perceived!

"One could not help admiring the colourful display shown by the lady members and it was possible to take one's choice from a range as wide apart as vivid contrasts and delightful studies in pastel shades. The main item in the competitions was the mixed foursomes. Miss Murphy and Mr. Lawlor first, Miss Stack and Mr. Kenny second, Miss O'Connell and Fr. Gibbons third."

The most exciting event of the afternoon was the ladies chipping and putting competition.It was run on a knock out principle.

"Miss O'Connells chipping being little short of marvellous during the qualifying rounds. She was only beaten into second place by the more experienced player , Mrs. Maher.

During the afternoon and evening the putting competitions were being run off. Mrs. Kenny and Mrs. Murphy tying for the ladies first prize with a score of 19."

Ladies Club Day continued merrily and foul weather never vanquished their enjoyment.

"In spite of the inclement May weather thirty ladies braved the elements. The "Drive" was tough but the "dykes" and "eagles" conquered "Old

A gathering of lady golfers and friends, circa 1960. Front, left to right:
E. Kelly, S. Malone, N. Golden, A. McCormack, M. Stack, G. Kelly, M. O'Connell, F. Rees.

Middle, sitting: L. Doherty, Mrs. Corbett, M. Kelly, Mrs. Mulloy, Mrs. Bourke, Mrs. Brown, L. Gill, M. Gill, J. McGreal, E. Joyce, E. Rabbitte, K. Staunton, B. Blennerhasset, R. O'Donnell, M. Mulloy.

Back: standing: M. Gillivan, U. Ashe, H. McMahon, E. Hughes, M. Nolan, P. Clarke, B. Kelly, A. Lydon, B. O'Malley, C. O'Connell, L. Hall (hidden), K. O'Malley, V. Shanley, K. Kelly, C. Martin, M. Gibbons, Dr. L. King, B. Wallace, Mrs. J. Dyar, M. McAleer, unkown, unknown, M. Jeffers, T. Tyndall.

Bogey" and the overall winner was Mrs. Evelyn Hughes." (1974)

The ladies were not just selfishly concerned with personal fun and enjoyment. They believed in the ethos of a Club. They were concerned with increasing membership and investing in the future.

"The ladies Committee of Westport Golf
Club are arranging golf lessons for
beginners, lessons which will help them
with their grip and swing. But the
beginners will not have to travel to
Carrowholly Links where they might have
to contend with strong winds and rain. The
lessons will be given indoors!"(1972)

In 1973 a golf clinic was conducted by Ireland's only lady golf professional.

"Mrs. Gwen Brandon of the Spawell Driving Range, Tallaght, Ireland's only lady golf professional, will hold a golf clinic. Members with problems are asked to turn out in force for this occasion. Mrs. Brandon does not discriminate between the sexes. She also provides instruction for the men." (1973)

In 1974 Mrs. H. McMahon expressed an interest in beginners.

"Prior to the commencement of the Committee meeting held in the Grand Central Hotel on 24/4/'74 the Captain, Mrs. Helen McMahon and committee met a number of ladies wishing to play golf. It was arranged that as many playing members as possible would take the beginners down on Wednesday evenings and give them instructions on how to swing a club and mark a card. Lady beginners present were:

Ms. May Conlon, Ms. Pamela Walsh; Ms. Anna O'Donnell, Ms. Ena Heneghan, Ms. Stephanie Quinn, Ms. Elaine Cahill, Ms. Mary Holland, Ms. Mary O'Connell, Ms. Bridie Hughes, Ms. Ann Colbert, Ms. Mary McGreal, Ms. Connie Coakley. Apologies from Ms Ann Hughes, Ms. Mary McBride, Ms. Laurie Henehan, Ms. Patricia Brown, Ms. Helen Farrell."

The Lady Captain was very pleased that 22 beginners had turned up on the 8/4/'74. She then

Circa 1975: Sinead Malone, Nuala Moran, Mrs B. Staunton, Mrs O'Regan.
Photo courtesy of Niall Staunton.

get another member and to look after that member personally. Then a new member would not feel lost or embarrassed to come down and play golf."

Mrs. Nora King appealed to mothers of young girls of twelve years and over to "take them down to the course to learn how to play golf."

The emphasis on investing in the future brought positive results. In 1977, 92 Lady Associate Members were listed:

Helen Bree, Shop Street; Brenda Blythe, Shop Street; Mary Browne, Shop Street; Nora Bresnihan, Castlebar; Mairin Byrne; Rosaleen Campbell, Tavern, Murrisk; Frances Campbell, the Grove; Ann Campbell, the Mall; Connie Coakley, Quay Road; Ann Colbert, Demesne; Angela Colgan, Castlebar; Kay Coe, James St.; Minnie Corcoran, Sheeaune; Chris Deane, Castlebar Rd.; Kay Downes, Castlebar Rd.; Mary Dolan, the Mall; Pat Dowling, Leenane Rd; Hazel Douglas; Anna Egan, Castlebar Rd; Helen Farrell, Newport Rd.; Ann Flanagan; B. de Ferranti, Pontoon; Mary Feeney, Cake Kitchen; Agatha Golden, Leenane Rd; Rose Golden , The Mall; Maura Gannon, Lecanvey; Ann T. Gaynor; Blanaid Hughes, Altamount St.; Evelyn Hughes, Castlebar Rd.; Bridie Hughes, The Pinewoods; Mary Hanlon, Kings Hill; Ann Hope, Newport Rd.; Rhoda Heverin, Castlebar; Marjorie S. Hillback; Rose Higgins, Castlebar St.; Pat Kelly, Belclare; Dr. Maeve Kilroy; Nora King, Ayle; June King, Newport Rd.; Anne Kilroy, Newport; Adrienne Lavelle, Lodge Rd; Brid Lee, Carrowholly; Nuala Moran, Mill St.; Eileen Moran, Kilmeena; Mary Mulloy, Shop St.; Moirin Murphy, Kings Hill; Hilda Morris, Rosbeg; Aine Murphy, Mary Murphy, Mary Moran, Castlebar; Kay Moran, Castlebar; Mary T. McDonnell, Castlebar; Eileen Mc Greal, The Quay; Jean McAleer, Newport Rd.; Peggy McAllister, Castlebar; Mary McCann, Skerries; Barbara McCormack, Castlebar; Anna May McCreave, Kilmeena; Annie McDonagh, Castlebar; Maureen McGovern, Newport; Claire McMyler, Kings Hill; Tilly McNeela, Newport; Helen McMahon, Altamont St.; Babs Nolan, James St.; A. Newell; Mary O'Brien, Rosbeg; Rita O'Donnell, Castlebar St.; Anna O'Donnell, James St.; Kay O'Kane, Belfast; S. Bean Ui Mhaoileoin; Kay O'Malley, Rosbeg; Loretta O'Malley, Bridge St.; Thelma O'Malley, Castlebar;

asked the ladies to volunteer to sit at a table in the clubhouse for one hour each day when ladies competitions were being played during Open Week. They were instructed to bring a beginner with them if possible as one felt it would be a good thing for them to learn something about the business side of golf. Duties to be:

1. Write name in competition book and cards.
2. Collect entry fee.
3. Check handicap and name of competitors home club.
4. Request ladies to order meal if desired before going out on course.

Mrs. Sinead Bean Ui Mhaoileoin then put it to the committee, "it would be a good thing to get a Junior Club going in Westport."

She suggested that the ladies might set an example by bringing their children down to play Golf and try to get the thing off the ground. The Committee agreed with this.

In 1975 the Secretary, Ms. Rose Golden posed the question, "How can we the Lady Associate members help?"

She answered the question as follows:

"We need more members and we need local members. Let us go out and look for them. Let's sell our Club and encourage others to join. Would each and every member take it upon themselves to

Nan O'Malley, The Fairgreen; Dr. B. O'Malley, Mill St.; Mary O'Connell, The Mall; Dr. Eileen Power, Irene Reidy, T.V.Mart; Sheelagh Ryan, Castlebar St.; Marine Ryan, Leenane Rd; Geraldine Ryan, Castlebar; Eleanor Staunton; Ita Sarsfield, Castlebar; Ita Staunton, Castlebar; Beda Tobin, Castlebar, Maureen Tobin, Castlebar; Ailbhe Tobin, Castlebar; Sharon Taylor, Maureen Walsh, Newport; Brigeen Walsh, Altamont St; Mary Walsh, The Mall; Pam Walsh, Leenane Rd.

Starting a Junior Club proved more difficult. In 1980 it was reported,

"No Juniors in the club presently."

This was in response to a letter from Mrs. Maire Dillon asking for the co-operation of the members in promoting "Junior Golf".

■ New Carrowholly.

The first ladies Committee Meeting held in the New Westport Club House took place on the 7th of May 1974.

The move to New Carrowholly did not proceed smoothly for the ladies club. In 1974 the Secretary reported a hesitant start to the year, "what with the New Constitution with its rulings on AGMs and Notices of Motion we were all at sea somewhat."

Major teething problems emerged for the ladies. These took the form of controversy over draws, internal discipline, a tough course and a changed relationship with the men.

The "draw" controversy and discipline led the Lady Captain to seek legal advice on the following question: What authority has the Lady Captain or Committee?

Legal answer: None.

Ladies for ladies only. Ladies can make rulings on competitions and any other matters or rulings which ladies made as a committee.

Procedure: Ladies Committee can recommend to Men's Committee.

On moving to New Carrowholly the ladies discovered they had to struggle to establish their identity with the Men's Committee. This was quite traumatic for the ladies as the atmosphere in Old Carrowholly was one of respect for the ladies. Friction soon emerged in the new relationship.

"Mrs. Hughes expressed her disappointment with the Men's Committee for their lack of appreciation of all the work the ladies did during Open Week and at other times. Other members present also joined in and referred to the non co-operation between Mens and ladies Committees. After a general discussion it was agreed to send a letter to the Secretary of the Men's Club setting out the complaints and improvements proposed in this regard. The Lady Captain agreed that this manner of approach was better than verbal."(1976)

Later the Secretary , Mrs. Rose Golden posed the following question: "Is the chip on our shoulders or the mens re. Lady Associate membership?"

She suggested the following response:

> "We, the ladies, can do something about it. We should be proud of our sex and remember that to ensure the smooth running of the Club the men need the ladies just as much as we depend on them. I realise we must look back in order to go forward but one look back is sufficient. It is the forward thinking and the forward looking that will either make or break this club.
>
> I would suggest that the Lady Captain and the Lady Vice-Captain arrange a meeting with their counterparts as soon as possible to iron out all the petty differences which have sprung up over the past few years and in doing so have now almost reached gigantic proportions in our minds.
>
> Dr. Farrell is a reasonable man, as indeed have all the other Captains been before him, but in the hope that his medical knowledge of the biological difference between male and female will help to eliminate our problems, let us strike while the iron is hot. Let us approach the men, talk to them, and having done so, let us work hard and in unity to make this Club a better one."(1976)

The out-going Captain said she would hope that there would be more co-operation with the men in arranging competitions for the coming year.

It was decided to ask the men for permission to play week-end competitions during March and April, as there would not be sufficient light to play 18 holes in the evening until late May.

A directive from the Men's committee did not help to ease tensions:

"The ladies were in future to begin all competitions from the 1st tee, from the 10th, at their own discretion but NEVER from the 7th tee!"

When the ladies were asked by the men if they would cater for the 23rd and 29th of May the affirmative only came after a lengthy discussion,
"After a lengthy discussion it was finally decided to submit a menu of soup, cold salad and cake." (1976)
In 1983 the men suggested that the ladies introduce a time sheet for all competitions.

"The men complained of slow play and the times for evening draws.
The majority of ladies did not favour a time sheet. The ladies explained that Tuesday was a social evening or day for the ladies and a time sheet would prevent them mixing.
They did not accept it. After discussion a number of draw times was agreed for approval by the men."

Gradually relations began to improve although there would later be occasional outbursts of hostility.

"Mrs. Bredin reported a very cordial meeting between the ladies and the men. The ladies to clean their own locker rooms, dining room and kitchen. The men clean their locker rooms, do the hoovering, bar , halls and stairs. Some ladies said they would not mind doing the hoovering but they were quickly told, "that would defeat the purpose of the meeting"(1983)

The men's tone continued to soften.
"On April 24th due to a large society of priests, approx. 150, the ladies may be inconvenienced. They were asked for

their understanding and co-operation as it was a large source of income to the Club."(1984)

The softened tone did not impress some ladies. They felt the ladies should draw up their own constitution:

"The Men's Captain requested that we should adopt their constitution as we had omitted doing this when they drew up their new constitution. Ms. Sinead Bean Ui Mhaoileoin proposed that we draw up our own constitution. Mrs. E. Hughes said the Western Executive were in favour of this. This proposal was defeated. Mrs. B. Walsh proposed that we adopt the mens constitution until such time as we draw up our own. This motion was passed." (AGM 1985)

In 1989 the ladies expressed gratitude for the vote of confidence in them by the men.

"We are grateful to the Men's Committee for agreeing to host the Irish Ladies Close Championship in May and the Home Internationals in September thereby expressing a vote of confidence in the ladies of the Club. Their confidence was well founded. Both events were a tremendous success.(1989)

The ladies continued to be grateful:

"We are very pleased to be working with the men in the House Sub-Committee and I thank Dr. Oliver Whyte for his attention to our viewpoint. He involved the ladies for the first time on this Committee."(1989)

■ **Full membership.**
The climax and end to this testy relationship occurred in 1991 with the announcement that women golfers were to be offered full membership and full rights.

The ladies took a cautious approach to this announcement,

"A letter to be written to the men's committee requesting confirmation in writing if full membership was available to Lady Associates in Westport Golf Club." (March 1992)

The ladies were anxious to weigh up the pros and cons before making a decision,

"After a lengthy discussion it was agreed that the ladies Officers have a meeting with the Men's Officers to discuss the following points:

1. Is full membership available?

2. Do the ladies have a choice?

3. What are the advantages of full membership over associate?

4. Do the ladies have a quota and are they combined with overall membership quota?

5. Can the fees be waivered?

In April 1992 at an E.G.M. the ladies opted to apply for full membership.

"After a lengthy discussion the Lady Captain asked for a show of hands.

Result: For: 40; Against: 3; Abstained: 1

The ladies included an appeal with their application: "So few of our ladies play regular golf we appeal to you and your fellow members to phase in the increased fee over five years."

The ladies club now adopted in full the New Constitution(1994) Three lady members were proposed for election at the inaugural general meeting of the Joint Club. They were Claire McMyler, Brigin Walsh, and Sheelagh Ryan.

The first insight the ladies had into their new status was the end to Vice-Captain's Day and their full participation in the President's Prize in 1995.

In 1996 they had to decide whether they would opt for an open time sheet or reserved blocks. In discussion they discovered that most ladies opted for the open time sheet and the reserved block was rarely used.

In 1997 by a vote of 17 for to 12 against the ladies opted for an open time sheet on Sundays. The reserved block was relinquished for green fees and societies. The days of competition draws for ladies was over.

Having established their rightful identity the ladies in 2000 focused their minds on the Office of President. In view of the *"Equal Status Act"* they felt that the Office of Club President should be held by a Lady say every 3rd. term.

"If the men are not in agreement with
this the ladies may decide to put up a
Lady for election."

This declaration appeared to cause some amusement to the men. But Gretta Murphy pointed out that under the present constitution ladies are entitled to put up a lady candidate for President. It was felt it would happen in the future at some date.

■ The Course.

The ladies always felt New Carrowholly was a tough course to play on. Consequently it was no easy task to bring the handicap down. They hoped to play on a short course which would help to reduce their handicaps.

Mrs Rose Golden said: "This would give us more confidence in ourselves and more important still give the opponents a better match."

In 1978, by 16 votes to 6, the ladies decided to send a recommendation to the Men's AGM that their course be shortened.

"That in order to attract more playing members both ladies and juveniles the course be shortened by forwarding the tees on the 10th and 18th holes and by altering the 8th hole to a par 5."

The reply to their request was abrupt.

A letter from Mr. M. Moran, Captain, re. shortening the holes.

" As he had not 7 days notice our request was not in order. Re-apply next year."

■ Lady Captain's Pln.

In 1974 a decision was made that the Lady Captain's Pin should be presented on the day the Captain assumes office.

"Mrs. Nuals Moran proposed, seconded by Mrs. O'Mhaoileoin that the Lady Captain's Pin should be bought now and presented to her on Lady Captain's Day and that all future Captains

Presentation of the
Fitzgerald Cup.
Front: Fr Paul Fitzgerald,
Bridget Gibbons,
Maureen Flynn, Fr Frank
Fitzgerald. Back: Kay
O'Briain, Anna May
McCreave, Maureen
Walsh, Francis Campbell.

be presented with their Pin on the day they take up office. This was passed unanimously."

Later…

"The Vice-Captain, Mrs. S.Ryan, then presented the Lady Captain with her Captain's Gold Pin for 1974. Sinead Bean Ui Mhaoileoin said it was interesting to note that Mrs. H. Mc Mahon first started her campaign for the Pin ten years ago in 1964. The ladies congratulated Mrs. Mc Mahon and agreed that she really did deserve the honour of wearing it."

Entry fees in 1974 for the first two competitions were fixed at 15p. Major competitions – 50 p and weekly competitions – 20p.

One of the major competitions for ladies was the Fitzgerald Cup. This is a splendid Cup presented by Rev. Fathers Paul and Frank Fitzgerald. The Landers Trophies were equally appreciated by the ladies.

The ladies were always conscious of charities that needed support. In 1997 the nominated charities were, Order of Malta; St. Vincent de Paul; Wheelchair Association and the Breast Cancer Research Institute, Galway.

Bridge was a major off course activity enjoyed by the ladies: "The open tournament at the Westport Golf Bridge Club attracted an entry of 64 players. It was played in two sections. There were numerous spot prizes and afterwards a

delightful tea was served by the Bridge Club ladies."(1976)

The ladies always enjoyed "friendlies" with other clubs.

"Mrs. Rose Golden asked that the friendlies be resumed. It was decided to send invitations to Connemara, Ballina, Ballinrobe and Castlebar with the suggestion that they might include a team of beginners if they wished."

Later…..

"We had a very enjoyable day with Connemara and as it was their first competition with an outside Club they were delighted to travel. We greatly enjoyed our return visit to them. We were unable to have friendlies with other clubs as all seemed to have full fixture lists." (1976)

In 1999 the ladies had a very enjoyable outing to Woodbrook G.C.

They travelled by train to Dublin. Green fees were not charged by Woodbrook.

An unusual ruling was sought in 1988. The question posed was, "Can your husband mark your card?"

"After discussion it was decided it was not a rule but that it should not be recommended. Number 21 in the bye-laws of the constitution states," in the event of a player being unable to find a partner in competition, the Secretary or Captain may appoint a special marker."

NOTABLE LADY GOLFERS (selected)

In 1938 the Ladies Captain's Prize was won by Miss Mercy Gibbons with a nett score of 62.

In 1939 Mrs. Maher, (26) Westport, with a 78 won the class B at the Ballyhaunis ladies Open Meeting.

In 1940 Miss Eldridge, Westport, won 2nd nett at the Claremorris ladies Open Tournament.

The Lady Captain's Prize for 1939 was played for in May 1940. The prize was presented by Mrs. Egan and was won by Ms. Nancy Murphy after a close finish by half(.5) a stroke from Mrs. Maher and Mrs. McGreal. Weather conditions confined the competition to half a round for which Miss Murphy's score was 38.

In June 1943 a prize presented by the Rev. Fr. O'Grady C.C. to Westport Golf Club, which took the form of a handsome silver mounted Biscuit Barrell, was won by Miss Girsha Stack. The Vice-Captain's prize, a beautiful silver cup presented by Mr. Mooney, Bank of Ireland, was also won by Miss Stack.

In 1944 there was a triple tie in the Lady Captain's Prize. Miss Canavan (29), Mrs. E.A. Maher (14) and Miss N.Murphy (33) brought in 65s. Miss Canavan won on the second nine holes.

In the final of the Lucan Cup in Castlebar, Mrs. McGreal, Westport, beat Mrs. Walshe, Castlebar, 4 and 3.

In the semi-final of the Carraholly Cup Mrs. McGreal(19) beat Mrs. E.A.. Maher (13) 2 up after a fine match. In ideal conditions the ladies of the Club turned out in large numbers for Mrs. Mooney's prize 1944. Mrs. McGreal (19) with a 67 won by three strokes from Miss N. Murphy (30).

In 1947 Miss Girsha Stack won the O'Connell Cup presented by Miss C. O'Connell, D.E.I. The Club prize for beginners was won by Miss G.Moore, Bank of Ireland. 13 competed.

In 1950 the Union Golf prizes (Western section) were played off on the Galway Course.

Most of the Clubs in the Western District were represented. Westport ladies featured in the prizes. Mrs. Maher, best nett, class A; Mrs. McGreal , third, class A; Mrs. O'Brien , 2nd, class B, 66 nett.

In 1952 there was one individual prize for the best nett score of the day in the County Cup played in Ballina. Miss Noreen Golden, Westport, won it with an excellent score of 57 nett. As a result of their high standard of play, Miss Golden's handicap was reduced to 21 and Mrs. Maher's, Westport, to 10.

In 1958 Mrs. Eileen Maher, who was Golf Secretary for twenty years, departed from Westport. She was presented with a valuable memento at a farewell function given by her comrades of the local ladies Golf Club.

On Sunday 14th September 1958 activities were resumed at the Links, Carrowholly, after the summer lapse. The ladies had a spoon competition and this was won by Mrs. McGreal. On Ladies Day the winner was Miss N. Golden and the runner-up, Miss Nuala Regan.

In 1965, with a score of 66, Sinead Bean Ui Mhaoileoin, South Mall, won the Fitzgerald Cup for the fourth time.

In 1966 the winner of the coveted prize – a gold charm bracelet with an inscribed gold medallion attached – was Mrs. E. Hughes, Castlebar Road.

"The victory will be a memorable one for the winner who now has the distinction of winning the last Lady Captain's Prize to be played for over the Carrowholly Links. The Club is being wound up at the end of this season. The lease of the Links is not being renewed."

1993: Maureen Flynn (back row, left) became the first ever Westport woman to capture the Connacht Ladies Junior Championship. She is pictured here at the 1993 Brenda Gibson Captain's Prize.

Back, Maureen Flynn, Nuala Hopkins, Bridget Gibbons, Maureen Gibbons, Kay Brown, Connie Coakley, Helen Twoomey, Marine Ryan, Maura Connelly, Mary Rowe.

Front: Kay O'Briain, Maureen Walsh, Brenda Gibson (Lady Captain), Loretto O'Malley, Bridie Moran, Brigin Walsh.

In August 1966 "in a simple ceremony in the club-house the ladies 'waked' the old club and hopefully toasted the 'new' one. The occasion marked the victory of Mrs. J. McGreal in the Carrowholly Cup, the last competitive game there."

In 1968 Ms. Rose Golden's prize was won by Mrs. Ann Lydon. The Fitzgerald Cup was won by Miss T. Landers (14), Rosbeg with a 65 nett.

In 1971 Mrs Peg Clarke's prize, a beautiful Waterford Glass Lamp, was won by Mrs. Rose Golden. In the six-hole competition for the very new beginners Ms. M. Gibbons was the winner. Seven beginners took part and each one was presented with a golf ball from the Committee.

"On Sunday Maureen Gibbons celebrated her 12th birthday by winning the stableford Silver Spoons Competition in aid of the Royal National Lifeboat Institute – open to men and women – with a suberb score of 34 pts."-

In 1972 Maureen Gibbons won the Fitzgerald Cup with a score of 70 nett and the Vice-Captain's Prize with a 65 nett.

In 1972 Miss Nan O'Malley became the first lady golfer ever to win the Rossyveragh Cup. In this competition the men outnumbered the ladies by at least five to one. Nan O'Malley brought in a score of 62 nett. Her nearest rival, Tony Joyce had a 64 nett. Nan was presented with the trophy by

Mr. Walter P. Curley (jr) Rossyveragh House, Newport, at a function where again the ladies were to the fore and served tea and snacks to the competitors.

The first major competition on the new course was the Fitzgerald Cup. The winner was Mrs. Maureen Tobin (23) with a nett score of 82. Runner-up was Mrs. Evelyn Hughes (35) with a nett score of 88.

In 1974 Mrs. Evelyn Hughes was elected to the Western District Council of the I.L.G.U.

"Some of the credit for this achievement must go to Sinead Bean Ui Mhaoileoin for attending the meeting and putting the case before them. Sinead must also be congratulated for fighting to have the Connaught Cup played in Westport. It is a fight to get such a major fixture for one's club."-

In 1978 the Rossyveragh Cup was won by Anna May Mc Creave with 67 nett beating Paul Bree by one stroke and thus maintaining the ladies fine record in this event.

In 1993 history was made at Westport Golf Club when Maureen Flynn became the first ever Westport woman to capture the Connacht Ladies Junior Championship.

Maureen defeated the former international, Rita McGoldrick, in the final. The Westport Club also had Maureen Walsh and Sheelagh Ryan in the semi-finals.

LADIES TEAMS
AND VICTORIES (selected)

1937 The ladies travelled to Claremorris to play the local club in the final of the County Cup. They were defeated by 4 matches to 2.

The Westport team comprised Miss Brady, Mrs. Kenny, Mrs. O'Regan, Mrs. McGreal, Mrs. Golden and Miss Dineen. Mrs. McGreal and Mrs. Golden won their matches.

Travelling to other courses to play golf improves one's game and this fact was underlined in 1940 when the Westport ladies achieved great success.

"In the current competition for the Connacht Trophy, Westport ladies, the babes in the competition, have swept all before them so far.

"At Tuam on April 20th they defeated the home club by 4 matches to 1. In the return meeting at Westport on May 3rd they were again successful by 3 matches to 2.

"On Sunday at Castlerea they beat a strong home selection by 3.5 matches to 1.5. "

The team was, Mrs. T. Maher; Mrs. G. Kenny; Mrs. P. Golden; Mrs. M.J. McGreal and Mrs. A. de Fleury.

Westport ladies crowned a highly successful season when on June 26th they won the Connacht Trophy at their first attempt.

In disposing of Ennis ladies by 4 matches to 1 in the unfamiliar surroundings of the Galway Club's Links at Salthill, they brought to a successful close a really remarkable campaign.

On their way to the final they disposed of Tuam, Castlerea, and Sligo, a truly remarkable performance by the babes of the competition.

They added the County Cup to their bag at Claremorris on Friday when they beat Castlebar and Claremorris. "(*Mayo News*, 1940)

1952 A team of five ladies travelled to Ballina to compete in the County Cup. The team was: Mrs. McGreal, Miss Noreen Golden, Mrs. J. Mulloy, Miss Mary Mulloy, Mrs. Maher.

1960 The Westport ladies won the "Mayo Golf Cup". The best nett, Mrs. Joseph King, Ayle. The following teams competed, Westport, Castlebar(2), Ballyhaunis, Ballinrobe, Ballaghadereen, Ballina and Claremorris.

Team: Mrs. C.Lydon, Mrs. J. Hughes, Mrs. Dr. McGreal, Mrs. E. Rabbette, Ms. Mary Mulloy (captain), Ms. Noreen Golden, Ms. Mary Burns, Ms. Eileen O'Malley.

1963 The ladies returned home from Castlebar with the coveted County Cup.

Team: Mrs. McGreal, Mrs. Wallace, Mrs. Malone, Mrs. Ashe, Ms. J.Ryan.

1974 **The Connaught Cup:**

" The 120 ladies who competed were not disappointed. The course was in perfect condition and all were loud in their praise of the new 18 hole Championship Course and the facilities available. The ladies added a delightful splash of colour to the scene and towards the end of the competition as the players came into the clubhouse the atmosphere was tense, and the cheers rang out long and loud as the Westport ladies were declared the winners.

The massive cup was presented to the Lady Captain, Mrs. Helen McMahon, on behalf of the ladies. The top scorers were, Mrs. Maureen Tobin, Mrs. Brenda Blythe, and Mrs. Evelyn Hughes who received suitable gold trophies for their very fine performance."

(*Mayo News*)

1974: The Countess of Granard Foursomes in Woodbrook:
"Congratulations to Mrs. Loretta O'Malley and Mrs. Marine Ryan for travelling such a long distance to represent this club. It matters not that they did not win. It is enthusiasm of this sort that puts one's club on the map."

1975 **The Landers Trophy:** "It was a pleasure for the ladies, especially the older members, to receive the Landers sisters, Pixie and Trixie, who travelled quite a distance to be with us for tea and to present the trophy to the winner in honour of their beloved father. (1975)

1975: The Carrowholly Cup:

"From reading the very worthwhile minutes written by the then Secretary, Mrs. Rees, in the

1978, Westport ladies win the Connaught Trophy for the first time since 1940. Front, Marine Ryan, Loretta. O'Malley, Maureen Walsh. Back: Sheelagh Ryan, Moirin Murphy, Bridie Hughes.

year 1929, I have discovered that this cup was presented to the ladies in that year. Furthermore, the decision to play a qualifying with the best 8 cards to qualify for match play was also taken in that year. It is interesting to note that the same system of play has continued for what will be forty-six(46) years in this the year 1975."

1977 **First Time Hosts:** "For the first time in the club's history Westport G.C. was host to the ladies Senior and Junior Connacht Championships and the mens Irish Close. These were major fixtures on the golfing calendar. These events were most successful with the ladies catering on each occasion."

1978 The Westport ladies won the Connacht Trophy by beating Athlone at Rosses Point (match play). The trophy had not been won by Westport since 1940.

Team: Ms. Sheelagh Ryan, Ms. Bridie Hughes, Ms. M. Murphy, Ms. Marine Ryan, Ms. Maureen Walsh.

The ladies also won the County Cup in 1978 after a lapse of 17 years.

Team: Ms. Brenda Blythe, Ms. Moirin Murphy, Ms. Bridies Hughes, Ms. Marine Ryan, Ms. Mary Hanlon.

1979 The ladies retained the Connacht Trophy. "Five ladies from the club won out over a gruelling 36 holes in Longford-the 50th year of the competition. The ladies defeated Athlone in the semi-final 3.5. matches to 1.5. in the morning. Because of the communications problem it was decided to play the final on the same day and at the same venue. Westport defeated Ennis by 3 matches to 2.

Team: Ms. Connie Coakley, Ms. Brenda Blythe, Ms. Sheelagh Ryan, Ms. Jean McAleer, Ms. Loretta O'Malley."

Mr. Pat Bree, Captain and Mr. Fergal Hope, Vice-Captain waited in the clubhouse till very late to congratulate the team and offer hospitality on arrival from Longford. Later the men hosted a celebration party to honour the occasion which was unprecedented in the club.

The ladies also retained the County Cup beating 11 teams in Mayo. Team: Ms. E. Hughes, Ms. Nuala Moran, Ms. B. Blythe, Ms. Loretta O'Malley, Ms. B. Hughes, Ms. S. Ryan, Ms. M. Hanlon. Sub: Ms. H. McMahon.

1980 The ladies travelled as far afield as Portnoo to Ennis. Sinead Bean Ui Mhaoileoin had a record score of 57 nett at Portnoo in the Connaught Cup. Loretta O'Malley and Thelma O'Malley reached the quarter-final and semi-final in the Connaught Championships at Ennis. Members also competed in Grange in the Granard Cup.

1981 The ladies put Westport on the golfing map by winning the Connaught Trophy, Connaught Cup and bringing the Australian Spoons across the Shannon for the first time.

The *Mayo News* reported that: "Two Westport ladies, Ms. Maureen Walsh and Ms. Marine Ryan brought honour to their Club on Monday last when they won the All-Ireland final of the Australian Spoons foursomes at Athlone Golf Club. Against opposition from all over Ireland they brought the title to Westport and for the first time ever West of the Shannon."

1982 The ladies brought the Connaught Trophy back again to Westport.

Team: Ms. Jean McAleer, Ms. Geraldine Kearns, Ms. Sheelagh Ryan, Ms. Bridie Hughes, Ms. Maureen Walsh.

1984 The Westport ladies played magnificent golf at Castlebar G.C. to win the County Cup.

Team: Ms. Ann Hope (captain); Ms. Valerie King, Ms. Bridie Hughes, Ms. Brenda Blythe, Ms. Marine Ryan, Ms. Maureen Walsh, Ms. Sinead Bean Ui Mhaoileoin, Ms. Evelyn Hughes, Ms. Connie Coakley, Ms. Anna May McCreave.

1985 The ladies won the "Lina Black" Trophy.

1987 The Huzzar Vodka Foursomes: " Maureen Flynn and Kay O'Briain qualified in Westport for the third successive year in the Huzzar Vodka Foursomes. They were runners-up in the All-Ireland Final in 1985 and beaten semi-finalists in 1986." (*Mayo News*)

The Ardmore Trophy and Donal Landers:

"Ms. Sinead Bean Ui Mhaoileoin asked for information on the Donal Landers trophies. This competition has now been superseded by the Ardmore Trophy and Sinead requested that the ladies retain the trophies for use in a competition."

1981: Connacht Trophy winners:
Front: Maureen Walsh, Francis Campbell, Jean McAleer.
Back: Sheelagh Ryan, Bridie Hughes, Loretta O'Malley.

1999: Connaught Cup winners: Joy Moran, Mary Barry, Mary Dolan (Lady Captain), Maureen Walsh
PHOTO: FRANK DOLAN

1989 The ladies hosted the ladies Irish Close. "All who attended – the visitors, the press, and the 120 plus players – were loud in their praises for the beautiful condition of the course and greens.

The winner was Ms. Mary Mc Kenna, Dublin."

In 1989 the ladies also won the County Cup and "Lina Black".

County Cup Team:

Ms. K. O'Briain, Ms. M. Walsh, Ms. M. Flynn, Ms. B. Hughes, Ms. B. Moran, Ms. K. Browne, Ms. N. Hopkins, Ms. B. Walsh, Ms. M. Rowe, Ms. M. Barry.

1991 The ladies captured All-Ireland Titles.

Jean McAleer and Sheelagh Ryan won the Australian Spoons title in Greystones.

Bridie Moran and Bridget Gibbons won the Daily Mail Foursomes title in Tralee.

They went on to represent Westport and Ireland in Leeds.

1995 The ladies defeated Swinford, Ballinrobe, Castlebar and Gort to reach the "Lina Black" final.

Team: Ms. Marie Farrell, Ms. Pat Kelly, Ms. Claire McMyler, Ms. Bridget Gibbons, Ms. Maura Connolly, Ms. Karen Cox.

1996 The ladies won the Connaught Trophy. The team captain was Ms. Bridie Moran.

1997 The ladies won the County Cup.

1999 The ladies won the Connaught Cup. Team: Ms. Maureen Walsh, Ms. Joy Moran, Ms. Mary Barry.

2007 The ladies won the Connaught Junior Cup, defeating Roscommon in the final.

Team: M. McDermott, A. Corcoran, T. Fahy, M. Duffy, M. Grimes.

1988 The ladies won the Connacht Trophy, County Cup and "Lina Black."

County Cup Team: Ms. M. Flynn, Ms. B. Hughes, Ms. B. Gibbons, Ms. B. Moran, Ms. J. Bolster, Ms. K. Browne, Ms. K. O'Briain, Ms. M. Walsh, Ms. M. Dolan, Ms. N. Hopkins.

Connaught Trophy Team: Ms. M. Flynn, Ms. K. O'Briain, Ms. B. Hughes, Ms. B. Moran, Ms. B. Gibbons.

This team beat Roscommon in the final at Tuam.

Above: 1986: Celtic International Sponsored Event.
Back: left to right: J. Cuddy, J. Bredin, F. Hope,
D. O'Sullivan, T. Browne, J. Healy, J. O'Donnell, Dr. H. Farrell.
Front: C. O'Connor jnr., B. Gibbons, M. Flynn,
P. Hopkins (captain).

Left: 2002: President of Ireland Mrs Mary McAleese with
Ms. M. Duffy (Lady Captain) and Mr H. Hoban (Captain).

Bottom left: A special visitor: Mary McKenna, who
represented Ireland in ladies golf for many years, with
left to right: Mary Dolan, Gretta Murphy and Bridie Hughes.

Below: Enjoying a social moment:
Karen Cox, David McDermott.

Christy O'Connor (snr) signing autographs for Neil O'Neill and Paul Navin in April 1992.

Chapter 9

The *Juniors*

OF WESTPORT GOLF CLUB

"MOL AN OIGE AGUS TIOCFAIDH SI."
"The Paddock Golfers"

The first reference to Junior Golf in Westport was noted in the *Mayo News* 1936. Under the heading,"Paddock golfers" the writer noted that upwards of 80 youths were to be observed "driving" in this unrecognisable Links on the long summer evenings. What is interesting here is that the Paddock/Horkans Hill area was the site of Westport's first golf course in 1908 and within walking distance of the town.

By 1936 the Club was situated in Carraholly nearly four miles from the town and thus travel wise out of reach to these young men. Can we take it that if the Club was still in the Paddock/Horkans Hill area that a vibrant junior section would have flourished? We can only surmise.

These young men were happy driving on this unrecognisable links and the world in the background was far away from their thoughts. Hitler invaded the Rhineland in 1936. The Spanish Civil War had just erupted. The King in England had abdicated because he loved a "commoner".

De Valera was merrily dismantling the Treaty with England and young men in Westport were instinctively swinging a club drawn by the colour of the earth on those long summer evenings.

1940s.

In 1940 the club membership file records two juvenile members, Mr. Patsy Golden and Mr. Liam Golden at 10s/6p fee. There was no official youth policy but young people were welcome.

1960s.

In 1966 there was a request to donate old clubs for the purpose of introducing young players to golf. 35 clubs were collected. In 1968 the minutes record two juveniles on the course and a request that "to regularise the situation they should be members."

Subsequently three juveniles applied for membership and were admitted – John and Michael O'Donnell and Michael Tiernan.

A competition was held for juniors offering a putter as the prize. This was won by Michael Tiernan. In the background a pitch and putt club had been established in Rosbeg by Aidan Clarke and Joe Higgins. This amenity introduced many young men to the game of golf and they subsequently played in Carrowholly. In 1970 Michael Tiernan won the Captains Prize.

1970s.

In 1971 the best junior in the Captain's Prize was Liam Gibbons (16) with a 71 nett.

In 1975 Mr. Michael Cavanaugh who owned the Railway Hotel presented the Cavanaugh Trophy for juveniles. The winner of this inaugural competition was Matt Farrell. Those who competed were Paul McAleer, Michael Ryan, Eamon Moran, Bernard Moran, Mark McAleer, Peter King and Bert Farrell jr.

In 1976 Alan Hastings of Castlebar St. was the winner with Michael Ryan also of Castlebar St. as the runner-up. In 1977 Peter King, Newport Rd. was the winner.

In 1978 a Boys 18-hole competition was part of Open Week.

The winner was Ray McCreave with Eamon Moran second and Hugh O'Donnell third. The best front nine was won by Bernard Moran (19 pts) and the 2nd nine by Tom Davies(17pts)

In 1979 fifty juniors partook in lessons conducted by golf professional Michael Ryan, and Tracy Ryan won a junior girls prize.

1980s.

In 1980 ten-year-old Jane Kelly won a junior girls prize in Open Week.

Boys who played in a 9-hole stroke competition during Open Week in 1981 were Peter Flynn, Alan Bredin, C. Murphy, N. Bolster, J. Mulroy, A. O'Malley, R. Coakley and M. Brennan.

In the early 1980's Donie O'Connor and George Reilly took charge of junior golf and a more organized structure was introduced.

A junior winter league was inaugurated.

In April 1983 a major difficulty for juniors was recorded:

"Not able to hit across the water at the 15th."

In that year Gerry McAleer gave Donie some trophies for junior competitions which included two cups that were extremely valuable!

Four juveniles qualified for a Connacht competition in Tuam but transport was a problem. Liam Walsh sr. undertook to assist in this regard. Juniors playing in 1983 were Paul Moore, Bernard Moran, Peter King, Brian Hope, Robert Flynn, Liam Walsh, A. O'Malley, Ben Walsh, and Frank Hastings.

In 1984 Donie requested that juniors be allowed the full week in which to play as it was not always possible for them to play on Saturday due to visiting societies.

Juniors qualified for the Connacht Close and played in the Connacht Matchplay Championship.

Junior girls playing in 1984 were Stephanie Hope, Bronwyn O'Malley, Sheelagh Bredin.

In 1985 the following featured in the boys/girls competition in Open Week: Brian Hope, Hugh Staunton, C. Walsh, C.Ryan and S.Hope.

Mini-golf and Westport Youth Activities.

In 1986 Westport Youth Activities organised mini-golf with transport from the Octagon on a Saturday. This was a wonderful success and introduced many future golfers to the game.

The following young boys participated every

PICTURE: GOLF IMAGE

Saturday; Colin Walsh, Darrell O'Toole, Raymond Gibbons, Brendan McKeown, Barry Halpin, Declan Cusack, Sean Walsh, Ciaran Clarke, Eddie Conway, John Conway, Martin Coughlan, Colin Halpin, Leslie Oosten, Frank Gill, Conor O'Neill.

Twenty-seven boys played in a two round competition and the winner was Frank Gill, Horkans Hill with Martin Coughlan, Rosbeg, second, Darrell O'Toole, Horkans Hill, third and Conor O'Neill, Moyhastin, in 4th.

The success of mini-golf was underlined in the desire to enter a good team representing Westport in the Community Games in 1988.

■ First Junior Team to contest Connacht Final.

In 1987 Tony Browne took charge of junior golf and he brought the first Westport junior golf team to a Connacht Final. In the Connacht Junior Matchplay Championship Westport defeated Claremorris, Castlebar and Ballinasloe to reach the final v Strandhill. Strandhill proved too strong on the day.

Team: Robert Flynn, Tom McHale jr., Brian Hope, Tom Browne, Killian O'Briain.

Liam Gibbons of Ashlawn Filling Station sponsored an u-18 junior competition. Brian Hope

qualified for the Connaught Close finals. John Harnett and Leslie Robinson conducted lessons and a request was made to low handicap golfers in the club to give 30 minutes per week to juniors.

In 1988 under-15s were offered free golf. The Captain Ollie Whyte had a special prize for juniors as part of his captain's day. Perry O'Reilly and Donie O'Connor conducted lessons for juniors.

■ 1990s.

In 1991 a new Junior Golf Committee comprising Paul Moody, Des Mahon, Gar Golden and Colam O'Neill was established. 30 juniors attended the first session of lessons.

The junior competition was won by Declan McNally with Dermot Kelly second and Colm Walsh third.

In 1992 Liam Halpin took charge of junior golf. He established a teaching course for juniors conducted by Alex Mealia and Mark Reid. In 1993 Alex Mealia, golf professional offered free coaching for juniors. The juniors playing in this year were Damien Fair, Liam O'Reilly, Shane Cunningham, Jamie Hope, Aidan Moran, Paul McDonnell, Ronan Mahon, Colm Walsh, Declan McNally, Joe Regan, Donal McIntyre.

In April 1983 a major difficulty for juniors was recorded: "Not able to hit across the water at the 15th."

■ Des Mahon and the County Mayo Junior Golf Tournament.

In 1993 Des Mahon established the County Mayo Junior Golf Tournament.

Des believed in encouraging a love for the game and that young Mayo golfers should have the opportunity to play a Championship Course for a nominal fee.

To sow the seed he ensured they played from the green and red tees depending on age in order to provide them with opportunities for eagles and birdies.

He wanted a young boy or girl to be inspired by the birdie or eagle they had in Westport. Westport juniors who featured in the inaugural tournament were;

Under-14 – Donal McIntyre; u-16-1st. Aidan Moran; 3rd, Jamie Hope; 6th, Joe Ryan; 8th, Paul McDonnell.

Under-18 – 2nd Colm Walsh ; 3rd. Ronan Mahon; 8th Declan McNally.

In 1993 junior golf was influencing sporting policy in the local schools.

Rice College finished 4th in the Irish Golf Foundation Connacht Schools

Championship. Team: Jamie Hope (14), Aidan Moran (13),Ronan Mahon (15),

Paul McDonnell (16).

In 1996 Tom McHale jr. took charge of juniors and dedicated efforts were also made by Sal O'Connor, Marion Duffy and Maire Connolly.

In 1997 Liam Friel, Captain, asked Pat Kearns, Sal O'Connor and Padraig McLoughlin to take an interest in juniors.

They were greatly helped in their efforts by Alex Mealia, Aidan Moran, Noel O'Connell (club secretary) and Margaret O'Grady (club administrator).

The arrival of Tiger Woods and Sky Sports led to a dramatic increase in Junior membership. The club officers were fully committed to junior golf and no expense was spared. In 1997 Westport

created a shock when defeating Co. Sligo 3/2 to reach a Connacht quarter-final.

■ Junior Competitions.

Junior competitions were played in Castlebar whenever the Westport course was unavailable and juniors played Ballinrobe, Strandhill, Enniscrone and Connemara.

In 1998 Westport juniors won every category prize in the inaugural Castle Trophies Competition in Ballinrobe: u-17: David Mahon; Jesse Kennedy. U-15: Tony Bree, Michael Kearns . U-13: Tom McLoughlin, Michael McGreal jr.

■ When We Were Kings: 1999-2002 7 Connacht Pennants, 3 National Finals.

In 1999 the Connacht Branch organised a Connacht under-15 inter-club competition. 21 Connacht golf clubs competed on the day and Westport stormed to victory by 14 shots from Strandhill. Tom McLoughlin brought in the best score of the day, a marvellous 64 nett. Cathal O'Malley had 76 nett and Patrick Collins brought in 74 nett. Westport had never won a Connacht Junior Pennant prior to this event.

This Pennant was quickly followed by the Connacht Junior Foursomes Pennant.

This was won amid tremendous drama and excitement at Ballinrobe G.C.

It also brought Westport to their first All-Ireland National Finals in Castlecomer. The Foursomes team was:
Noel Kavanagh(4)/ Tom McLoughlin(11),
Jesse Kennedy(8)/ Michael Kearns(9).

Cahir Park defeated Westport by 3 holes in the All-Ireland semi-final.

The Connacht Junior Inter-Club Pennant followed in more dramatic fashion. This final was played at Strandhill versus Athenry. A large group of supporters travelled from Westport. With three holes to play Athenry were leading by 2

Westport junior 2000:
Connaught champions,
Fred Daly Junior
Foursomes,
Inter club under 18,
All Ireland finalists:
Fred Daly junior
foursomes:

Back, P. McLoughlin,
N. Kavanagh, T. Bree,
N. Halpin (capt),
S O'Connor (lady
captain), P. Kearns,
C. Hughes (President),
M. Kearns,
T. McLoughlin.

Front: C. O'Malley,
M. McGreal,
N. McNulty, A. Mealia
(professional).

matches to 1 and Cathal O'Malley was 1 down as also was David Mahon. Westport had to win these two matches which they duly did. Cathal O'Malley sank an unbelievable putt on a green full of contours to win his match.

Then David Mahon emerged heroically to win the vital match. Who will ever forget the pandemonium that broke out when David sank the winning putt?

In the Connacht Close Finals Westport had more qualifiers than any other club in Connacht. Westport juniors really arrived in 1999 and they always looked very well in their club jerseys.

2000 proved to be an even better year for Westport juniors.

In March they received a Mayo Sports Star award in recognition of their achievements in 1999. Tom McLoughlin was selected for the National u-15 panel following trials in Royal Dublin where he shot 75 gross.

By the end of the year three more Connacht Pennants had been won and two All-Ireland Finals lost by the narrowest of margins.

The Fred Daly is the premier junior competition in Ireland for low handicap juniors.

Westport defeated Ballinasloe by 6 matches to 4 to win the Fred Daly Connacht Pennant for the first time.

The National Finals were held in Strandhill and Westport defeated Stackstown 3 matches to 2 to reach the All-Ireland Final of the Fred Daly versus Banbridge.

Padraig Harrington's father Paddy (R.I.P.) was captain of the Stackstown team. When congratulating Westport he said he had never heard of Westport in junior golf circles before. The Westport team felt this was a tribute to all the captains and officers in Westport who supported junior golf down the years.

Banbridge boasted three Irish Internationals, Conor Doran, Ciaran Mc Aleavey and Richard Kilpatrick. Westport were leading by 2 matches with the the other 3 matches going down the 19th.

Surely Westport would win a third match? But it was not to be. Two matches were lost on the 20th hole.

The gallant Westport team of Noel Kavanagh, Neil McNulty, Cathal O'Malley, Michael Kearns, Tom McLoughlin and Tony Bree had lost a second All-Ireland Final in the space of twenty-four hours by the equivalent of a short head.

The captain of the Banbridge team, Mr.Doran, felt Banbridge had stolen the title and sportingly he insisted that a photograph be taken with the two team captains holding the Green Pennant.

Earlier in the year Westport won the Connacht Junior Foursomes Pennant once again.

The qualifier was played on a turbulent day in Strandhill. Westport pairs of Neil McNulty/ Michael Kearns, Tom McLoughlin/ Cathal O'Malley were leading qualifiers and they defeated Co.Sligo in the final.

In the national finals Westport defeated Lisburn to reach the final versus Castletroy. This

Above: Winning team for the First Connaught Junior Pennant:

Back: Tom McLoughlin, Cathal O'Malley, P. Collins.
Front: S. O'Connor, B. Burns (Captain of Westport GC), P McLoughlin, P. Kearns.

Right: The Connaught inter-club winning side with the same officials:

Back, C. O'Malley, D. Mahon, J. Kennedy, M. Kearns, T. McLoughlin, T. Bree, N. McNulty.
Front, S. O'Connor, B. Burns (Captain, Westport Golf Club), P. McLoughlin, P. Kearns.

final went to the last green and the last putt where Castletroy emerged victorious by 1 hole. Their final pairing had chipped and putted five times in the last five holes!. Westport juniors could so easily have brought home two Green Pennants from Strandhill but such is sport.

The Connacht under-18 Inter Club campaign began with a late night drive to Adare to bring back Westport members who had not made the cut in the Munster Boys. It was an early start in Claremorris the following morning.

Westport defeated Ballinrobe, Strandhill, Castlebar, and Tuam to reach the final versus Ballinasloe in Belmullet. Westport won the final 4 matches to 1 but this scoreline does not reflect the tension, excitement and the closeness of the matches.

The Westport team was Cathal O'Malley, Neil McNulty, Tom McLoughlin, David Mahon and

Michael McGreal Jr. (reserves; Michael Kearns, Tony Bree).

Westport juniors also formed the backbone of the Mayo u-18 team in 2000.

In 2001 the Westport "Fred Daly" team was expected to reach the National Final once again. However this team failed to win Connacht. This was a major disappointment to all involved.

■ Connacht Close U-16 Champion 2001.

Tom McLoughlin won the Connacht Close U-16 Championship hosted by Carrick-on-Shannon G.C. when he shot a gross 73. This was the first time a Westport junior won a Connacht Close title.

■ "Fred Daly " Connacht Final 2002.

Westport defeated Roscommon, Co. Sligo, Strandhill and Carrick-on-Shannon to reach the Connacht final versus Athenry.

Tom McLoughlin, the Connacht Close Under-16 champion in 2001. He shot 73 gross at Carrick-on_shannon.

Over the two legs Athenry emerged victorious by 6 matches to 4. Team: Cathal O'Malley, Tom McLoughlin, Michael McGreal jr., Cormac O'Halloran, Anthony Browne, Keith Ruddy.

■ Irish Schools Connacht Matchplay Champions 2003.

The management of Rice College Westport and teacher Mr. Joe Cuddy had persevered with golf as a sporting outlet for boys for many years. Their reward finally arrived in 2003 when a team from the school won the "Tony Kearney" Cup for the Connacht Schools Matchplay Championship. The Rice College team were leading qualifiers in Strandhill and in the Connacht semi-final they defeated St.Josephs, Galway 4 matches to 1 and in the final they defeated Marist College Athlone 3 matches to 2.

Team: Cathal O'Malley, Tom McLoughlin, Michael McGreal jr., Cormac O'Halloran, Anthony Browne.

■ Provincial and Irish Championships.

Between 1999 and 2005 Westport juniors travelled Ireland playing in the various boys and youths championships.

There was always great joy when they made the "cut" and great personal disappointment when they failed. The young men involved in this circuit were, Noel Kavanagh Jr., Cathal O'Malley, Tom McLoughlin, Michael Kearns, Tony Bree, Neil McNulty, Michael McGreal Jr., Cormac O'Halloran, Anthony Browne.

The cut and thrust of boys and youths championships led to a raising of standards and a determination to work hard and improve.

This in turn resulted in Connacht and Irish Caps coming to Westport for the first time since Liam Golden received Connacht Caps in 1959 and 1960. Noel Kavanagh Jr., Cathal O'Malley and Cormac O'Halloran received Connacht Boys Caps; Cathal O'Malley received a Connacht Youths Cap; Noel Kavanagh Jr. received Connacht Senior Caps and Cathal O' Malley was honoured with an Irish Youths Cap. Cathal also received the Junior Golfer of the Year Award(Connacht) in 2004.

Noel Kavanagh Jr. and Cathal O'Malley received American golf scholarships. These young men brought 7 Pennants, Connacht and Irish Caps and major media publicity to Westport Golf Club between 1999 and 2005.

Junior golf is now a major component of Westport G.C. and at present is in the very capable hands of Liam Friel, Ger Needham, Sal O'Connor, Alex Mealia, and Aidan Moran.

■ Rules for Juniors.

In 2001 a comprehensive set of rules for juniors was drawn up by Liam Friel. The G.U.I. said these rules were "as comprehensive and fair as they had seen." They have been adopted by Ballinrobe G.C. They are a "common sense" set of rules that

The first girls team.
Front:
S. Murtagh, L. Friel,
M.S. McLoughlin,
C. O'Connor, A. Duffy.

Back:
P. McLoughlin,
A. McLoughlin,
Liam Friel,
K. Reddington,
P. Kearns, S. O'Connor.

encourage juniors to enjoy golf in a safe way and to respect the honesty of the game. These rules cover competition,conduct in the club house and on the course and also safety for the junior golfer.

■ First Junior Girls Team.

In 2001 the junior girls made history when they represented the club for the first time in a Connaught Junior Girls competition in Claremorris.
Team: Carmel O'Connor, Mary Susan
McLoughlin, Laura Friel.

■ The "Super-Valu" Golf Scheme.

In 2002 the Super-Valu Golf Scheme was initiated and sponsored by Mr. Noel Kavanagh, Managing Director of the O'Connor Group. The scheme was designed to promote and develop underage golf by providing lessons and coaching for junior members of Westport Golf Club. Hundreds of awards have been made to juniors under this scheme.

These awards entitle them to individual coaching from a professional.

Juniors have to earn these awards by showing that they have a genuine interest in golf and the ability to enhance their skill. Mr. Kavanagh's vision and the financial support underlying that vision is a major benefit to junior golf in Westport.

■ Junior Girls Representing Connaught.

In 2003 three girls from Westport represented Connacht in a match versus Munster. They were Carmel O'Connor, Laura Friel and Mary Susan McLoughlin. Although losing the girls learned much from the experience.

■ 163 Juniors.

In 2003 there were 163 juniors in Westport Golf Club. Juniors played in 13 National events and 16 local and Provincial events. In 2003 the junior convenor was Liam Friel assisted by Pat Kearns, Sal O'Connor, Mary McDermott, Mary Rowe and Alex Mealia.

■ Junior Club 2004.

In 2004 a junior club was established. This club has a captain, vice-captain, secretary, treasurer and a committee comprising four boys and four girls.

They work with the junior convenor, officers and committees of Men's and ladies clubs, staff, professionals and members. They promote junior golf in the schools and amongst their friends. They assist in helping to organise junior golf in the Club.

On the 14th of May 2004 the first junior committee met. The attendance comprised Carmel O'Connor (Girls Captain), Tara Fahey, Laura

Friel, Mary Susan McLoughlin, Cormac O'Halloran, Anthony Browne, Shane Collins, Sal O'Connor, Ger Needham and Liam Friel. Some interesting suggestions emerged. For example, to speed up junior competitions it was felt junior markers should be placed on the course 100 yards forward and the ladies tees on the 6th, 7th, 9th and 15th should be utilised.

It was also suggested that the competitions should not be all stroke/ stableford but that there should be some scrambles, Scotch foursomes and mixed competitions. Ger Needham introduced the idea of a golf camp for juniors.

■ The Liam Walsh Bursary:

In 2005 the Liam Walsh Bursary for junior golf was established by the Walsh family in memory of their father, Liam. Five promising junior golfers were selected for intensive golf coaching.

This bursary is a major boost to the development of junior golf in the club. Liam Walsh sr. was a great supporter of juniors in the club through the years. He was the first to telephone congratulations when the club won its first Junior Pennant.

■ Major Breakthrough for Girls:

In 2006 two Westport girls were selected on the Connacht team to contest the Girls Interprovincial Championship held in Kilkenny.

Tara Fahey (14) and Carmel O'Connor (14) represented their club and province with pride, courage and golfing ability. Later in the month (April) both girls combined to win the May Fitzgibbon Foursomes Connacht Title.

This success is a great reward in particular for

Lessons to be Learned

Juniors grow up eventually. they become captains, committee members, team members and they introduce their own children to the game.

Juniors need time, patience, travel and money. juniors need regular competitions as these play a vital role in a juniors development. The benefits come back to the club in many different disguises. The club gains increased profile in golf circles. The club gains publicity. Pennants are won, caps awarded and scholarships received. Low handicap juniors provide a club with a Senior Cup team, a Barton Shield team and they give a competitive edge to many other teams within a club.

In Westport Golf Club the age profile of the members is getting older. A G.U.I. fact is that by 2015 the average age of those playing golf in Ireland will be 65 years. This is a sobering fact. The club must continue to develop and promote junior golf for the survival of clubs financially and for the continued well being of the game.

Money invested in junior golf is money well spent.

Sal O'Connor . Sal has championed girls golf down the years with very little return. A major obstacle facing Sal was girls did not see golf as a "cool" game to play.

Thanks to Sal this attitude has changed with the arrival of Tara, Carmel and Laura Friel. Alex Mealia and Aidan Moran are also due recognition for the ongoing development of girls golf.

Liam Friel

It would be remiss not to recognise the extensive work of Liam Friel in the area of junior golf in the club since 1997. As already detailed junior golf is a major growth area. It demands time and energy of epic proportions. Most of this work is invisible to the ordinary member. Liam has not alone served as junior convenor but he has continually produced and administered a junior golf philosophy in the club.

1977, Irish Close Championship: Winner Mark Gannon with
V. Coakley (Westport GC Captain), B Staunton (president) and M. Moran (Secretary).

Chapter 10

Championships
AT WESTPORT

I f Westport G.C. was to have the prefix "Championship" appended then championships would have to be played on the course. More importantly the course would have to show its true championship character by producing a stern test of golf and worthy champions. Westport officers and committees knew they had a fledgling championship course but could they convince the G.U.I.? One man who was already convinced was Christy O'Connor Jr. "I had heard Westport had a Championship Course but in no way did I imagine it was as good as it is. The fairways and greens are as good as, if not better, than some of the courses I've played. The first eight holes are relatively easy and possibly give false security. The 9th is a very interesting hole. The back nine are of championship standard. The scenery is really beautiful." (1976: Christy Jr. shot a 3-under 70).

■ The Irish Close 1977.

The man who was largely responsible for convincing the G.U.I. to give this prestigious championship to Westport was Mr.Gar Golden. There was opposition to giving this championship to a fledgling course. But the G.U.I. were assured that the course was a true championship test and the organisation would be top quality. The captain and committee responsible for delivering this assurance were: Mr.Vincent Coakley (Captain), Mr. Michael Moran (Vice-captain), Mr. Denis Egan (Hon.Sec.), Mr. Gerard Colbert (Hon.Treas.) and committee members: D. Blythe, M. King, C. Lavelle,

A. Malone, H. Murphy, Bro. P.K. Maher, G. McAleer, H. Ryan, S. Walsh.

At the AGM for 1976 there was a degree of nervousness about the forthcoming championship. Everyone knew how symbolic it was going to be for the future of Westport G.C.

"It will be the first championship played on our course and that will certainly justify the use of the label championship.

"Our top amateur golfers will be playing here and they will be looking for perfection. If it is a success the club will benefit enormously from it. If it is a failure it could be the beginning of the end for Westport Golf Club."

The top amateurs did not get their version of perfection. Few of the trees on the course had reached maturity and the G.U.I. was fearful that the top amateurs would burn it up. As a consequence they encouraged the growth of the rough. The course inspection by the G.U.I regarding the setting up of the course is interesting.

It was decided that the maximum width of a fairway would be 35 yards and the apron surrounding each green would be a maximum of 6 feet.

It was decided that the crown and rear of all banks on the sides or back of greens should be closely trimmed so that an inaccurate stroke would

result in the ball running to the bottom of the outside slope. The front greenside of all banks on the sides or back of greens should not be too closely trimmed so that an inaccurate stroke would not roll down to the green.

It was decided that all rough from the edge of the fairway should be graded outwards with the first semi-rough grading a 5 gang (12 feet) mower width.

It was not intended that the "semi-rough" should be unplayable but it was intended that a player should not be able to use the same club for a stroke from this rough as he would on the fairway.

On the 13th hole the instruction was to bring in rough by the width of a 5-gang mower on the left hand side beyond the trees to prevent players seeking to carry the trees on the left.

On the 14th hole the banks around the green were to be trimmed so that an inaccurate shot would finish in the bunker.

On the 15th the instruction was to let the rough grow in on the left of the green to prevent a ball running down the slope and out-of-bounds.

The result of all this preparation of the course was that the test was possibly the toughest ever in this Championship.

■ Day 1.

The papers reported that the rough had been allowed to grow in unusual vast quantities for an Irish golf course and countless balls had been lost by players paying severely for their waywardness. The reigning champion. Declan Brannigan, commented:

> "The course is difficult enough as it is without the introduction of tiger rough. You would get the impression that the lay-out was designed by a golf ball manufacturer."

Other noteworthy features of the day were Paddy Mulford of Delgany driving the green at the 17th and Des Mahon (Mayo County Manager) defeating T. Smith 2 and 1.

■ Day 2.

Des Mahon (Mayo County Manager) was defeated by the eventual champion, Mark Gannon by 1 hole.

■ Semi-Finals.

John Redmond (journalist) reported as follows- "After all the ballyhoo about the new Westport Club being allocated this most important championship in Ireland, officialdom, and the course itself has been vindicated as the cream has come to the top in the person of three established inter-nationals and Tony Hayes who is accepted as one of the best young players in the country."

A noteworthy feature was the incorrect rules decision which helped Mark Gannon ultimately win his match on the 15th. He was 3-up playing this hole.

He was in rough left of the 15th green and his ball was lying on recently cut scattered grass. He looked for a decision. After much delay he was allowed to drop two club lengths distance which gave him a perfectly good lie but afterwards it was generally agreed that a player is allowed to drop from greenkeepers cuttings only when the grass is piled for the purpose of being eventually collected.

■ The Final.

Tony Hayes was dormie 3 up against Mark Gannon. He had played the outward nine in two under 34 to Gannon's 39. People who had backed Gannon had already paid up. But Hayes scored 5,5,6, for the last three against Gannon's level par run of 4,4,5. The match went to the 19th where incredibly Gannon won.

Mark Gannon said, "I never gave up trying but I felt I had little hope coming down the 17th hole. It just shows you should never give up in a golf match."

Westport's 17th Hole (index 17):
Winner Mark Gannon said: "I never gave up trying but I felt I had little hope coming down the 17th hole. It just shows you should never give up in a golf match."

On Day 1 of the Championship, Paddy Mulford of Delgany drove the green.

Westport Championship Course had produced a true champion with pedigree.

In 1977 Mark Gannon was the only golfer to have won the boys, youths and Irish Close Championships. He had also won the West and South and lost to Ray Kane in 1974 in the final of the Close.

He had been two years in the wilderness because of a stomach muscle injury.

He had a masterful touch from 40 yards in and when beating Barry Reddan and Tony Heverin he got down with a chip and putt on at least a dozen occasions.

This uncanny ability saw him beat Reddan with figures of 3-under par and he was level par when beating Heverin.

■ Aftermath.

Members of the Golfing Union of Ireland gave it as their opinion that this was the most successful Close ever run in the country.

Mr Vincent Coakley said:

"The benefits from the Championship have yet to come. The result of the event has proven to all that Westport has a golf course comparable to the best in the country."

The staging successfully of this prestigious championship underlined the tremendous organisational ability within the club.

The 1977 Irish Close Championship was to be the fore-runner of the many championships yet to come.

In 1981 the Irish Youths Open Championship was hosted by the club.

The winner was John McHenry, Douglas, Co. Cork. His four round scores were, 75,75,77,76. He had ten shots to spare over runner-up Noel McGrane, Greenore, Co. Louth.

The condition of the course, greens and fairways received glowing tributes from G.U.I. officials and competitors.

In 1982 the Connacht Boys Open Championship was hosted by the club.

The winner was I. O' Neill.

■ The Irish Close 1985.

When the Irish Close was hosted by the club in 1985 there was no need for any trickery with the rough. The course had grown into a fine championship lay-out in its own right.

The Close Committee began preparations in January 1985. A second meeting was held at Bertie Farrells house on Wed. 30th January. Those present were L. Walsh (Chairman); D. Blythe, V. Coakley, B. Farrell, G. Golden, P. Hopkins, C. Hughes (Captain).

The G.U.I. were leaving the preparation of the course to the discretion of the club.

This was significant recognition of the golfing expertise available in Westport G.C. The Close Committee was adamant that all visitors, from G.U.I officials to the players and spectators must be made to feel very welcome.

The matters discussed at this meeting were, course preparation, car parking, stewards and marshalls, referees, sponsorship, communication system, public relations, reception, lockers, press invitations, office accommodation, flags and telephones.

■ Day 1.

The opening 64 matches involved the higher handicap players ranging from 5 down to some two's with the winners going forward to meet the lower handicap players. 192 golfers were competing including six Westport golfers, Liam Gibbons, Perry O'Reilly, Shane Underwood, Donie O'Connor, Liam Halpin, and Aiden Redmond.

The main talking point was the weather. The course became a monster to play due to the fierce winds that were at times accompanied by rain. Many players could not get across the water at the 15th so the front tee was used. Pat Mulcare lost two balls at the now very difficult short 14th. Liam Gibbons, Shane Underwood, and Aiden Redmond won through to the second round. Donie O'Connor was beaten at the 21st hole. Liam Halpin was beaten 3/2. Perry O'Reilly had a bye.

■ Day 2.

The weather was still making matters most difficult. One of the interesting matches of the day was

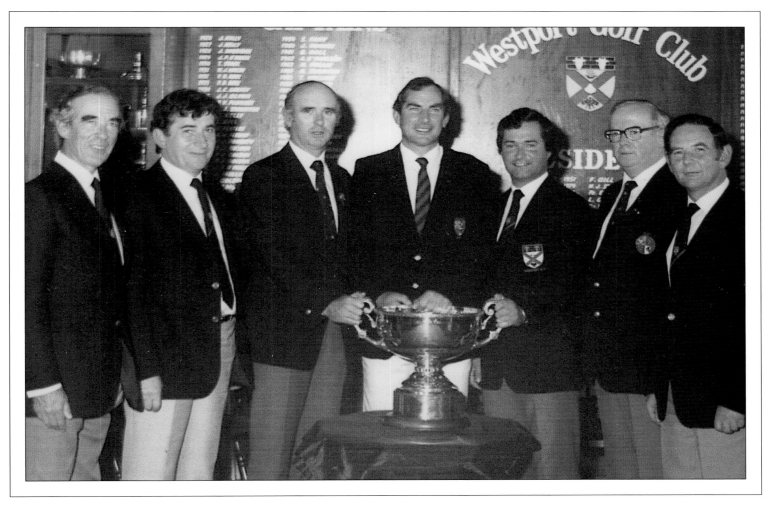

1985, Irish Close:
Left to right, P. Hopkins
(vice captain),
Dr H. Farrell (Westport
President), Frank Bowen
(GUI President),
Dennis O'Sullivan
(winner),
Cathal Hughes (Captain
of Westport),
G. Golden (Chairman,
Connacht GUI),
P. Murphy (secretary).

that between Mark Gannon and Juan Fitzgerald of Limerick. Fitzgerald was named after motor racing legend Juan Fangio. He defeated Gannon 4/3. This was the Juan Fitzgerald defeated by Perry O'Reilly in the All-Ireland final of the Junior Cup in 1980. Shane Underwood, Aiden Redmond and Perry O'Reilly won their matches. Liam Gibbons was defeated at the 19th.

■ Day 3.

This day was notable for the rules rumpus in the match between Arthur Pierce (Tipperary) and Pat Lyons (Nenagh). Paul Mc Ginley had earlier been defeated by Lyons 5 and 4.

The match between Pierce and Lyons was all square playing the 13th when Lyons carved a three-wood second shot into the trees.

He advised Pierce that he would hit a "provisional" in case his ball was lost. Then from 220 yards and with the same 3-wood he hit the second ball into the hole. After a brief look into the trees Lyons proclaimed that he was declaring his first ball lost and that he was therefore in the hole for a par-four, taking into account the penalty for a lost ball.

Pierce objected as he believed that his opponent was obliged to look for the statutory five

minutes for the ball which was found well within the time limit. But Ivan Dickson G.U.I. Secretary ruled in favour of Lyons. The G.U.I. man said "Under rule 27 Lyons was entitled to abandon his ball as a player is not required to search for a lost ball."

An angry Pierce felt he was robbed. He maintained his opponent should not have an option when he found his first ball. That is the one he should have been required to play and the provisional ball ruled out. Pierce was beaten 3/2 still seething at the rule decision given against him.

Perry O'Reilly and Aiden Redmond won their 3rd round matches but Shane Underwood was beaten. In the fourth round both Perry O'Reilly and Aiden Redmond were beaten by one hole.

■ The Final.

Denis O'Sullivan defeated Declan Brannigan by one hole mainly due to a magical short game. This was a sweet victory for O'Sullivan as he had lost to Brannigan in the 1976 final. Denis O'Sullivan was an Irish International and later he was to play successfully on the European Seniors Tour. Once again the Westport course had produced a worthy champion with golfing pedigree despite the vagaries of the weather.

In 1986 the Connacht Youths Championship was hosted by the club. The winner was G. McNeill (Royal Portrush). The leader after 36 holes was Darren Clarke (Dungannon) on 155.

In 1988 the Irish Seniors was hosted by the club and the winner was B. Buckley (Grange)

In 1989 the Ladies Home Internationals were hosted. Ireland lost to Scotland and England but defeated Wales.

Irish International Anne Ferguson said:

Being selected to play for your country, on 'home ground' is as good as it gets in sport.

Westport was an inspired venue. The 15th hole – striking out over the inlet's sparkling Atlantic waters.

Croagh Patrick towering in the distance, inspired perfect fairway positioning. Local caddy John left me in no doubt I'd be 'giving it the full treatment'. A birdie followed. A neat wedge into the short but tricky 17th-match all square. Pressure point on 18. A tight drive near the out of bounds, but made the green in regulation. A slippery four-footer to halve. 'No break-back of the hole' said John. And so it was. The crowd cheered, John smiled, job done. Strong memories, great people, ONLY Westport.

Thank you."

In 1989 the club also hosted the Irish Amateur Ladies Close. The winner was Mary McKenna in a sudden death finish with Carol Wickham. This was Mary McKenna's eighth title.

In 1990 Westport hosted the Irish Cup and Shields All-Ireland Finals.

The Senior Cup was won by Warrenpoint G.C., the Barton Shield by Cork G.C., the Junior Cup by Waterford, Jimmy Bruen by Ardee, and the Pierce Purcell by Oughterard.

The Youths Interprovincials were also held in 1990. The winners were Leinster. Padraig Harrington and Richie Coughlan (Birr) were members of the Leinster team. David Higgins was a member of the Munster team and Raymond Burns (Banbridge) the only player to have won four Provincial Youth Championships in the one year (1989) was on the Ulster team.

In 1994 the Senior Interprovincials were hosted. The Ulster team was victorious. The following top golfers participated-Walker Cup players Garth McGimpsey and Padraig Harrington, David Higgins, Denis O'Sullivan, Ken Kearney, Liam McNamara, Tom Cleary, Eddie Power, Jody Fanagan.

In 1995 the club hosted the Connacht Seniors. The winner was B. Wallace.

In 1997 the club hosted the Irish Seniors. The winner was D. Jackson.

■ The Irish Close 1997.

In 1997 the club once more hosted the Irish Close Championship. 192 top amateurs entered. The field included Walker Cup players Jody Fanagan, Garth McGimpsey and Peter Lawrie (winner in 1996). Three Westport golfers were also in the field: Perry O'Reilly, Liam Halpin, and Donie O'Connor.

The Westport Officers in 1997 were Liam Friel – Captain; Noel Connell Hon. Sec.; Tom Walsh, Hon.Trea.; Dermot Blythe, President; The Joint Club Committee: D. McDermott, L. Campion, P. Duffy, A. Duffy, M. Grimes, M. Dolan, G. Golden, C. Pigot, D. Ruddy, K. Cox, B. Hughes.

A Close Committee was established by Liam Friel. Close affairs concerning house were to be the responsibility of David McDermott. Course affairs the responsibility of Gar Golden. Administration to be looked after by James McNamara and protocol and press by Noel Connell. A Championship brochure was produced which included the draw for the championship. Eddie Connaughton examined the greens for the Close and he expressed satisfaction with their condition.

Large crowds attended the Close and they were not disappointed. Quality ball striking and exciting matches were abundant. In the second round out went Noel Fox to Kieran McCarthy (Kinsale) along with Andrew McCormack (Scrabo) and Michael McGinley (Grange). The defending champion, Paul Lawrie, got through. So too did Garth McGimpsey, an impressive 4 under for 14 holes. Arthur Pierce escaped on the 24th.

The fourth round produced even more drama. Dermot Snow (Portmarnock) was 4 under and 1

Above: The Home Internationals 1989. Captain Aidan Redmond and Lady Captain Maureen Walsh with the England winning team.

Left: 1997 Irish Close Championship: Winner Ken Kearney (Co. Sligo) second left, with (left to right) Liam Friel (Westport Captain), Peter O'Hara (GUI President), and John Keaveney (Bank of Ireland).

Below: Pictured at a reception hosted by the Bank of Ireland during the 1997 Close Championship. Left to right: Jackie Bolster, Noel Connell (Hon. Sec. W.G.C.), Brendan Bolster, Liam Friel (captain), Marie Grimes (lady captain).

up playing the 18th against Peter Lawrie. Snow birdied the 18th but Lawrie eagled from 12 feet to send the match down the 19th. Here Snow found the trees with his drive and Lawrie had escaped.

Jody Fanagan was two down with two to play against S.Maloney. But Fanagan birdied 17 and 18 and eventually won on the 20th.

Pat Murray went to the 21st in defeating Jim McClure. Garth McGimpsey was defeated by Gary O'Flaherty (Cork)

The course was sun drenched for the final between 23-year-old Paul Lawrie (U.C.D.) and Ken Kearney (Co.Sligo). A borrowed putter from Tom Ford weaved magic for Kearney. He had five birdies on the first nine holes and a total of 12 putts. He was 4 under after 14 holes and won 5 and 4. Lawrie was 1 over. Ken Kearney added the Irish Close Title to the West of Ireland Title he had won in 1992.

Once again Westport G.C. had proved itself a true championship course. A worthy champion with golfing pedigree had emerged from the 192 strong field. The course produced golf of the highest quality and a host of exciting matches. It was only right and fitting that the grounds staff and the Close committee were complimented in the aftermath.

In 1998 the club hosted the Connacht Youths Championship. The winner was Lee Dalton (Waterford) 288 who won on the first tie hole from Michael Hoey (Shandon Park). Third in the u-18 boys was Justin Kehoe (U.C.D.) 300.

In 1999 the club hosted the Irish Ladies Senior Cup finals and also the Connacht Ladies Championships.

In 2001 the Connacht Boys Amateur Open Championship was hosted. The winner was Michael Mulryan (Athenry) with 292. 168 boys had entered and six of these were from Westport. Conditions were tough on Day 1 and only 12 golfers broke 75. One of those was Westport's Michael Kearns. 51 players made the cut and four of them were Westport's Noel Kavanagh, Michael Kearns, Tom McLoughlin, and Cathal O'Malley. As a result of his play during the year and in this Championship Cathal O'Malley was chosen on the Connacht Boys Interprovincial Team.

■ The Irish P.G.A.

In 2002 Westport hosted the Smurfit Irish P.G.A. Championship. Initially it was expected that 6 Irish Ryder Cup players, Padraig Harrington, Darren Clarke, Des Smyth, Eamonn Darcy, Philip Walton, would be in the field. However Padraig Harrington and Darren Clarke were unable to play. The total field comprised 102 professionals. The April weather was foul and the last day's play was cancelled. The winner was Paul McGinley.

In 2004 the Club hosted the Connacht Veterans Championship and the winner was Bob Wallace .

■ The Irish Close 2005.

The big story surrounding this Irish Close was the performance of Rory McIlroy (Hollywood).

At 16 years and 42 days old McIlroy became the youngest Irish Close Champion.

He was fully six months younger than Ronan Rafferty who turned 16 in January 1980 and won the Close at Royal County Down.

Brian McElhinney arrived on the 1st tee as holder of the British Amateur Championship for 2005. He brought the British Amateur Cup with him to Westport and it was a wonderful trophy to behold. He was quickly into his stride and shot a new course record 68.

However his record did not last long.

Sean McTernan (Co. Sligo) tore it to shreds with a stunning 61 comprising 10 birdies and an eagle for 12 under par.

Modestly he said he just pitched close every-time. One wonders how can this course record ever

Paul McGinley receives the 2002 Irish PGA Trophy from Westport Captain, Haulie Hoban, who also received, on behalf of the club, a commemorative plaque for staging the event (inset) from Dr. Michael Smurfit.

Letter from Paul McGinley

I would like to chronicle and share my memories with a golf club that has a soft spot within the McGinley family.

My first memory is of the Irish Close Championship in 1977.

All the talk that week was of a U.S. Open setup and of how difficult the course was playing with its high rough! I was eight years old at the time, caddying for my Dad and I didn't know a U.S. Open from an open fourball!! My Dad was beaten in one of the earlier rounds as Mark Gannon staged a great comeback to beat Tony Hayes.

My second memory is of my wife to be, Ally, and her visit to Ireland for the first time to play for England in the Home Internationals in 1989. I was playing elsewhere that week and recall tales of Knock Airport, Irish Hospitality and Guinness as England won and Ally went unbeaten.

Westport had played its part in introducing Ally to my home country!

My most recent visit was the Smurfit P.G.A. Championship in 2002. I was on a roll with my game as the two previous weeks I had finished 16th in my first U.S. Masters at Augusta and helped G.B. and Ireland beat Europe in the Seve Trophy at Druids Glen.

Unfortunately the early date in the golfing season brought some very strong winds and the last round was "winded' out. Fortunately I was leading after 3 rounds and was declared the winner.

I look forward to my next visit to Westport and playing one of my favourite par 5s in the world, the 15th hole.

Best wishes to all the members and thanks for many great memories.

A Chara, Paul.

be beaten or even equalled given the nature of the course and the weather generally in the West?

It is more true to acknowledge that Sean McTernan has achieved immortality with his outstanding 61.

Another marvellous highlight was McIlroy's match against McTernan in the quarter-final. This match featured the courage and tenacity of McTernan against the unbridled optimism of teenager McIlroy.

The shotmaking and ball striking by both players was superb. McTernan found himself 4 holes down after 13. He won the 14th with par and the 16th and 17th with birdies.

A real highlight here was McTernan driving the par 4 uphill 16th and then scoring birdie after a wicked 30 ft. downhill first putt.

But McIlroy was never flustered.

One up playing the 18th he birdied the hole as also did McTernan after his eagle chip just came up short.

McTernan was three under for the last 5 holes and McIlroy level par.

McIlroy played Conor Doran in the semi-final

and was 7 under after 11 holes and six under when they shook hands on the 15th. Conor Doran was suffering from a stomach bug and really was in no position to do himself justice.

Rory McIlroy defeated Eddie McCormack of Galway in the final by 3 and 2. He thus added the Irish Close title to his West of Ireland title for 2005. He had previously won the Irish Boys, Irish Youths and Ulster Boys titles.

So Westport Colf Course had produced another worthy champion and a golfer with proven pedigree.

It will be fascinating to watch the progress of this young man in the years to come.

Rory went on to win the Silver Medal for the highest placed amateur in the 2007 British Open Championship at Carnoustie.

■ Some interesting sidelines.

Banbridge defeated Westport in the Fred Daly 2000 All-Ireland final. Five of those participants played in this Close and one was a reserve – Conor Doran, Rory Kilpatrick, Ciaran McAleavey from Banbridge and Noel Kavanagh jr., Cathal

2005 Irish Close
Championship.
Winner, Rory McIlroy
receives the trophy from
Mr. L. Shanks (president
G.U.I.), watched by
C.O'Malley (captain
W.G.C.) and P. Murphy
(president W.G.C.).

O'Malley and Michael Kearns (reserve) from Westport.

Westport had a number of local players in the 150 player field.

Liam Halpin shot 75 on day 1 and 80 on day 2. Noel Kavanagh Jr. shot 78 and 77; D. Stapleton shot 80 and 78; Padraic Walsh shot 83 and retired sick on day 2; Cathal O'Malley shot 77 and 74 to make the cut. He was defeated in the 1st round matchplay by J. Waldron (Muskerry).

From June 11th to the 15th the weather was excellent. The course looked wonderful and the organisation was superb. Captain Christy O'Malley, Vice-Captain, Willie Elliot, Hon. Sec; John Collins, Hon Treas. Dave McDermott and the Club Committee can be very proud of a job well done.

In 2008 the Club will continue its fine tradition of hosting Championships. Both the Irish Ladies Close Championship and the Irish Seniors Championship will take place on Westport's true champions course.

There can be no argument now. Westport G.C. is a true Championship Course. It is a course with a proven ability to produce great matchplay situations and great champions. It is a terrific venue for championship play. Long may the greats of Irish golf continue to pump the adrenalin on this truly fine golf course.

■ **Postscript.**
The following Irish international golfers (selected) have played Championship golf in Westport. Many of them are now playing on the various professional tours.

They fly the Irish flag on the P.G.A. Tour, the European Tour, the Challenge Tour, the Nationwide Tour and the Seniors Tour.

Some of them have performed heroics in the Ryder Cup and will continue to do so in the future. These names stamp "Championship" on every blade of grass in Westport:

Paul McGinley; Des Smyth, Eamon Darcy, Padraig Harrington, Philip Walton, Michael Hoey, Peter Lawrie, David Higgins, Darren Clarke, John McHenry, Brian McElhinney, Christy O'Connor Jr, Ken Kearney, Rory McIlroy, Raymond Burns, Richie Coughlan, Sean McTernan, Justin Kehoe, Gary McNeill.

Gar Golden: Captain of Westport Golf Club 1975; President of Westport Golf Club 1990-1992; President of the Golfing Union of Ireland 1990-91.

Chapter 11

Gar Golden

A golf club only becomes successful because great administrators emerge and give generously of their time and knowledge. One such person is Mr. Gar Golden who has played a major part in mentoring Westport G.C. over the past 38 years. The list is endless where Gar's knowledgeable mentoring has been. At various times through the years he has been active in club development, course development, major championships, ladies golf, junior golf,, inter-club golf, club administration, club marketing, the club professional and the organisation of groundstaff. Add to this list the administration of Connacht golf as Council member and Chairman of Connacht Branch, G.U.I. Finally add administration of National Amateur golf as President of the Golfing Union of Ireland and then one may appreciate the treasured fountain of golf knowledge available to Westport G.C. in the person of Gar Golden. The wonder is during all this time Gar has retained a single-figure golf handicap!

■ Learning Golfing traditions and values, 1963-1990 :

Before attaining the highest office in amateur golf Gar spent 27 years learning the traditions and values of golf. His education involved the intense study of the spirit of the game which he garnered by playing golf and from golf administration.

■ Playing the Game:

In 1963 Gar was a member of the Westport County Cup team who finished runners-up in the competition. He played alongside M. Henehan, E. McCrea, T. Joyce, M. Mulloy,

G. Hall, J. Kelly, G. McAleer, F. McMahon and D. Landers. Before the year was out Gar was to experience a major personal success when he won the Boyden Cup in Castlebar.

The *Connacht Telegraph* reported as follows:

> "For the first time in its history, the Boyden Cup left Castlebar when it was won by Gar Golden of Westport, who returned a sensational 62 for a total of 132. The winner hit a long ball of the tee, played accurate iron shots to the green and putted boldly. Mrs. Joan O'Malley, whose father presented the cup to the Club back in 1935, presented the cup to the winner."

In 1970 Gar was a member of the winning County Cup team playing off 9.

He played alongside Tony Joyce (5); John Farrell (8); Gerry McAleer (9); Maurice Mulloy (15); John Kelly (16); Hugh Murphy (17); Padraic Higgins (17); Perry 0'Reilly (18); and Niall Halpin (19).

In 1975 Gar was a member of the first team in the history of the Club to reach the Connacht Shield Final but this team was defeated by Strandhill. The members of that team were:

Tony Joyce(5); Gar Golden(8); Perry O'Reilly(5); Gerry Hughes (14); Gerry McAleer (7); Michael Moran (12); Michael Henehan(12); John Farrell(10); Jackie Morris(14); John O'Hanlon(17).

In 1979 Gar was a member of the Connacht Shield team defeated in the final by Co.Sligo. The Westport team experienced the agony of losing on the last green in three of the five matches. His playing companions were; Perry O'Reilly/ Liam Gibbons; David Joyce/ Tom McHale; Tony Joyce/Hugh Murphy; J.O'Meara/M.Moran; Donie O'Connor/Gar Golden.

Later in the year Gar went on to win the Carrowholly Cup.

In 1980 Gar won the Donal Landers Trophy and the President's Prize with 41 pts playing off 8. Gar also won the golfer of the year in 1980.

But his golfing memory for life will be the winning of the All-Ireland Junior Cup as a playing member of that brilliant team. His contribution as selector and playing member to that team was vital and it is to his credit that he did not hesitate

to cry off the final team after he lost his match in the semi-final.

In 1982 he won the President's Prize.

In 1983 he had the pleasure of being Captain of the Mayo Golf Team defeated by Louth in the All Ireland Final of the Inter-County Championship.

Reaching this final was a major first for Mayo. The Mayo team was: V. Freyne (Ballyhaunis); J. McVeigh (Ballyhaunis); H. McKinney (Dun Laoighre); Tony Maher (Woodbrook); Joe Corcoran (Ballina); M. Lynott (Enniscrone); P. O'Reilly (Westport).

In 1985 he was a member of the Junior Cup Team that reached the All-Ireland Finals in Kilkenny alongside Tony Joyce, Liam Walsh, David Joyce, Tom McHale and Martin McIntyre. In 1988 he won the Hughes Cup.

By 1990 Gerard D. Golden (Gar) was more than familiar with the rules and honour demanded by the game.

As a single figure golfer he had won major Club competitions and played on successful club teams climaxing with the All Ireland Junior Cup win in 1980.

■ Golf Administrator.

In 1970 the move to the new course was a live issue and this was a busy year for all concerned. Gar became very involved in getting the infant course on its feet and trying to solve its teething problems. These problems were myriad and concerned the access road, finance, water leakages, faulty stopcocks, rota system to water greens and the sheer frustration in getting Bord Fáilte officials to make decisions. These problems involved many meetings and multiple heated discussions.

When play started draws became a controversial subject:

> "The controversy regarding being in time for draws on Sundays led to heated discussions and much time was wasted in long drawn out arguments."

This question of draws led to resignations, fines and threats of legal action.

In 1973 Gar was elected a Trustee of the Club.

Club Captain Gar Golden with Taoiseach, Liam Cosgrave, at the opening of the new course.

When he became Vice-Captain in 1974 the reality of financing the new course had a sobering effect. The focus was on how to raise money. The Officers had to become familiar with the new constitution. The deed of covenant, lease and contract for the road was signed.

The main event of his Captain's year was presiding over the official opening of the new Westport Golf Club by the Taoiseach, Mr. Liam Cosgrave T.D.

In 1977 and 1985 Westport was the venue for the Irish Close Championship. Gar was instrumental in bringing this major event to Westport.

In 1985 he was elected Chairman of the Connacht Branch G.U.I. However he continued to serve his club on committee and as a Trustee. In 1986 and 1987 he remained on committee and discussed issues such as marketing the club, a secretary manager, stolen trophies and damage caused by hares and rabbits. In 1989 he expressed concern about the future development of the club. At the AGM he proposed "That Westport Golf Club be directed to get a ground development report from a competent golf course architect to plan the future development of the golf course with a view to improving the golf course." This motion was adopted.

By 1990 Gar had played his part in estab-lishing the new course from virgin earth. Here he cut his teeth as a golfing administrator dealing with Bord Fáilte, a new constitution and numerous problems. He had served his club on committee, as Vice-Captain, Captain, and Trustee.

His golf-politics skills had been sharpened from the cut and trust of club affairs.

He had played an active part in organising the Irish Close of 1977, 1985 and many other Championships played at Westport. He knew how a course should be set up for championship play. He knew what was required to run a successful champi-onship. As Provincial Golf Officer he had reached the highest office, Chairman of the Connacht Branch.

All this depth of golfing knowledge and golfing administration knowledge was behind Gar when he became President of the Golfing Union of Ireland in 1990.

■ Gar Golden, Westport, President G.U.I. 1990.

On Friday 23rd of February 1990 Gar Golden was elected President of the Golfing Union of Ireland. His year was to be a busy cycle of club openings, annual dinners, centenary celebrations, amateur golf championships and a number of "firsts".

In another life Gar had been Chairman of Westport Urban Council and President of Westport

Chamber of Commerce. During his term of office on both bodies Gar had championed the cause of industrial, social and commercial development in Westport. The greatest honour for any man is to be honoured by his own. A Civic Reception hosted jointly by the Westport Urban Council and Westport Chamber of Commerce was convened to celebrate Gar's achievement. Westport Golf Club also hosted a reception in his honour.

His first official function was to be guest-of-honour at Royal Belfast G.C. annual dinner. His first centenary function was at the Island G.C. He attended centenary celebrations in Sutton G.C. where the legendary Joe Carr officiated. His visit for the centenary celebrations at Ballycastle G.C. proved memorable as he had the double pleasure of playing golf with Joe Carr and meeting Darren Clarke's father who was looking after the course. Whilst off course activities do provide highlights for Presidents it is the on course activities which fuel the memory for life.

■ The Amateur Golf Championships.

Gar had the pleasure of watching Niall Goulding win his first West of Ireland Championship at Rosses Point.

The Junior Inter-Provincials followed in Westport and here he witnessed Leinster and the young Padraig Harrington emerge winners. He presented Raymie Burns with a memento in recognition of his great achievement in winning all four Boys Championships in the one year.

The East of Ireland followed at Baltray. Here Gar watched his friend Denis O'Sullivan, Cork G.C., triumph. The Carrolls Pro-Am at Portmarnock G.C. was next on the agenda.

This was followed by the North of Ireland Championshp at Royal Portrush G.C. where Gar was to experience a magical golfing moment intertwined with a scary one. A crowd estimated to be 5,000 watched the final between Darren Clarke and Paul McGinley.

Gar, as referee, walked around with the match.

After 17 holes the match was all flat. The 18th hole was opposite the clubhouse. Both Paul and Darren played two great drives. Paul missed the green but chipped and putted for a four. Darren found the green but was 30 feet short of the pin.

Earlier Gar had noticed a number of dogs amongst the crowd.

On enquiry he was told they were police sniffer dogs as two bomb threats using a special code had been received by police. The police believed the bomb would be in the vicinity of the clubhouse. If Darren missed his putt the clubhouse would have to be passed to reach the first play-off hole and it was still been searched by police!

Darren sank the putt for a dramatic end to a memorable final.

The police then took over and asked everyone to stand in open ground. The all-clear came after an hour.

The first all-Ulster final in the South of Ireland at Lahinch saw Darren Clarke defeat Jim Carvill.

The Irish Close was hosted by Baltray and here Darren Clarke defeated Padraig Harrington in the final.

Gar had the pleasure of presenting Darren with his last amateur trophy as he turned professional the following morning.

Darren had a wonderful golfing year. He had won the North of Ireland, the South of Ireland, the Spanish Amateur and finally the Irish Close.

Belvoir Park hosted the Irish Mixed Foursomes. Here Gar witnessed a Galway win. He travelled to the British "Open" for blind golfers at Donaghadee where he observed some great golf. He travelled back home to Westport for the All-Ireland Cups and Shields. He was particularly proud of the excellent organisation displayed by his home club.

He presented Green Pennants to Cork, Waterford, Warrenpoint and Oughterard.

■ "Golden" Memories.

Gar was a guest at a lunch for the World Presidents of Golf given by the Royal and Ancient during the "Open" at St. Andrews. He watched Nick Faldo, playing with Greg Norman, produce a fantastic round of golf on Saturday which enabled him to win comfortably on Sunday.

The main agenda for the President of the G.U.I. in 1990 was the Home Internationals at

The 1990 Irish Home International Team, winners of the Triple Crown and Championship at Conwy Golf Club, Wales.

Back: H. Bennett (coach), Paul McGinley, K.Kearney, G. McNeill, Gar Golden (President of the GUI), Padraig Harrington, D. Errity, N. Goulding, J. Fanagan.

Front: L. McNamara, N. Anderson, G.F.Crosbie (Captain), G. McGimpsey, M. Gannon.

Conwy in Wales. A star-studded English team was expected to win. However Liam McNamara sank the vital putt on the 18th green in the final match to give Ireland victory by 8 matches to 7. The Irish team had made history by winning the Triple Crown for the first time outside the country. Padraig Harrington was the youngest member of the team at 19 years old and he came through his six matches without defeat.

The Irish team members were, Paul McGinley, Padraig Harrington, Garth McGimpsey, Neil Anderson, David Errity, Jody Fanagan, Mark Gannon, Niall Goulding, Ken Kearney, Gary McNeill, Liam McNamara with Francis Howley of Sligo flown out as cover for Garth McGimpsey who was feeling unwell.

It was a proud moment for the President of the G.U.I. when the Irish team led by their captain, George Crosbie, entered the hotel dining room to a standing ovation which lasted at least ten minutes.

A notable guest was Robbie Lowry, Lord Chief Justice, N.I. He followed Padraig Harrington every day and forecast a bright future for him which is evident today.

The Lord Chief Justice had four Special Branch men guarding him night and day. In the midst of the revelry they burst in and lifted a fellow who was sitting just three places away from Robbie Lowry. In a flash they were gone with the words, "It's all right! Have a good night!"

In October Gar led the first Irish team to America for the inaugural Metedeconk International Challenge Cup match between Ireland and the Metropolitan Golf Association.

It was to be an eye-opener for all concerned. Metedeconk National was designed by Robert Trent Jones. A member is expected to be a gentleman before he plays, while he plays and after he plays.

The course was magnificent. The tees and fairways looked good enough after one more cut to qualify as greens at almost any venue in Ireland. Holes had been cut on some of the tees so that players could practice their putting if delayed by the group in front.

The cup played for was a 17-inch silver cup made by Weirs of Dublin and created in 1912. The Irish team was defeated. Padraig Harrington came unstuck at Metedeconk. He lost his first three matches and was dropped for the final round of singles.

What was apparent from this result was that Irish players needed world stage opportunity to develop their game.

Gar reported to the G.U.I. that the most desirable move after this experience would be to field our own Irish team in the World Championships for the Eisenhower Trophy.

The Irish party was invited to play Pine Valley G. C. at the invitation of Ernest Ransome 111. While looking at the members board Gar noticed the name "Kelly, Ballybunion G.C."

Joe Carr told Gar the story behind this man's membership. Years earlier an American had arrived to play Ballybunion but there was no one around to take his green fee.

A man approached on his bike and said to the Yank, "Go ahead, I'll see you when you come in and enjoy your golf."

When the Yank finished his round he was greeted by the same Kerryman.

"Hope you enjoyed your game?"

"Fantastic, absolutely fantastic!"

The Yank proceeded to sign the green fee book.

"Ernest Ransome, U.S.A."

"Jeepers!! exclaimed the Kerryman, "we have a machine with that name on it."

"It must be one of mine," replied Ransome

"Forget the green fee," said the Kerryman. "I'm making you an honorary member of Ballybunion."

"Fantastic, absolutely fantastic," cried Ransome, "and I'm making you an Honorary member of my club, Pine Valley G.C."

Gar's year of golf was nearly over when in November an invitation arrived from Buckingham Palace. The Queen and Prince Philip required Gar and his wife, Agatha, to attend a ceremony honouring the game of golf.

The Master of the Household arranged the group in order to meet the Queen. Amateurs appeared to rank higher than the professionals in the eyes of the monarchy. First was the President of the English Golfing Union, then the Presidents of the Scottish, Welsh and Irish Unions. Next was Nell Bruen, the President of the Ladies Golfing Union and the widow of the late Jimmy Bruen, followed by the President of the R. & A., the President of the P.G.A. and the secretary of the R. & A. The Queen then met the members of the Walker, Ryder and two Curtis Cup teams.

Now when he looks back on this wonderful year of "firsts" in golf his first thoughts are with his family. He is particularly grateful to his wife, Agatha, for the family support he received. He considers it strange that it should have been a Westport man who was there for all those "firsts" in golf. But his overriding emotion is how lucky he was indeed to experience all those wonderful days.

Did Gar gracefully disappear having served in the highest office open to golf administrators?

It can be recorded with pride that Gar Golden continued to serve golf in Westport and in Connacht. Westport G.C. always came first with Gar and in true "covie" spirit he quickly immersed himself once more in the continual development of Westport G.C.

From 1991 onwards both as Trustee and Committee member Gar has been involved in the following club happenings.

In February 1992 he was part of a delegation to Bord Fáilte to try and get Bord Fáilte to change the format of their relationship with Westport.

In 1993 he served on the committee dealing with the lease with Bord Failte and full membership for ladies.

In 1995 at the inaugural general meeting of the Joint Club he was elected an Honorary Life Member and he served on the management committee.

In 1996 he remained on the management committee and discussed the development of the clubhouse and the decision of Ireland West to sell the course to Westport G.C.

In 1997 he played his part in organising the Irish Close hosted by Westport.

In 1998 he was honoured for 25 years service to the G.U.I. He helped to organise the Irish P.G.A. tournament in 2002 and the Irish Close in 2005. He has been involved in the development of water features and new greens on the course. He was a member of the Junior Cup team defeated by Portumna in the Connacht Final of 2002.

He continues to mentor. He is always available for advice, guidance and information.

It would be impossible to quantify the man hours given so generously by Gar Golden to the development of golf in Westport.

Suffice to say that in this centenary year it is only fitting and just to salute Mr. Gerard D. Golden (Gar) for his ongoing contribution to the development of golfing excellence in Westport G.C.

Gar Golden presents Raymond Burns of Banbridge Golf Club with a plaque to acknowledge his winning of the four Irish Boys Championships in one year.

Christy O'Connor senior with Jim Kiely at the Allergan special outing to celebrate his retirement.

Woodbrook's President exchanges ties with Gar Golden to mark the twinning of the clubs.

Past president; Dennis Egan raises his glass to Westport Golf Club.

"Length should have its own reward and youth will out but old foxes should still be given the chance to play. We simply can't be designing courses for the best players in the world because what happens the other 51 weeks of the year when they aren't competing? For me that's why club championships and matchplay, the truest form of the game, among friends is when the real game is on."

Robert Trent Jones jr.
(golf architect)

Chapter 12

Cup Winners
THROUGH THE YEARS

■ **The Captain's Prize.**

Picture this. It is Captain's Day 2004. The car park is bulging. The sun glints of myriad clubs swung with grave intensity on the practice ground. The putting green is awash with Pro-V's stroked lovingly into cups. The atmosphere is pregnant with anticipation. Each golfer secretly hopes it is going to be "my day!" A flutter at 33/1 has been wagered. The Captain, Liam Walsh jr. is congratulated by outgoing golfers. He is wished a lovely day.

Early scores have been posted. The bar sighs and groans with hard luck stories. "I was going great until I took an eight at the eighth!!" "I went out of bounds at the 15th only for that…"

As the stories thicken with drama John Kelly with his friend, Maurice Mulloy, ambles in. They take their coffee out to the balcony beside the diningroom. They sit quietly watching various groups approach the 18th hole. Occasionally they glance at Croagh Patrick towering over the course. Sometimes their eyes stretch towards the 15th tee where a group are about to hit screaming drives over the Clew Bay inlet. On other occasions they pass a greeting to golfers who have finished their round.

"Any joy cove?"

Memories awaken from the slumber of years. The old days and the old ways come flooding back. Maurice says quietly, "remember the suckling pig cove?"

"Will I ever forget!" John replies.

It is Captain's Day in Old Carrowholly. The year is 1958. It is John Kelly's day. He has a surprise for the members – a suckling pig! And don't they need it. The weather is foul. The greens sodden. What a saga! There it stretches, a deep golden brown, a succulent whisper of the goodliness to come. John turns the spit. Jim Warde, chef de cuisine, prepares the rum sauce. The ladies have laid a magnificent table... it is a sweet memory...

Oh! Oh! the joy and glory of Captain's Day!

1938 P. Dempsey
1944 C. McKinney
1947 P.J. Golden
1948 M.J. Sugrue
1950 S.W. Johnston
1951 G. Murphy

"that was the day when there was salt in the air and the sun shone."

1952 L. Golden

This is the prize of the golfing year in Carrowholly, when hopes rise high and mighty in the heart of the long handicap man, and when the expert to meet him nervously practice swings his club and prays that the reward for constant endeavour should now be his.

Every evening now there is the thud of clubs on the grass outside, the clatter of men into the pavilion , the shuffle of chairs and the soft question in the candlelight, "how did you do?"

The laugh and the talk and all the time the hope rising higher in the hearts of some and dead in the hearts of others. The Nazis had a name for it. They called it the Nervenkrieg. This enabled them to get what they wanted without fighting. The Russians then took it over in 1945 and in 1952 it reached Carrowholly in a big way in the Captains Prize.

But with this difference. Here we have the nerves and the fighting. Every match has been a struggle to the last hole of the eighteen and even of the thirty-six and now D.P. Landers meets Liam Golden in the final. Mr. Landers probably knows every blade of grass on the fairway, every undulation of the greens. Liam Golden is the newer style of golfer, magnificent driving, get your second up to the pin. We shall therefore see golfing craft matched against flashing brilliance.

Through the years at Carrowholly there has grown a legend about one man. He can do this. He can do that. There is nothing he cannot do and the story is he can do it better with a jacket and an empty pipe. On Sunday he stood on the Kilroy with the match all square and two holes to go. He played to the green 190 yards away. His drive hit the wire going in and the ball trickled onto the green. Local rules allow a substituted shot. No golfer in his place would tempt fortune by taking the second shot.

But the jacket and the empty pipe came into play, the shot was taken, the ball landed ten feet from the pin and was duly sunk for a two and a win. All Liam Golden could do was win the next hole and the match was squared and both players live to fight it out again.

In the replay dykes were sometimes not sufficient to guarantee a win. D.P. put the whole game in a nutshell when he said, "Liam could beat me anytime when playing the kind of golf he played to-day. He was unbeatable."

1954 J. Rafferty
1955 L. Golden
1956 Norman Ashe
1957 D.P. Landers

" D.P. Landers has attained legendary status in the club. A foundation member, a golfer of about 40 years standing with an uncanny ability of getting into the tin without fuss,without labour and with a smile in his eye he pits his know-how with deadly accuracy against the free-swinging younger generation. He brought home the prize to the delight of all the members and to his own pipe-smoking infinite content."

1958 Frank O' Callaghan

"Conditions and weather foul, sodden greens, quaking fairways, hell and high water. The rest of the field a sorry motley crew of sweaters, corduroys and wellingtons (note wet gear!!!).

Brian McElhenny, British and Irish Amateur Champion in 2004, brings both trophies to Westport in 2005 during the Close Championship.
Also in the photo: left to right: Clair McMyler (lady captain), Pat Murphy (president) Charity O'Malley (captain) Gar Golden.

Prizewinners in the Ardmore Mixed, 2000: L. Friel, C. O'Donnell, T. Walsh, P. Moran, T. Whyte, N. Halpin (Captain, Westport Golf Club), A. Duffy, and J. Regan.

1959 D.P.Landers.
1963 G.McAleer.
1964 F.McMahon
1966 F.Hope

"Michael Henehan and Fergal Hope returned all square with a score of 60 but the prize went to Mr.Hope on the last nine of the 27 holes. The runner-up lost a ball in the rough dropping two points."

1967 J.Kelly	1986 Frank Fitzgerald
1968 T.Joyce	1987 Michael Langan
1969 J. Farrell	(Castlebar)
1970 M. Tiernan	1988 Tom McHale jr.
1971 Dr. Bert Farrell.	1989 Pat Griffith jr.
1973 Mick King	1990 Joe Moran Mill St.
1974 Liam Golden	1991 N.McSweeney
1975 Thomas Higgins.	1992 Pat Griffith jr.
1976 Dr. John	1993 G.Hughes
Coughlan-(120	1995 H. Staunton
played-70% up on	1996 Hugh Murphy
previous year)	1997 D.McLoughlin
1977 Fr. John	1998 Noel Feeney
Cosgrave	1999 P.Kearns
1978 Liam Walsh	2000 V. O' Malley
(Newport)	2001 M.Groden
1979 Martin McIntyre	2002 J.Collins
1980 Gar Golden	2003 Ronan Mahon
1981 Tony Joyce	2004 Diarmuid
1982 Dermot Blythe	O'Keeffe.
1983 Des O'Leary	2005 John Golden
1984 John O' Meara	2006 Liam Friel
1985 John Kearns	2007 Eamon Canning

■ The Rossyveragh Cup

Major Walter J. Curley, Pittsburg, P.A. presented the "Rossyveragh Cup".The Curley family called the cup the "Carrigahowley Cup." It was designed and produced by a silversmith in Limerick. The trophy was stolen during a break-in and the tournament was not continued. Walter J.Curley sr. and Walter Curley jr. bought Rossyveragh House in 1958. Walter jr. and his wife joined Westport G.C. in 1959 and they have been members ever since. Walter Curley sr. was an officer in the American army in France, Luxemburg, Belgium and Germany during World War One. He was the founder of a railway tank car company, served on a number of business and philanthropic boards and served in the U.S. Department of Commerce in President Eisenhower's administration. He was a keen sportsman with a love of golf, riding, skiing and shooting. Ireland and especially Mayo held strong places in his heart. He died of a stroke in 1970. He would have loved the new course.

In 1976 Walter J.P.Curley jr. was the Ambassador of the United States to Ireland. He was made an honorary member of Westport G.C. during his term of office. He appreciated this courtesy because of his family's close ties and affection for the Westport Golf Club and community.

In May 2006 he presented an architectural plan of the proposed "new" Westport Golf Course designed by Fred Hawtree and Son as a valuable historical source to the club.

■ Naming the trophy

"The Chairman read a letter received from Mr. Walter J. P. Curley, 630, Fifth Ave, New York. The Hon. Sec. had been instructed to thank Mr. Curley for his kind offer.

Of the three names mentioned in the letter it was proposed by Mr. Gill, seconded by Mr. Gilmartin that the new trophy be called the "The Rossyveragh Perpetual Cup". The Chairman asked if it would be possible for the ladies to partake in the competition for the Cup. Mr. Gill said that the ladies handicaps were completely different to the mens and would be extremely difficult to arrange for both men and ladies to play in the same competition. It was then decided to make it a men's competition.

The Chairman stated that the difficulty of ladies and gents competing against one another in the same competition could be overcome as this type of competition was quite common in Dublin Clubs. Mr.Golden said that as we were a struggling club it would be for the good of the club if most members took part in our competitions and he proposed that the ladies be allowed to play in the Rossyveragh Cup.

Mr.Stephen Walsh seconded this proposal and it was carried unanimously." (1960)

Enjoying a celebratory moment 1989. Back: left to right: P. Quinn, O. Whyte, J. Gibbons, M. McDonnell, M. Walsh, M. Henehan, P. Hopkins, P. Kennedy, P. Bree. Front: B. Bolster, M. Cavanaugh, A.Redmond (captain), C. O'Neill, D.O'Sullivan.

Men at leisure 2005. Back: left to right: P. Moody, J. O'Donnell, P. Kearns, L. Walsh, P. Cawley, R. Mahon, L. Gibbons, P. O'Neill.
Front: P. Murphy (president), W. Elliott, C.O'Malley (captain), J. Collins (hon.sec.).

The Rossyveragh Cup

1963 Tom Kelly	1980 Bridie Hughes
1964 Tony Joyce	1981 John G. Moran
1967 Fr.M.Golden	(runner-up-Bridie
1968 Sean Tobin	Hughes)
1970 Capt. D. O'Regan	1982 David Joyce
1971 Hugh Murphy	1983 Liam Gibbons
1973 Hugh Murphy	1984 Anna May
1974 Aiden Redmond	McCreave
1975 Liam Walsh	1985 M.Brady
1978 Larry Hingerton	1986 Kay Brown
1979 Bridie Hughes	1988 Jack Bredin

■ The Phillips Cup:
Presented By E.R. Phillips In 1935.

"A golfers first love, gleaming silver on shining ebony plinth. Confined to handicaps of 18 +. It causes more discussion in the club than any other cup. Members who have grown grey in the service of the game have had a belt at this in their younger years, they have lost it, they have won it and all the time with or without blue ribbons, it is there gleaming in its silver brilliance challenging you to come and get it if you can." (1952)

1944 E.Roycroft	1987 M.Heraty
1947 James	1988 A. Brennan
McLoughlin	1989 C.Madigan
1948 M.J.Sugrue	1990 C.Madigan
1950 P.O'Driscoll	1991 J. Cox
1951 Joe Mulloy	1992 D.McNally
1952 E. L. Hynes	1993 C.Madigan
1960 Larry Hingerton	1995 Liam Campion
1968 Cecil Adams	1996 Liam McNamara
1969 Cecil Adams	1997 Declan Quinn
1970 A. O'Mhaoileoin	1998 Harry Herterich
1971 Phillip	1999 Jack Bredin.
McLaughlin.	2000 Michael Groden
1975 Liam Walsh	2001 Sean Hoban
1977 S.Malone	2002 Kevin Cusack
1979 Greg Dyar	2003 Philip McGinnity
1981 George Reilly	2004 Redmond Lyons
1982 D.O'Flaherty	2005 David Scott.
1983 T.Walsh	2006 David Newton
1984 J.Foley	

Carrowholly Challenge Cup 1929

1936: D.P. Landers	1986 S.Underwood
1944 P. Gill	1987 P.Kennedy
1947 P.Flanagan	1988 F.McHale
1949 G.Murphy	1989 P.O'Reilly
1950 D.P.Landers	1990 C.Hughes
1952 L.Golden	1991 D.O'Connor
1954 John Kelly	1992 T.McHale
1958 L.Golden	1993 P.Griffith
1961 L.Golden	1994 L.Halpin
1963 T.Joyce	1995 L.Friel
1967 M.King	1996 M.Loughrey
1968 M.Henehan	1997 M.Halpin
1969 T.Joyce	1998 T.Walsh
1970 L.Walsh	1999 S.Fitzgerald
(Newport)	2000 J.Bredin
1974 M.Moran	2001 M.Halpin
1975 P.Hoban	2002 J.O'Haire
1979 Gar Golden	2003 M.Halpin
1981 P.O'Reilly	2004 E.Groden
1982 John Kelly	2005 A.Browne
1984 G.McAleer	2006 T. Lyons
1985 G.Golden	2007 B. Burns

The Gill Cup:

In 1933 twenty members played paying an entry fee of 3s/6p each.

1954 M.Golden	1972 A. Redmond.
1959 Martin Cox	1973 P. Higgins
1961 J.Kelly	1974 N. Halpin
1963 E.McCrea	1975 V. Coakley
1964 F.McMahon	1976 P. Hoban
1967 G.Mc Aleer	1977 Greg Dyar
1968 P.Cox	1979 John Moran
1969 M. Henehan	1980 Martin Halpin
1970 M. Tiernan	1981 Martin McIntyre.
1971 J. Farrell	

The Carrowholly Stakes: 1953

This is confined to all who failed to qualify for the Phillips Cup and all other members with handicaps of 18 and over. The contest is mainly devised for the newcomers. Entry fee is 1s and the only condition laid down is that each contestant must finish the course of 18 holes.

Donal Landers with his wife.

The Malone-Landers Cup: Played For In 1934:

Presented to the club by Rev. M. Malone and D.P. Landers.

"It has seen the passage of time and a full length World War and still retains its pristine elegance and charm." In 1960 "the Chairman stated the Malone-Landers Trophy was inscribed, 'Mulranny Cup' and these words were inserted in the minutes and the words Malone-Landers deleted."

"The trophy that was presented for the Malone-Landers was I believe 'borrowed' by a commercial traveler from Mulranny Golf Club. It had a long holiday in W.G.C.!!"
(John Kelly/Capt.1958)

1947 G. Murphy	1967 G. McAleer
1948 G. Murphy	1970 Maurice Mulloy
1954 G. Hall	1971 P. O'Reilly.
1958 Tom Kelly	1973 N. Halpin
1960 Pat Golden	1974 M. King
1964 P. Cox	1980 Gar Golden
1966 J.Kelly	

The Cavanaugh Trophy:

In 1969 Mr.Michael Cavanaugh, The Riverside Hotel (Railway Hotel), presented a magnificent trophy to the Captain.

> "Mr.Cavanaugh to be asked on what lines he would like the trophy to be played for."

1970 Capt. D.O'Regan
1971 Niall Halpin (12)
1973 Tony Joyce
1974 Vincent Coakley.

In 1971 a letter was received from Miss Teresa Landers of Galway offering, subject to the committee's approval, a perpetual trophy in the form of a silver salver in memory of her father,the late Mr. Donal Landers. The committee were unanimously in favour of accepting this trophy.

1971 Liam Walsh/Mrs. Rose Golden
1972 N. Halpin/Jean McAleer
1973 Phillip McLaughlin/Mrs. Maureen Walsh
1974 Gar Golden/ Mrs. Maureen Walsh
1975 John O'Hanlon/Mrs. Rose Golden
1976 A. Redmond/Mrs. Jean McAleer
1977 J. O'Sullivan/Mrs. Bridie Hughes
1978 D. Carroll/Ms . Beda Tobin
1979 T. Joyce/Mrs. Bridie Hughes
1980 G. Golden/Ms. Loereeta O'Malley
1981 Ms. Sheelagh Ryan
1982 Ms. Maureen O'Hara
1983 Ms. Francis Campbell

The Guinness Masters:

1971 Mickey Hastings	1980 John Kelly
1972 P. Higgins	1981 P. Higgins
1973 G. McAleer	1982 Martin McIntyre
1975 Tony Joyce	(12) –with 47 pts
1976 Br. L. K. Walsh	– a record stable-
1977 G. Hughes	ford score.
1978 Liam Walsh	1983 Perry O'Reilly.
(Westport)	

The Presidents Cup:

1944 P. Gill
1947 P. Gill
1948 A. de Fleury
1949 E. L. Hynes
1958 P. Cox
1965 P. Cox
1968 M. Henehan
1969 G. McAleer.
1974 M. King
1975 A. O'Mhaoileoin
1976 R. McCreave
1977 R. Neville
1978 V. Coakley
1979 Bro. Murphy
1981 D. O'Connor
1982 Gar Golden
1983 R. McCreave jr.
1984 C. Hughes
1985 Neil O' Donnell
1986 Perry O' Reilly
1987 G. Reilly
1988 F. McMahon
1990 J. Gibbons
1991 P. Farren
1992 P. McAleer
1993 F. Hope
1994 D. Joyce.
1995 V. Farrell (men's medal)
       H. Piggot (ladies medal)
1996 M. Heraty
1997 N.Feeney
1998 V. Rigney
       Brigin Walsh
1999 Sean Walsh
2000 J. O'Haire
2001 Liam Walsh jr.
2002 Liam Walsh jr.
2003 Ronan Mahon
2004 Jack Dunne.
2005 Martin Brennan
       Bridie Moran
2006 Vincent Farrell
2007 John Gibbons
       Mary Dolan

Bertie Staunton Trophy:

1981 Perry O' Reilly (1st winner)
1982 Jack Bredin
1983 Paul Bree
1984 M. Heneghan
1985 G. Boylan
1988 P. Walsh
1989 M. J.Mc Donnell
1991 A. O'Toole
1992 J. Bredin
1993 W. Golden
1994 T. Reilly.
1995 L. Halpin
1996 Pat Moran
1997 M. Kirk
2001 B. Burns
2002 Noel O'Malley
2003 H. Golden
2004 B. Hopkins
2005 Anthony Doyle.
2006 V. O'Malley
2007 T. Canning

T.V. Mart Trophy:
Kindly Donated By Mr. Jim Reidy.

1974 Joe Higgins
1975 Liam Walsh
1976 Liam Gibbons
1977 Liam Walsh (Newport)
1978 P. O'Reilly
1979 V. Coakley
1980 Scott Fishbeir (New York)
1981 Liam Halpin
1982 Niall Halpin

James Murtagh Foursomes:

1994 M. Walsh / J. Finn
1995 T. Browne / J. Coyne
1996 C. Piggot / P. Kearns
1997 T. Joyce / J.G. Moran
1998 P. Kearns / M.Kearns
1999 C. Rose / C. Brown
2000 P. Higgins / N. McNulty
2001 J. Regan / R. Barry.
2002 I. Carroll / E. Cranley
2003 L. McNamara / P. Carroll
2004 B. Duffy / V. O'Malley
2005 Colin Cameron / Patrick Collins.
2006 Eddie Groden/ Eugene Lavelle.
2007 L. Campion/M. Murray

W.J. Walsh Trophy

Presented by the Walsh family in
memory of their father, W.J.Walsh,
captain in 1944.

1975 Michael Henehan :
       18 holes stableford
       competition(inaugural)
1976 Perry O'Reilly
1977 Liam Gibbons
1979 P. O'Reilly / Niall Halpin
1980 P. O'Reilly / Dr. H. Farrell
1981 P. O'Reilly / D. Flaherty
1982 G. McAleer / F. Hope
1983 D. Carroll / M. King
1984 S. Walsh / M. Halpin
1985 A. Redmond / M. Loughrey
1986 P. O'Reilly / J. Ryan
1987 M. Loughrey / J. O'Donnell
1988 M. Loughrey/ P. McLoughlin
1989 Denis Kendricks/ P. McLoughlin
1990 F. McDermott/ J. Moran
1991 F. Fitzgerald/ P. O'Reilly
1992 D.A. Sullivan/ M. Hastings
1993 P. Moran / J. O'Sullivan
1994 P. Murphy/ J. Cox
1995 L. Gibbons/ P. Farren
1996 P. Higgins/ C. Pigott
1997 P. Higgins/ D. Browne
1998 B. Hopkins/ N. McHugh
1999 N.Kavanagh / D. Blythe
2000 L. Campion / N. McNulty
2001 D. McDermott/ N. Halpin
2002 D. O'Regan / D. McLoughlin
2003 L. Friel/ G. O'Shaughnessy
2004 T. McLoughlin/ R. Barry
2005 R. Flynn / T. Canning
2006 D. Mahon/ P. Collins
2007 N. P. O'Malley/G. O'Shaughnessy

1985: Semi-finalists of the Junior Cup played in Kilkenny: Front, Dennis Carroll, Liam Gibbons (team captain), Cathal Hughes (Westport Captain), Martin McIntyre.
Back: Tony Joyce, Liam Walsh (Newport), Gar Golden, Dave Joyce, Tom McHale.

1987, Winners of Connacht Shield:
Back, Shane Underwood, Tony Joyce, George Reilly, Liam Halpin, Perry O'Reilly, Donie O'Connor, Liam Gibbons, Ray McCreave (team captain), Tom McHale snr, Tom McHale jnr, David Joyce, Brendan Frost, S. Goggins, M. Loughney.
Front, Frank Kelly GUI, P at Murphy (club captain), Gar Golden (President, Connacht branch GUI), Val Ganning (Calor Gas, sponsors), J. Higgins (Calor Gas), and Denis Egan (club president).

1987: Senior Cup winners.
Back, Liam Gibbons, Donie O'Connor, Tony Joyce, Shane Underwood, Laim Halpin, Perry O'Reilly.
Front, Pat Murphy (Westport captain), and Ray McCreave (team captain).

The Hughes Cup

presented by the Hughes family, Westport.

1983 Liam Gibbons ~(inaugural)
1984 M. Halpin
1985 M. Kearns
1986 D. O'Connor
1987 J. Lyons
1988 G. Golden
1989 L. Halpin
1990 C. Hughes
1991 N. McSweeney
1992 N. Halpin
1993 P. Griffith
1994 T. McHale
1995 L. Gibbons
1996 V. Rigney
1997 N. Halpin
1998 D. Browne
1999 P. McLoughlin
2000 P. Griffith
2001 E. Cranley
2002 F. Hastings
2003 B. Burns
2004 T. Bree
2005 T. Reilly
2006 D. Mahon
2007 D. Scott

Past Captains Perpetual Trophy:

- presented by Mr. Vincent Coakley
1993 G.D. Golden--inaugural
1994 G. McAleer
1995 M.B. King
1996 V.F. Coakley
1997 D. Blythe
1998 H. Murphy
1999 P. Murphy
2000 G.D. Golden
2001 L. Friel
2002 N. Halpin
2003 V.F. Coakley
2004 N. Connell
2005 L. Friel
2006 L. Friel
2007 C. O'Neill

The Ardmore Trophy:
(Mixed Foursomes)

-presented by Pat Hoban.
1985 D. Carroll / M. Tobin
1986 D. O'Connor / C. Henehan
1987 T. Brown / B. Moran
1988 S. Walsh / F. Campbell
1989 D. O'Connor / B. Hughes
1990 D. O'Connor / S. Ryan
1991 G. Golden / M. McDermott
1992 T. Joyce/ B. Gibbons
1993 D . O'Connor / C. Fleming
1994 F. Fitzgerald / J. Moran
1995 D. McDermott/ M. Walsh
1996 V. Rigney / N. Hopkins
1997 D. O'Connor/ K. Cox
1998 P. Healy / L. O'Malley
1999 B. Hopkins/ M. Barry
2000 P. Moran / T. Whyte
2001 L. Friel / M. Dolan
2002 P. Moran/ M. Madigan

The Golden Matchplay Trophy:

-presented by Mr. Gar Golden
1998 P. Kearns
1999 N. Connell
2000 C. O'Malley
2001 P. McLoughlin
2002 A. Browne
2003 J. Finn.

Donie O 'Connor Memorial Trophy

2004 Thomas McLoughlin
       (inaugural)
2005 Eugene Patten
2006 Sean Kelly.
2007 S. Duffy

Golfer Of The Year
(sponsor G. Golden since 2004)

1970 P. Higgins (gold)
N.Halpin (silver)
G. McAleer v M. Mulloy in play-off
for Bronze.
1971 Niall Halpin.
1973 P. O'Reilly)
1974 P. Bree
1975 P. O'Reilly
1976 Bro. L.K.Walsh
1977 L. Gibbons
1978 M. Heraty
1979 J. Devanney – Castlebar
1981 P O'Reilly
1982 P. O'Reilly
1985 J. Kearns
1986 D. Kendricks
1987 N. Connell
1988 Tom McHale jr.
1990 L. Halpin
1992 V. Farrell
1993 L. Gibbons
2004 B. Hopkins
2005 M. McGreal Jr.
2006 B. Hopkins
2007 P. McLoughlin

The Fitzgerald Perpetual Cup

1988 Maureen Flynn
1989 Kay O' Brien
1990 Mary Barry
1991 Claire McMyler
1992 Nuala Hopkins
1993 Loretta O' Malley
1994 Bridget Gibbons
1995 Jackie di Lucia
1996 Ina Hennelly
1997 Brigin Walsh
1998 Gretta Murphy

Castlecourt Mixed Trophy:

2005 Martin Brennan/ Carmel
       O'Connor.
2006 Richie Barry/Bridie Moran
2007 Freddie Molloy/Carmel
       O'Connor.

1989: All Ireland runners-up in Mixed Foursomes at Castleroy: Back, Tom McHale snr, Tony Joyce, Liam Halpin, Maureen Walsh (Lady Captain), Liam Gibbons, Donie O'Connor, Perry O'Reilly. Front, Kay Browne, Nuala Hopkins, Maureen Flynn, Aiden Redmond (Captain), Bridie Moran, Bridget Gibbons, Bridie Hughes.

Westport Golf Club – Ladies Challenge Cup:

1959 Mrs. M.J. McGreal
1960 Mrs. M.J.McGreal
1961 Ms. Eileen O'Malley
1962 Mrs.M.J. McGreal
1963 Ms. Judy Ryan
1964 Mrs.M.J. McGreal
1965 Ms.Teresa Landers
1966 Mrs. M.J. McGreal
1967 Mrs.M.Rafferty
1968 Mrs. R. Clarke
1969 Bean Ui Mhaoileoin
1970 Sinead Bean Ui Mhaoileoin
1971 Sinead Bean Ui Mhaoileoin
1972 Mrs. Jean McAleer
1973 Mrs. Maureen Walsh
1974 Mrs. Maureen Walsh
1975 Mrs. Mary O'Hanlon
1976 Ms. Sheelagh Ryan
1977 Mrs. Loretta O'Malley
1978 Mrs. Jean McAleer
1979 Mrs. Bridie Hughes
1980 Dr. G. Kearns

1989: Connacht winners of the Jimmy Bruen competition: Back, Tony Joyce, Dave Joyce, George Reilly, Denis Kendrick, Joe Cuddy, Noel Connell, Laim Walsh (Newport). Front, Denis Carroll, Tom McHale, Aidan Redmond (captain), Fergal Hope, Tony Browne, Tom McHale snr, Tony Fitzpatrick.

Westport Golf Club Senior Perpetual Trophy:

-presented by Liam Walsh (W/port) in 1993.
1993 Peter O'Rourke
1994 Paddy Hopkins
1995 Peter O'Rourke
1996 John Kelly
1997 Tony Browne
1998 Joseph O'Haire
1999 Gerry McAleer
2000 Gerry McAleer
2001 Joseph O'Haire
2002 Dermot Blythe
2003 Dermot Blythe
2004 V. Coakley
2005 Brendan Murphy.
2006 Gar Golden.
2007 T. Joyce.

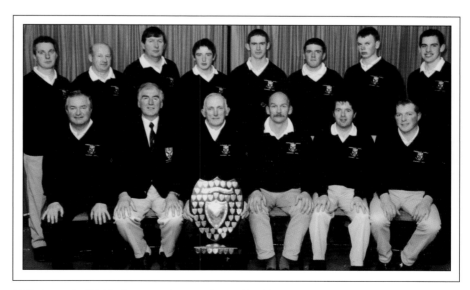

2000: Connacht Shield Winners: Back, Sean Fitzgerald, Bill Hopkins, Padraic Walsh, Cathal O'Malley, Michael Kearns, Neill McNulty, Tony Bree, Thomas McLoughlin. Front, Cathal Hughes, Pat Kearns, Niall Halpin (captain), Pete Healy, Liam Friel, Pat Griffith.

Presentation to our Greenkeepers 1997.

Back: N. Connell, A. Fadian, A. Garavan, J. Joyce, M. Grimes, (lady captain), T. Walsh.

Front: L. Friel (captain), P. Fadian, J. Garavan (head greenkeeper), T. Joyce, D. Blythe (president).

Chapter 13

WESTPORT People

■ **Groundstaff.**
Charles (Chas) Cannon- Head Greenkeeper 1973.

■ **John Garavan – Head Greenkeeper from 1974.**

"In 1973 there was no proper road to the golf course. This was the case until 1975 when the new road was opened. This road was maintained for several years by the groundstaff. In 1973 there were no trees on the course and no sand in the bunkers. Some of the tees still had to be built and some of the greens re-shaped. There were many rocks in the fairways and they were dug out by hand resulting in a few spades-being broken.! Chas Cannon (R.I.P.) was head greenkeeper in 1973. Paul Cook left abruptly in 1972.

The machinery we used in 1973 was as follows:

2 Hand mowers for cutting greens
2 Matadors for cutting tees
1 Fly mower for cutting around bunkers
2 Gang mowers, one for fairways, one for the rough
2 Tractors, which are still in working order
1 Walk-behind spiker.

Machinery has changed so dramatically we can now do more in one hour than we could do in a day with the old machinery. All our machines are now hydraulically driven and all mowers are ride-on

> *Machinery has changed so dramatically we can now do more in one hour than we could do in a day with the old machinery.*

and more efficient. Parts are more readily available to-day compared to thirty years ago. In those days we often had to wait several weeks.

A typical days work then comprised cutting on a daily basis. Fertiliser was mixed by the ground-staff. It was a mixture of dried blood, meat and bone meal, sulphate of iron, ammonia, potash and compost. This was weighted for each green to the exact amount. If the weather was bad, there was always the machinery to be maintained on a regular basis.

The biggest nightmare for a green-keeper is an oil-spillage on a green. Also disease might be discovered on a green after the weekend. Livestock breaking in and tramping on the greens would be a major problem. A greens mower that might break down on a Friday evening with no part available until Monday, that's another headache!

During the seventies and eighties we had to fight hard to get a much needed machine. It was always a case of insufficient funds. Staffing levels were low with just three permanent staff for 25 years or more.

The Leenareevagh area caused much grief. The flooding was so severe there was water at the 9th tee and beside the old 8th green.

Drainage of Leenarevagh and a new barrier at the Churns resulted in the drying out of the course. Hundreds of trees were planted all over the course.

The building of the club-house, machinery shed, and the installation of a telephone line were big events.

Until then we had no phone to ring for parts etc. and we had to go to Westport to make the calls. In 1992 an automatic irrigation system was installed and officially switched on by Padraic Flynn, Minister for the Environment.

In 1977 we had the Irish Close Championship. This was quite an undertaking at the time with no modern machinery and few staff who worked long hours for no extra pay.

In 2002 the Smurfit P.G.A. Championship took

On course

Tony Joyce- worked on the Old Course in 1961 and started on New Course in 1971.
Pat Fadian- 1974-
Colin Brown
Kevin Corcoran-2001
Patrick Collins -2004
Noel Heacy -2003
Seamus Higgins- 2006

place. This was a hectic time with only two months to prepare and the weather so bad with strong winds and rain.

In my 34 years working on the course I have found 99% of members to be understanding of work being carried out.

Over the past 34 years I have seen huge changes and improvements on the course. We re-built some tees and re-shaped others. We built three new greens and made three beautiful lakes. There were 90 new bunkers built and the most recent addition has been the driving range which adds greatly to the course.

I believe that Westport Golf Club is one of the finest courses in the country and I am proud of my small part in it's history.

*We built
three new
greens
and made
three
beautiful
lakes.*

A view of the 7th
green (index 10)
and lake, and the
construction of
the 8th green
and lake.

The Professionals

■ **Keith Mongan 1988.**

McGregor Golf owned the rights to the pro shop and Keith was the professional representing McGregor Golf.

■ **Alex Mealia – from 1991.**

Alex is from Skerries in Dublin. He trained in Dun Laoghaire for 3 years, Royal Dublin for 2 years and qualified as a professional in 1989.

Alex spent two seasons in Austria working for the government golf programme.

On returning home he worked in Celbridge Driving range until May 1991.

On arrival in Westport he met the then Captain, Mr. Jack Bredin, Vice-Captain, Mr. Vincent Farrell, Hon. Sec. Pascal Quinn, Hon. Treas. Mr. Terry Sheridan and President, Mr. Gar Golden.

A one-year contract was agreed – 16 years ago!! Alex has contributed to the introduction of a green fee book and daily time sheets, systems for competitions and general administration, hotel open weeks, the mentoring of his assistant professional, Aiden Moran, the club AM/AM and Open Week. He has observed the course mature to become a tighter and longer course.

Over the years he has been lucky enough to meet the following well-known characters who came, played and enthused about the course....Jack Charlton, Pakie Bonner, Rory Bremner, Keith Allen, Gary Kelly, Joe Dolan, Steve Staunton, Sir Alex Ferguson, Patrick Kielty, and the great Christy O'Connor Sr.

Major highlights for Alex have been his marriage to Susan in 1992, Kelly Ann his daughter arriving in 1994, his son, Sam Alexander, arriving in January 2007, watching Aiden progress from a young junior to a P.G.A. qualified professional, observing Close Championships, Irish P.G.A. Championship, G.U.I. and I.L.G.U. Championships hosted by the club.

A disappointment for Alex was that serious illness prevented him from competing in the P.G.A. Championship. Alex is extremely grateful to the general membership, the various Captains,

officers, committees, ladies section and Margaret for the help and kindness conveyed to himself and his workers in the professional side of the club.

■ **Aidan Moran – from 2002.**

"My association with Westport Golf Club started in August 1991 when I was 13 yrs old. A new golf professional, Alex Mealia, had arrived in the club. He employed me in the pro-shop for open week 1991. Over the next few years I continued to work in the Pro-Shop.

I started playing golf and I developed a keen interest in the game. In turn this keen interest aroused my ambition to become a professional golfer. Between 1992 and 1997 I reduced my playing handicap from 20 to 4. A handicap of 4 was the requirement in order to turn professional.

I signed my contracts in February 1997. Over the next three years I trained under the guidance of Alex. Throughout each year I completed assignments in swing, club repairs, merchandising and the rules of golf. These assignments were posted to the PGA in the U.K. for correction and once a year I travelled over to the PGA National Training Headquarters based at the Belfry in Birmingham to undertake my 1st and 2nd year exams. In October 2000 I sat my final exams.

In 2001 I went to work in the Galway Driving Range to gain some more teaching experience. I became a fully qualified PGA Professional in March 2002. I returned to Westport Golf Club. In 2005 the Driving Range Golf Academy was built and this facility had enabled Westport G.C. to become a premier teaching college. The progressive move to introduce a beginner membership category has increased the number of people starting to play golf.

The role of the golf professional has changed dramatically since 1997. In the old days the Golf Professional's syllabus involved three areas, teaching, club repairs and the running of the golf shop.

The massive boom in the golf industry has led to golf professionals developing roles as golf managers/directors , golf course designers/ archi-

tects, golf psychologists, green keepers/ agrono-mists and media gurus.

To help the professional improve the PGA are currently conducting the PDP (Professional Development Programme). Seminars range from the latest advances in coaching involving the use of psychology, fitness and nutrition, to coaching the varying levels of golfers and to courses in business performance and management. P.G.A. qualifications differ to-day.

The levels of qualification range from a Class A Professional who is a member qualified for 3 years to a Master Professional who is a member with a minimum of 15 years experience. Currently I am classed as a Class AA Professional which means I am qualified for over 3 years and currently participating in the PDP.

Westport Golf Club has been my life. It is also where I met my wife. In the summer of 1998 a local girl Sarah O'Connor started working in the kitchen of the golf club and the rest is history. Seven years later we got married. Westport Golf Club has given me the opportunity to start and develop a career.

It has helped develop my social skills through meeting so many varying personalities and having to deal with many different situations. Finally it found me a soulmate for life. Westport Golf Club.

Thank you!

Professional golfers at Westport Golf Club: Alex Mealia (left) and Aidan Moran.

Management at Westport Golf Club: Margaret Walsh, Karen Walsh, and manager Paul O'Neill.

General Managers

James Mc Namara 1992
Pat Smyth 1996-2000
Paul O'Neill 2000-

Paul said: "I spent 12 years in the hotel and beverage industry. Manager of Westport Golf Club covers the A to Z of club golf. The big attraction with the job is that every day is unique-different people, different competitions and of course, different weather. A former captain whispered to me in week one, " You're very welcome, best of luck- you'll be blamed for everything!!" But I have no complaints. There are great people in the club. This is their club, in their town, in their county- they want the best and they demand it. They are very proud of what they have created.

The job covers many different aspects of man management, whether dealing with staff, members or the public. I remember meeting John Garavan for the first time: "Hello John, I'm Paul O'Neill. Have you worked here long?"

"About 35 years," was the reply.

As manager it is obvious to me the non-golfing role the club plays in the local community and even more importantly in the region. Its contribution in attracting in excess of 13,000 visitors annually to Westport must not be overlooked. In high season employment can rise to in excess of 25 staff- thus playing a notable role in the local economy.

Club Secretary :

Margaret Walsh (nee O'Grady) became club secretary in June 1991. There was no office as such before her arrival. Her working space was a small corner where the pro-shop is now. The first administration purchase then was a typewriter, a red chair and a filing cabinet. These were purchased from Berry's shop.

Margaret has worked with three dedicated managers, James McNamara, Pat Smyth and Paul O'Neill. The major changes in the club impacting on Margaret's work load have been, full membership for ladies, building changes, consti- tutional changes, and the joint club.

The most dramatic change from a secretarial viewpoint has been the computer. Margaret is married to Martin and the couple have three sons, Stephen, Conor and Raymond.

Assistant Secretary 2006: Ms. Karen Walsh.

WESTPORT *Moments*

Castlecourt Trophy winners, 1999: G. Murphy, M. Grimes, N. Hopkins, A. Corcoran (sponsor), A. Duffy, M. Dolan (Lady Captain), J. Moran, M. Wilson.

Sisters: Mary McDermott and Ann Corcoran enjoying a round of golf.

Here's to the next 100 years: Back, left to right: L. Gibbons, P. Gallagher, J. Collins (Hon Sec), S. Larkin, S. Walsh, C. Walsh.
Front: S. Fitzgerald, R. Mahon, D. Scott, W. Elliott.

Club Captains

1908/11	H. D. Livingstone	1951	P. J. Golden	1981	D. Blythe
1912	A. J. Simpson	1952	J. F. O'Malley	1982	N. F. Connell
1913	J. Murray	1953	N. Gill	1983	M. Cavanaugh
1914	H. Yelverton	1954	F. Callaghan	1984	L. Walsh
1915/16	H. J. Tiernan	1955	M. Gilmartin	1985	C. D. Hughes
1917	J. Kelly	1956	P. Cox	1986	P. A. Hopkins
1923	M. J. Henehan	1957	M. J. McMahon	1987	P. Murphy
1926	J. Kelly	1958	J. Kelly	1988	R. McCreave
1927	J. W. Kelly	1959	S. Fahy	1988	Dr. O. Whyte
1928	J. Sheridan	1960	J. Hughes	1989	P. A. Redmond
1929	J. P. O'Brien	1961	G. Hall	1990	C. O'Neill
1930/31	T. Stack	1962	A. Malone	1991	J. Bredin
1932/33	D. Rees	1963	M. Mulloy	1992	V. Farrell
1934	J. C. Garvey	1964	M. Staunton	1993	T. Sheridan
1935	J. J. Glynn	1965	T. Wallace	1994	M. J. McDonnell
1936	P. V. Plunkett	1966	G. McAleer	1995	V. Murray
1937	H. J. Staunton	1967	M. King	1996	P. Duffy
1938	J. Kelly	1968	Fr. M. Tobin	1997	L. Friel
1939	L. Gill	1969	H. Murphy	1998	D. McDermott
1940	J. Flatley	1970	P. McLaughlin	1999	B. Burns
1941	T. F. Maher	1971	Fr. E. O'Malley	2000	N. Halpin
1942	Fr. O'Grady	1972	M. Hastings	2001	P. Kearns
1943	Mr Mooney	1973	E. McRea	2002	A. Hoban
1944	W. J. Walsh	1974	Comdt. D. O'Regan	2003	J. Gibbons
1945	A. De Fleury	1975	G. Golden	2004	L. Walsh
1946	E.J. Timoney	1976	Dr. H. G. Farrell	2005	C. O'Malley
1947	C. J. Doherty	1977	V. F. Coakley	2006	W. Elliott
1948	L. Golden	1978	M. Moran	2007	T. McCabe
1949	P. Gill	1979	P.A. Bree	2008	S. Walsh
1950	P. J. Dempsey	1980	J. F. Hope		

WESTPORT Moments

Past Captains P. Hopkins and D. Blythe.

Past Captains M. Moran and C. Hughes

Fianna Fail Golf Classic winners 1999: Front: Cllr Declan Dever, Cathy O'Donnell, Frank Murray, Mary Dolan (Lady Captain), John Grant, Cllr Sean Staunton. Back: Joe O'Donnell, Christy O'Malley, Eamon Moran, Brendan Bolster, Hawley Hoban, Liam McNamara, Jack Bredin, John Meaney.

Successful again: Left to right: C. O'Malley, G. McAleer, L. Walsh, M. Loughrey, J. O'Donnell, P. Murphy.

Honours list

Ireland Representation:
Cathal O'Malley
(Youths-European Youth Championship)

Connacht Representation:
Liam Golden
Noel Kavanagh Jr.
Cathal O'Malley
Cormac O'Halloran

Presidents

1926-1951	F. Gill	1992-1994	S. J. Walsh
1951-1979	H. Staunton	1994-1996	P. Hopkins
1979-1981	Fr. E. O'Malley	1996-1997	D. Blythe
1981-1984	L. Golden	1997-1999	L. Walsh
1984-1986	Dr. H. G. Farrell	1999-2001	C. Hughes
1986-1988	D. V. Egan	2001-2003	C. O'Neill
1988-1990	M. J. Cavanaugh	2003-2005	P. Murphy
1990-1992	G. D. Golden	2005-2007	P. Duffy

The 3rd (index 16), the first par 3 on the course known as the Judge's Tower.
Inset: The Judge's Tower, which is located to the left of the green.

Lady Captains

1929	Mrs M. Duncan	1958	Mrs E. Hughes	1984	Mrs A. Hope
1930	Mrs E. Ryan	1959	Miss M. Burns	1985	Mrs J. Bolster
1931	Mrs J. J. O'Regan	1960	Miss M. Mulloy	1986	Mrs J. King
1932	Mrs K. McGing	1961	Miss E. O'Malley	1987	Mrs B. Gibbons
1933	Miss E. King	1962	Mrs L. Hall	1988	Mrs B. Walsh
1934	Miss E. King	1963	Mrs S. Mhaoileoin	1989	Mrs M. Walsh
1935/36	Mrs B. Golden	1964	Mrs M. J. Wallace	1990	Mrs J. McAleer
1937/38	Mrs J. McGreal	1965	Mrs F. Rees	1991	Mrs K. O'Briain
1939	Mrs M. Egan	1966	Mrs E. Rabbitte	1992	Mrs M. Flynn
1940	Mrs M. J. Kenny	1967	Mrs A. Lydon	1993	Mrs B. Gibbons
1941	Mrs M. Murphy	1968	Mrs M. Golden	1994	Mrs T. Whyte
1942	Mrs G. Stack	1969	Mrs N.H. O'Malley	1995	Mrs G. Murphy
1943	Miss M. Gill	1970	Mrs B. Nolan	1996	Mrs B. Ruddy
1944	Mrs Mooney	1971	Mrs P. Clarke	1997	Ms. M. Grimes
1945	Ms V. Carroll	1972	Mrs J. McAleer	1998	Mrs K. Cox
1946	Miss C. O'Connell	1973	Mrs N. Moran	1999	Mrs M. Dolan
1947/48	Mrs E. Maher	1974	Mrs H. McMahon	2000	Mrs S. O'Connor
1949	Miss M. Mulloy	1975	Mrs S. Ryan	2001	Mrs A. Duffy
1950	Mrs E. J. Gill	1976	Mrs N. King	2002	Mrs M. Duffy
1951	Mrs R. De Fleury	1977	Mrs M. Murphy	2003	Mrs M. Barry
1952	Mrs E. J. Gill	1978	Mrs L. O'Malley	2004	Mrs M. Rowe
1953	Mrs K. Staunton	1979	Mrs M. Ryan	2005	Mrs C. McMyler
1954	Mrs Blennerhassett	1980	Mrs B. Blythe	2006	Mrs B. Moran
1955	Miss N. Nestor	1981	Mrs F. Campbell	2007	Mrs K. Brown
1956	Miss N. Golden	1982	Mrs B. Hughes	2008	Mrs N. Hopkins
1957	Mrs F. Rees	1983	Mrs H. Bredin		

Looking to the future...

CATHAL O' MALLEY – FROM LISCARNEY TO ALABAMA

Cathal is a product of the junior golf programme in Westport G.C.

He is one of the leading golfers and best prospects from Westport G.C. In 2004 he received a golf scholarship to the University of Alabama as a result of his golfing displays in Ireland. In 2004 Cathal reached the last 16 in the West of Ireland and he made the top 10 in the East of Ireland. Consequently he was selected for the Connacht Senior Inter-Provincial team. Due to the excellence of his golf he was selected for the Irish Youths team to contest the European Youth Championship. He was selected in 2005 for the Irish Senior training panel in Portugal. In 2006 he shot a course record 65 in the Mullingar Scratch Cup. He currently plays of + 1.

Once Cathal had represented Ireland he was considered for a golf scholarship. It takes 8 to 9 nine hours to reach Alabama. It is a 7 hour journey to Atlanta and another hour for a connecting flight. He found it a surreal experience living in an apartment. The Americans had difficulty with his name but most people like the Irish. However he discovered others didn't know where Ireland is.

One culture shock for Cathal was the disciplined society in America.

"No real binge drinking over there because of the age limit to drink. Society is definitely more disciplined there than in Ireland."

A typical day for Cathal would be:
College: 8.00a.m. to 11.30.
Golf: 12.00 to 7.00 p.m.
Gym/Study: 7.00 to Bedtime.

Coaching is very similar to the approach in Ireland. The student visits the teaching professional and he helps him to work on his swing.

It is extremely difficult to be selected for the College team. The competition for places creates a pressurised atmosphere. The format is a five-member team selected from a 12-man squad. Four scores to count out of the five over 3 rounds.

The best course Cathal has played is Shoal Creek. It was designed by Jack Nicklaus and has hosted two USPGA Championships.

The most famous Alabama student on Tour at present is Graeme McDowell.

■ In June 2007 Cathal became the first Westport golfer in 99 years to reach a handicap of plus-2. This was his reward for shooting 9 under par in a club competition and shooting 4 under par in the Captain's Prize. For the record books he was also the first Westport golfer to reach a plus-1 handicap.